*The Way
the Wind
Blows*

The Way the Wind Blows

An Autobiography
by
LORD HOME

COLLINS
St James's Place, London

William Collins Sons & Co Ltd
London · Glasgow · Sydney · Auckland
Toronto · Johannesburg

First published October 1976
Reprinted October 1976
© Lord Home 1976

ISBN 0 00 211997-8

Set in Bembo
Made and printed in Great Britain by
William Collins Sons & Co Ltd Glasgow

To Elizabeth

Contents

	Early days in the Borders	page 11
II	School and University	22
III	A beginning in politics and Parliament	43
IV	Neville Chamberlain and the approach of war	58
V	A declaration of faith	76
VI	Time for thought	84
VII	Scottish prelude to the Commonwealth	102
VIII	Africa	119
IX	The diplomacy of Suez	138
X	Foreign Secretary under Macmillan	142
XI	The Soviet Union and the United Nations	156
XII	The strategic scene	167
XIII	The succession to the Premiership	176
XIV	The office of Prime Minister	191
XV	Scotland's government	205
XVI	General Election 1964; resignation of party leadership; shadowing foreign affairs	212
XVII	The Foreign Service	241
XVIII	Once again at the Foreign and Commonwealth Office	248
XIX	China	263
XX	45 years of politics	276
	Appendices	287
	Index	315

Illustrations

The author with his mother   *between pages* ⎫

Douglas Castle

The five brothers

The author's father with Neville Chamberlain   ⎬ 24–5

The author in 1943 with his three daughters

Dr and Mrs Alington

Springhill and Castlemains   ⎭

With Sir Denis Greenhill   ⎫

With James Stuart

Croquet at Hatfield

With Harold Macmillan   ⎬ 104–5

Reading telegrams on holiday

State Service in St Giles

Electioneering in 1963   ⎭

Test Ban Treaty in Moscow   ⎫

Guest of Chou En-lai

With Willy Brandt on the Berlin Wall

With Dean Rusk, Harold Macmillan and President
Kennedy   ⎬ 152–3

Ian Smith

President Sadat

Sir Abubakar Tafawa Balewa   ⎭

The Hirsel   ⎫

A family Christmas

Fishing on the Tweed   ⎬ 280–1

On my seventieth birthday   ⎭

I

Early days
in the Borders

When I succeeded Mr Harold Macmillan as Prime Minister in 1963, an inquisitive journalist sought out our head game-keeper and asked him, 'What do you know about the Homes?' He was probably bamboozled by the reply: 'Oh, the Home boys always seem to know which way the wind blows.' Our game-keeper was not thinking of me as a political trimmer, but simply stating a fact of our family life; for my father was a countryman, and a naturalist, and on the right interpretation of wind or weather depended the action of the day. So every morning, as soon as we could walk, our first conscious act was to look and see which way the wind blew. It mattered a lot. When the wind blew icy from the north, he would take us to find the woodcock hidden under evergreen, juniper, holly, yew or rhododendron, beside the springs which never froze. Sometimes we could not see it, but we learned to listen for the unmistakable 'flip' as the bird takes to the air – a sound which is just as reliable as sight.

When the wind blew from the west, we would go down to an embankment running along the River Tweed, which was built by French prisoners after the Napoleonic war, and is still called the 'Maigré'. There we would lie at dusk and my father would tell us that we need not be really alert until the first star could be seen in the sky, and the green plovers came flopping over, for they always preceded the ducks in the evening flight. I had the keener eyes, and my brother Henry the quicker ears. We could at an early age identify all the birds in the Border country by sight or sound. I can still remember the almost suffocating excitement of seeing a Roseate starling sitting on the lawn a few yards outside our drawing-room window, to which my sister Bridget was a witness.

As a treat we would sometimes go out at dawn. It might be to see the young badgers tumbling over each other outside their wide-mouthed sett; or the otter lying on his rock holding a glistening salmon, taking the epicure's bite out of the back of the neck, and disdainfully leaving the rest for the greater black-backed gulls.

We learned the broad truth of the saying 'A red sky in the morning is the shepherd's warning'; but we found that it is not always true; for when the dawn spreads its rosy fingers over the sky and the colour does not come back to the sun, then the day ahead will be miraculously fine.

When the east wind blew from the North Sea we took cover, but if the wind was soft from the south, my father would initiate us into the art of fishing for trout. A fly for each season (worm was forbidden). March Brown, Greenwell's Glory, Olives, Blue Dunns, each in the right conditions, would work its magic, and the signal for the pulse to quicken was when the lesser black-backed gulls took to the air, and then dipped to the surface to catch the natural hatch of flies. At that time we had a chauffeur whose joy in life was to sit on the bank of the Tweed, fishing for eels with long strands of red wool. I can see two vivid pictures of him to this day. One, in his uniform, with his moustaches waxed, sitting on the driving-seat of an early Renault; the other thrashing around in a seething mass of eels which obstinately refused to die.

Fishing is unquestionably a form of madness but, happily, for the once-bitten there is no cure.

So at Springhill – on the River Tweed – the small house in which we lived on The Hirsel estate, the whole wide field of nature was our playground; and when we visited our grandfather at Douglas

Castle in Lanarkshire for the summer holidays we would add to our bird knowledge a fresh vocabulary for there were the grouse and the blackcock, the peregrine falcon and the hen-harrier, the ring ousel, and among the animals the shy elegant roe-deer of the forest, and the hares which turned white in winter. We came to know them all. Birds and beasts, butterflies and flowers, in all their beauty, were our daily companions.

Of course, no one who lives close to nature can be wholly starry-eyed, for its ways are also cruel. Both faces of it were known to us as children; for we would watch the stoat hypnotizing the rabbit for the kill, the hawk poised for the strike, and the fox stalking its prey. I once met a stoat with its coat completely white, carrying a woodcock in its mouth. Such experiences were a salutary preparation for some of the shocks of life.

The same dichotomy was present in our egg-collecting, or in later years in our enjoyment of shooting, yet we were never vandals nor wantonly cruel. On the contrary we were conservationists. It would be a point of honour never to take more than one egg from a nest for our collection, and then only when the clutch was so big that the parent birds would not notice its absence. We would bend my mother's long-shanked egg-spoons and insert them with a surgical precision into the small hole in the dome of the nest of the long-tailed tit, probing gently among the three thousand feathers of the lining for the coveted prize; we would put a drop of Seccotine on the end of a twig to raise the tiny egg of the golden-crested wren from the miraculously woven mossy cradle in which it nestled, under the branch of the yew or the spruce tree. And we would treasure and gloat over our trophies like any miser who had struck gold. At that time, Bridget, Henry and Rachel were the collaborators.

My sister Rachel recalls asking me one day if she could see my egg collection. My answer was, 'Yes, if you don't touch them.' As ill-luck would have it she poked a finger through the shell of the chief prize – a kingfisher's egg. She made herself scarce for some time after that.

Eventually three more boys were added to our number. William in 1913, and Edward and George after the 1914–18 war was over. We were numerous enough to entertain ourselves, and all took to the open air like ducks to water.

After living with nature one can never again be bored. On many a train journey I have marked the likely pools in a river in which salmon or trout might lie; the field of lucerne or clover where the Clouded Yellow butterfly might be on the wing in August; and the fields, woods and valleys where the pheasants and partridges might best be driven to test the skill of the guns.

Later, much of my life was to be spent in politics and in London. When I could not escape further afield, I would go to St James's Park and watch the ducks. When I was with Mr Neville Chamberlain we identified a scaup blown in from the sea by a storm. When times were hard in politics my refuge was a day or two in the Borders – once so harsh, now so calm. The healing balm 'Peace be still' never failed to cure and bring content.

The Borders had not always been peaceful. For centuries it was the debatable land between England and Scotland, and the respective Kings were not averse to keeping the local feuds going so that the Border families should not gang up against the one kingdom or the other.

From the fourteenth to the end of the sixteenth century, the whole Border area was a wasteland, as the reivers and cattle thieves went about their business of arson and loot. 'Blackmail', which is about the nastiest word in the English language, originated in the Borders at that time.

Douglases and Homes were, in their different ways, above the local family quarrels, and were more concerned with the international scene. The Douglases were the warriors, always harrying the English, while the Homes were the peacemakers, being for long periods Wardens of the Eastern Marches, charged to concert with their English opposite number to keep order.

The Black Douglas, who was a mighty fighter in the armies of

King Robert the Bruce, was the terror of every Englishman. Under the direction of his King he was constantly attacking the English garrisons. One night, at Roxburgh Castle, the wife of an English soldier was lulling her child to sleep with the topical song:

> 'Hush ye, hush ye, little pet ye,
> Hush ye, hush ye, do not fret ye,
> The Black Douglas shall not get ye.'

Out of the night came a hand on her shoulder, and a voice – 'I am not so sure of that.' It was Sir James (the Good!) His home was Douglas Castle – the Castle Dangerous of Sir Walter Scott's novel, and it saw some grisly sights. On Palm Sunday in 1307 he trapped the English, who literally met their God in St Bride's Chapel, for they were massacred to a man as they worshipped there. Sir James and his followers then proceeded to eat the lunch which had been cooked for the English occupiers of the Castle. The 'Douglas Larder' was not a joke.

The Percys of Northumberland were the chief rivals of the Douglases, and perhaps the most famous of their meetings was the Battle of Otterburn in 1341. The fight swayed to and fro and the Percys' forces were severely shaken, but by no means beaten, when the Douglas was mortally wounded. Hidden under a bush by his friends, he recalled an ancient prophecy –

> 'I had a dream, a dreary dream,
> Beyond the Isle of Skye,
> I saw a dead man win a fight,
> And I think that man was I.'

He died as the Scottish reinforcements arrived which swept the Percys from the field.

Another of the early Douglases would invite his acquaintances to dinner, and having dined and wined them well, negotiate for the transfer of their properties to his name. Those who were not wise enough to conform, he would hang from a tree outside his bedroom window, 'to remind himself' as he was reputedly wont to say, 'of the dangers of over-indulgence' and to save his guests the inevitable anti-climax of the morning after the night before. When I was a boy we still – until the castle was pulled down – ate off a sideboard carved from the 'Hangman's Tree'.

Douglas Castle was sacked and burned many times, but perhaps the most curious episode of all had nothing to do with fighting.

The Duke of Douglas of the day had a beautiful and talented sister called Lady Jane. He was jealous for her and suspicious of the many suitors who aspired to her hand. He actually went so far as to kill with his own hands a Captain Kerr of whom he disapproved. It is not surprising that the potential husbands kept away. But in the absence of an heir the Douglas properties would have gone to the Duke of Hamilton, who was his next-of-kin. At the age of 53, and still a virgin, Lady Jane in desperation eloped with and married in Paris a Scottish adventurer, a Colonel Stewart, and produced male twins. Such a feat was judged to be medically impossible, and confirmed her brother in his now righteous indignation against her. The estate was alienated. Meanwhile Lady Jane had died and so had one of the twins; and a legal battle-royal began over the future of the 'Heir of Douglas'.

The Duke of Douglas and the Hamiltons maintained that the boys had been bought in the market in Paris; and there was circumstantial evidence that a red-faced Scotsman had been trafficking in children about that time. Rumour went further and asserted that the children were the sons of a certain Parisian glass-blower. But the Duke had calculated without his Duchess. We have a picture of her by Gainsborough and she is portrayed as she certainly was, a masterful woman. She fought the case. It took ten years and cost each family a fortune for those days. She lost the fight for legitimacy in the Scottish Courts on the casting vote of the Lord President of the Court of Session, but undaunted, decided to appeal to her peers. In the House of Lords the verdict was reversed, and the lands and possessions reverted to the Douglas family. That Lady Jane had been in life beautiful, talented, virtuous and romantic certainly counted with their Lordships, but did it sway their judgement? The evidence brought by the Hamiltons was certainly circumstantial. My guess is that Lady Jane had a child which died at birth, and that Colonel Stewart seized the chance to acquire male twins to make the succession doubly sure.

The feud with the Hamiltons was only ended when my grandfather entertained the Duke of Hamilton to luncheon at Douglas Castle in 1920. There was a picture of the 'Cause' showing Justice holding the scales with her foot on the Duke of Hamilton's neck, who was represented as a serpent. My grandfather took a pair of scissors and cut her short at the ankle. So was the hatchet buried; so was a unique work of historic art lost to posterity; so chivalry gained the day.

The Homes, who in the early years lived at Hume Castle, which is about eight miles from The Hirsel and now a ruin, were less colourful, but much more responsible and respectable; even so one of them became notorious.

The third Lord Home was a turbulent fellow, and in 1513 led a raid into Northumberland and devastated much of the country. He was, however, ambushed by English archers ten miles from home, and the expedition was named the 'ill raid'. As a result he became so poor that the Scottish Council gave him a grant of £300 for his house, 'because he had no goods undestroyed to furnish the same'. Later in that year he was among the forces mobilized by James IV of Scotland, to try to stem the advance of a punitive expedition sent by King Henry VIII of England to teach the Scots a lesson. The Earl of Surrey – the English general – fought a classic battle. He made a feint past Berwick-upon-Tweed, as though marching north on Edinburgh, and the Scots deserted their safe line of retreat into the Cheviot Hills and committed themselves to the plain. It was the move for which the English commander had been manoeuvring and waiting, and he attacked the Scottish vanguard with his main army, pinned the troops back on to the banks of the Tweed, and inflicted a crushing defeat in which King James was killed with the larger part of his army.

The lament for the Scottish nobility who fell at the Battle of Flodden is sung in Sir Walter Scott's 'Marmion'.

> Their King, their Lords, their mightiest low,
> They melted from the field as snow,
> When streams are swoln and south winds blow,
>   Dissolves in silent dew.
> Tweed's echoes hears a ceaseless plash,
>   While many a broken band
> Disorder'd, through her current dash,
>   To gain the Scottish land;
> To town and tower, to down and dale,
> To tell red Flodden's dismal tale,
> And raise the universal wail.
> Tradition, legend, tune and song,
> Shall many an age that wail prolong;
> Still from the sire the son shall hear
> Of the stern strife and carnage drear;
>   Of Flodden's fatal field,
> Where shiver'd was fair Scotland's spear,
>   And broken was her shield!

'Marmion' is often criticized as jingly poetry, but Sir Walter Scott composed it at the canter as he rode his horse at Abbotsford, and it ought to be read at that pace.

Lord Home's rôle was to deal with Surrey's flank-guard and then to hold the ford at Wark Castle over the River Tweed. The first task he fulfilled, literally wiping out the English contingent. It was a misty day and, not suspecting that the main Scottish army was hard-pressed in battle, he then proceeded to his second duty – to secure safe passage for the Scottish armies across the River Tweed;

but no army came, for there was none left to come. Home and his men survived the slaughter, and were accused of deserting the rest at a critical moment of the fight. A survivor, named Fletcher, who returned to Selkirk, coined the ditty:

'Up with the Soutars of Selkirk,
And down with the craven Lord Home!'

The Homes were only forgiven when the citizens of Selkirk conferred on me the Freedom of the Burgh in 1963. It was a happy ending to a long, long feud.

In the year 1832 the eleventh Earl of Home married the Douglas heiress and the warriors and the peacemakers were joined.

Nothing in the Douglas or Home family trees had so far suggested that an active Party politician might emerge; but my mother was a Lambton, and politics were strong in the blood, and they were Whig and Radical.

The family were based on County Durham where they were countrymen and later coal-owners, and they were full of charm, good looks, hot temper and eccentricity. The famous 'Red Boy' by Lawrence gives a good idea of the dashing aristocratic grace which came out in generation after generation.

The most famous of them was the first Earl of Durham – a member of Lord Grey's Cabinet in the 1830s, and the will behind the Reform Bill.

As a politician he possessed great ability, but he was at times so erratic, irritable and irascible, that even his closest friends and colleagues found him almost impossible to work with.

The Prime Minister who was Durham's father-in-law was sorely tried by him, but recognized the value to the Whigs of a man who was a hero in the whole of the North of England for his reforming zeal.

No doubt his cantankerous behaviour can be explained and partly excused by the atrocious health which constantly plagued him, but he tried even the Prime Minister's patience too high and he was sent overseas first as special envoy and then as Ambassador to Moscow. In that post he showed himself to be a master of diplomatic skill.

Lord Melbourne, when he succeeded as Prime Minister, had less reason to be patient. He sent Durham even further afield, and on an even more difficult assignment, to settle an incipient revolt in the colony of Upper and Lower Canada.

Here again Durham was high-handed but successful. The Durham Report of 1840 was responsible not only for the Constitution of Canada, but it was the model for the transition from colonial status to equal partnership within the British Empire and Commonwealth. He foresaw the inevitable trend some ninety years before the Statute of Westminster became a fact. He was a man of vision and a statesman of the first rank.

There is a double dose of Grey blood in my veins, in that Lord Durham's wife was a daughter of Lord Grey, whose great-niece May married my Home grandfather.

My Lambton grandfather, Freddy, was for a short time a Member of Parliament, but unlike his ancestor he was a quiet countryman who took little active part in the controversies of the day.

His wife was a Bulteel, and she was the life and soul of Fenton, the Northumberland home in which my mother grew up. We would often drive over from The Hirsel, in a pony cart, and she would send us away loaded with enormous black peppermint bulls' eyes and Berwick cockles. It was a sure way to our hearts.

Freddy's twin brother Jack was a more active politician. On one occasion when the real targets were Joseph Chamberlain and Mr Gladstone, he was the object of lampoon at Blackpool by Lord Randolph Churchill.

He said, 'Just look at Mr Chamberlain himself. He goes to Newcastle and is entertained at a banquet there, and procures for the President of the feast a live Earl – no less a person than the Earl of Durham. Now Lord Durham is a young person who has just come of age, who is in possession of immense hereditary estates, who is well-known on Newmarket Heath, and prominent among the gilded youth who throng the corridors of the Gaiety Theatre, but who had studied politics about as much as Barnum's white elephant . . .'

The poor young man who had just come of age had to suffer much more, but he snatches a small corner of history, for the peroration of that speech was the famous caricature of Gladstone cutting down trees at Hawarden.

Against the Whig Lambtons and the Greys, the Tory Homes could only field the ninth Lord Home, who was for a short time an Under-Secretary in the Foreign Office; and my father who unsuccessfully contested Berwick and East Lothian in the Conservative cause. He was the most reluctant politician I have ever known, and was immensely relieved when he was beaten by a handsome majority by one of the Liberal Tennant family.

My father strongly advised me against politics as a career. He also told me that no Home could drink champagne. Otherwise a dutiful son, on both these points I disagreed, and proved my point.

II

School and University

In 1963 my mother was asked whether I had shown any precocity as a child. She said, 'Oh no, he was a very ordinary little boy.' She knew all right, because she exercised discipline in the home, and gave my sister Bridget, my brother Henry and me our earliest education. I recall our Sunday evening religious teaching. She would read to us from a book of simple instruction called *Line upon Line*. There was a God. Jesus was His Son. We were all born in His image, and He watched us individually at work and play. He was to be loved and feared, for He would approve of us if we were good and punish us if we were naughty. So my mother taught us the difference between right and wrong as contained in the Christian code of conduct, and when we fell from this standard, we would be appropriately and immediately punished. The cynic will say that this was dope for the young and propaganda for the establishment. I can only testify that I have been deeply thankful for this early guidance in elementary Christianity. With hindsight too I am grateful that the penalty was directly related to the crime, and promptly executed. It left us rebuked – unlikely to repeat the misdemeanour – but with no lingering sense of guilt and inferiority.

My father was the nearest thing to a saint. He could not bring himself to think ill of anyone. When in the last war, my brother Edward was a prisoner of the Japanese in the notorious camp in which so much cruelty was inflicted, someone said to my father, 'Never mind, one day we will have our revenge.' His reply was, 'What would be the point of that?'

He was sometimes gullible. I was once accused of belonging to a notorious Communist organization. I could not understand how this originated, and made some enquiries. I found that my father had subscribed to it, because the word 'peace' appeared in the title of the prospectus.

But he gave me the most valuable advice which I have ever received, and it sprang from his own Christian living. 'Remember,' he said, 'to ask yourself before you act, what the effect is likely to be on the other fellow.'

At the age of five or six, our education was handed over to a governess. Miss Triplow had firm views about curriculum. First we were grounded in the three Rs and then, because Henry and I were due to go to school at Ludgrove and Eton, we had to learn Greek and Latin Grammar.

The Foreign Office once said that it was better to have no French than that taught at Eton. Miss Triplow's French was like that. But she endeared herself to us because, while she kept our noses to the desk for a long morning, she would come rat-catching with our Border Terrier in the afternoon. She must have taught us reasonably well for, although neither Henry nor I aspired to scholarship, nevertheless we got into Ludgrove and Eton fairly near the top of the list.

Of course at The Hirsel and at Douglas there were not only parents and relations. There was a host of attendants who were our friends and allies.

Mr Macmillan, the gardener at Douglas, who would hold us back after the family inspection of the greenhouse on a Sunday afternoon, and give us a large bunch of white muscat grapes, with the caution not to let our elders see.

Mr Froode, my grandfather's butler, who once a week, when the housekeeper was bending into the linen cupboard, would push her in and lock the door. She regularly gave notice to my grandmother, who gravely turned it down, knowing that for the housekeeper to leave would be to admit defeat, which she would rather die than do.

Mr Telfer, the head game-keeper, who was once asked by Mr Baldwin his opinion of a speech which he had just delivered at Douglas. 'I've no doubt', he said, 'that it was very good. But, hoots man, what would the poachers be doing with me at political meetings?' After walking fifteen miles a day he would sit down of an evening and study the gold market.

My father's butler, Collingwood, who was faithfully produced in my brother's play *The Chiltern Hundreds*. He would tip us when we were short of pocket-money. His vocabulary was unusual. For example a 'quandary' was always a 'quadrangle', while he enjoyed making heavy weather if he could. On the outbreak of war in 1939 he was on holiday in Carlisle, which is about seventy miles from The Hirsel with a good road. He sent my father a telegram which read, 'As the emergency has broken out I am making my way back to The Hirsel across country overnight.' He was a splendid character and what we should have done without him I do not know.

And there was Jimmy Scott, the fisherman, who as a young man had hooked a salmon which had on it 'a back like a huge black Sow'. It used to be a point of honour that guests should extract from him the story of how a well-meaning man on the opposite bank had given him bad advice which led the fish among the rocks and to the inevitable cut line. At ninety his language was as lurid as it had been at nineteen.

We were all a very happy family.

Life at home had been so idyllic and carefree that one was bound to be let down with a bump, and for a young boy who had led a sheltered life, the impact of boarding-school was a shock.

For me perhaps it was less so than for some of my contemporaries; for, although my father and mother were well-off, they insisted on a disciplined home. None of us was spoiled; living was good but frugal (my mother turned an imaginative cook into 'good plain' in

The author with his mother.

Douglas Castle (demolished 1938).

The brothers who knew which way the wind blew: (l. to r.) Alec, Henry, William, Edward, George.

My father and Mr Chamberlain: this picture was taken in the autumn of 1938 just after Munich.

First steps back to health. This photograph with (l. to r.) Meriel, Diana and Caroline was taken in 1943 after two years' confinement to bed.

Elizabeth's father and mother, Cyril and Hester Alington.

Our first two homes, Springhill and Castlemains.

no time). After we married, Elizabeth noticed that I never took a second helping at meals. The simple reason was that in our family unless you took what you wanted on the first round, there was nothing left to take.

Pocket-money was for thrift, and only in the last resort for spending. Prayers and Church were a 'must'. We were brought up to obey the authority of parents, nanny and butler or, in modern jargon, to 'respect the establishment'. Some of us were more law-abiding than others – my brother William was scarcely one to conform – but home was a happy place and a safe haven.

At the start of every term at Ludgrove I was homesick, but was soon caught up in the work and play of school life, and there was little time for moping.

Ludgrove was a privately run school, which was approved by my father's friends, and it was undeniably very well conducted. The first Headmaster had been Arthur Dunn, the famous international footballer, but he had retired when I arrived and had been succeeded by G. O. Smith, who had the distinction of having been English centre-forward, and having made a hundred for Oxford in the University cricket match. He was sustained by a supporting staff most of whom were kindred spirits, for they played games well and taught more than adequately.

Coming from Scotland where, because of the climate, cricketers were thin on the ground, I had never seriously considered the possibility that I could compete with my English contemporaries at the game. It was a master, W. S. Bird, later killed in the war, who had kept wicket for Kent, who banished that particular inferiority complex. I was playing 'stump cricket' (one stump to bowl at with a softish ball) when I overheard him say to the Captain of the XI: 'That boy is worth watching – he can bowl.' That modest encouragement was enough. I decided then and there to try and be an all-rounder, so as to get the maximum enjoyment out of the game.

The master to whom I and countless others were most indebted was a non-games-playing teacher of classics, who for some forgotten reason we christened 'Bunko' Brown. He was a rather forbidding figure, invariably dressed in a greenish-brown herringbone tweed suit, and a stick-up collar which, with a large drooping moustache and plastered-down hair, produced a portrait of unrelieved gloom. But as an interpreter of Virgil and Ovid, Homer and Plato, he was a genius. He could even bring alive the interminable campaigns of Caesar. As a politician, where above all an accurate use of language matters, I gladly acknowledge my debt to 'Bunko' Brown. At any rate Ludgrove enabled me and four brothers after me – for by then William, Edward and George had arrived – to enter Eton, reasonably able to hold our own intellectually with our contemporaries, and more than adequately coached at games.

One year at Ludgrove was much like another; but there was one event which was unique. In 1916 we were woken and told to go downstairs, because a German zeppelin was due to fly right over the school. We were scarcely out of our beds when the whole sky was illuminated with a flash, and the huge flaming torch fell to the ground about two miles away at Potters Bar. It was an awesome sight, and I still have a piece of the frame collected from the scene on the following day. That, and the growing list of relations and friends killed, introduced us as small boys to the follies, cruelties and sorrows of this world. The death in action of Geoffrey, my mother's second brother with his dashing good looks and irrepressible sense of fun – my favourite uncle – left me with a sick and empty feeling which I remember to this day.

If Ludgrove was a shock, Eton was an earthquake. One House was as large as Ludgrove. The whole school numbered a thousand, and from the first week as a 'fag' the new boy was in contact with the most senior boys. No preparation could adequately arm one for so dramatic a transition to independence, self-reliance and self-preservation within a largely self-governing structure.

Each boy from the start had a room of his own, small but undeniably his territory, into which nobody, not even his House Master, could come without knocking. Years later I took the wife of the President of Pakistan to see a typical boy's room at Eton. She was disbelieving and was sure that it must be the clothes' cupboard. We were guided, but certainly not coddled, and a judicious balance was held between the individual's rights and public order. The responsibility for maintaining discipline out of school was very largely placed by deliberate policy on the shoulders of the senior boys. The House Master would naturally keep an oversight to prevent abuse, but the boys were encouraged to work out a code of living for themselves and to administer justice.

There have been many critics of the boarding and public school system, and tales of bullying, and of small boys whose lives have been warped by the punishment meted out by their elders. In any large company of boys there will always be the lout who tries to throw his weight about at the expense of weaker brethren. There were such at Eton, but they always managed to mobilize public opinion against themselves and were invariably marked down and defeated by it before they could reach the age and position of authority. I remember only one boy who looked as though he was constantly expecting the enemy, but that was totally deceptive for he became at his weight the boxing champion of the school and of his University, and was the first man to fly solo over Mount Everest.

I arrived at Eton in 1917, and although many of the younger masters had fallen in war, and many more were absent in the forces, the standard of teaching was high and given by some scholarly men.

I went to P. V. Brooke's House, but it was his last 'Half', and while he was kind and helpful to a new arrival, there was no time for him to make much impression on me or I on him.

In September A. W. Whitworth took over, and I like to think we were soon on each other's wave-length. Scrupulously fair to all the different types in his House – a light but persuasive disciplinarian, a classical scholar and first-class amateur footballer and a keen sportsman, he was loved and respected by all of us. Happily he shared my total dislike of mathematics, an understanding which saved me many frustrating hours which a mathematical tutor might have inflicted upon me.

He disliked having to punish, and would invariably use one argument which was almost naïve, but so devastatingly logical, that it deterred us from the worst. I recall the first occasion on which he used it. One of us had poured a jug of water over the stairs, and the contents had landed on his head. 'Hm,' he said, 'suppose the whole House had done that?' He seldom had need to set us the penalty of transcribing five hundred lines of Virgil, which was the heaviest punishment which a House Master could inflict. Senior boys could use the cane for breaches of internal discipline, and the Head Master the birch for crime. There was, in fact, little physical punishment, but it was a deterrent and if it had to be given was quickly over and done with.

Whitworth was a companion as well as schoolmaster, and for that and much else I and many others are thankful.

He taught classics, but one did not necessarily, except for general oversight, sit under one's House Tutor for any particular subject. There were plenty of masters, characters and personalities in their own right, among whom we were distributed.

A. S. F. Gow and C. M. Wells for classics. G. W. Headlam and C. H. K. Marten for history; to say nothing of Dr Alington for both; while always ready to entertain us was the Provost, Monty James, with his ghost stories washed down with port. These and others were household names in academic circles, and each contributed a lot to our learning.

Andrew Gow was an acknowledged Greek scholar, and ever since his instruction it has been my favourite 'dead' language. He made it exciting and vivid, and with his caustic wit added a lot to the amenity of the life of the elder boys. The highest praise which he ever bestowed was 'not utterly bad'. He collected pictures from the Impressionist School and his taste was immaculate.

He once visited us at Douglas during the grouse-shooting season and, tired of walking, lay down where he could see over the valley of the Douglas Water. When we returned to him he asked if the local Territorials were manoeuvring, and he described in detail where he had seen men marching along the hillside and down the valley to the village. The Lanarkshire Yeomanry were not in the area that day, but he had described exactly the route taken by the Covenanting army as they marched to fight and win over their oppressors some hundreds of years before.

After leaving Eton and becoming a Fellow of Trinity College, Cambridge, he had to sign a form for an undergraduate who wished to qualify to fly. He felt bound to learn to fly himself, so that he would really know what he was doing when he signed or declined to do so.

'Tuppy' Headlam used also to come and stay with us. He disliked the colour of heather, and great care had to be taken to select a green place for our picnic lunches. At Eton he would instruct us in Dicey and the Constitution, and we learned much about Parliament and the structure of British democracy. He was one of three Headlam brothers who were known as 'Sometimes angry', 'Always angry', and 'Furious'. 'Tuppy' was the 'Sometimes' of the trio. True he could be angry, but it was usually assumed, and his teaching was laced with racy anecdotes and a mordant wit which made even early morning school a hilarious and unforgettable experience. He once began a period of tuition with 'I am told on good authority that there will shortly be an internecine struggle between the white races, the black races and the yellow races. My prayer is that we shall draw a bye in the first round.'

C. H. K. Marten was of course a great historian. I began to specialize in history at the age of sixteen plus, and thereafter sat at his feet at least once a week. He was the first of my teachers to make me realize that the characters of history had once been human beings like us. The picture gallery in the Provost's Lodge was filled with portraits of famous men painted in their Eton days, and as C. H. K. Marten talked, the statesmen and politicians, the financiers, soldiers, sailors and philosophers came out of their frames and were alive.

Marten had a raven which used to sit on the back bench of the Division. If anyone was inattentive or slow, at a signal from him the bird would nip the offender's ear. There were not many laggards in that class.

I suppose that the most eccentric of the wartime masters was John Christie of Glyndebourne fame. His even odder father had left it in his will that John must adopt some profession in order to inherit his fortune, and when invalided out of the army he came to Eton as a master. His subject was science, although I suspect that this was never proved. I was 'up' to him for Early School once a week for almost a year. The routine was this. He would appear late in a dressing-gown, distribute a book on 'Levers' and then ring the bell for his butler. He would say to him, 'Childs, entertain the young gentlemen while I have my bath.' By the time he had washed, and Childs had provided us with coffee and biscuits, John Christie was ready for a short dissertation on the magic of leverage. He never questioned us, which made us suspect that it was ground which was too dangerous for the teacher. Alas, it was too good to last. Childs's intelligence network had for once become rusty, and Christie over-confident, and the Head Master walked in unannounced. He took in the situation at a glance, and that was the beginning of the end of John Christie's professional career. He would sometimes regale us with the tale of how he successfully contested his father's will, on the grounds that when he made it he was not in his right mind. According to John, the turning-point in the case came when he said to the judge, 'If you have any remaining doubt, your Honour, as to my father's madness, you have only to look at me.' The judgement went in his favour.

C. M. Wells – small and square – was a fine classical scholar, and he played football and cricket for Cambridge and England. A famous rugger match against Scotland was subsequently called 'Wells's match'. With all of that he was shy and would rather have died than reveal emotion. There was an occasion when he and Mr Austen-Leigh (then Lower Master) went on a Hellenic cruise, and were over-persuaded by the captain of the ship to see the sun rise over the Acropolis. They duly emerged from their bunks, and dutifully waited for the magic moment. When it arrived Wells turned and said, 'An extraordinary thing – the pattern of our pyjamas is exactly the same'; and they went back to their cabins.

Wells was not at his best with women, and when Mrs Alington came to dinner, he would put the clock on one hour, so that, when the ladies left the dining-room, his male guests had time to savour his incomparable port, and put an end to the whole business at a reasonable time. He knew everything there was to be known about wine; while his stamp collection was second only to that of the King. He was, too, a keen and skilful fisherman. Every year he used to visit Norway, and caught, I believe, more salmon of forty pounds and over than anyone before or since. Once when he was over ninety he fell into the river Test and found it difficult to get out. His fellow anglers insisted that he should in future be accompanied by a ghillie. A friend a year later enquired whether he had fallen into the Test again. 'Yes,' he said, 'I did so the other day. I thought that I must give that fellow something to do.'

Wells was a very good cricket coach, and his ability to press his thumb on the wicket and say, 'That is how it was at the Oval in 1900, or Lord's in 1906 – boy, put them in' carried the authentic ring. He retired just as I was approaching the fringes of the Eton first XI, and was succeeded by R. A. Young who for a number of years kept wicket and went in Number 3 for Sussex. He was the cricketer who was judged to have kept his pads on in the pavilion longer than any other first-class batsman. It was doubtless true as Numbers 1 and 2 in the batting order were occupied by Ranjitsinhji and C. B. Fry! Young was also quoted as proving the rule that an English side should never play the second-best wicket-keeper for his batting in a Test Match. I suppose that he had dropped some vital catch, but I suspect that he was maligned, for he was a really first-class batsman, making, I recall, a century for Sussex in each innings against Warwick Armstrong's side of 1921. Having coached boys all May, June and July it was no mean feat to achieve that, and against the fastest of bowlers – Macdonald and Gregory.

Wells and Young were reinforced by a canny Yorkshireman – a professional whose name was Matt Wright. Woe betide the batsman at the crease who had not reached double figures in the first quarter of an hour. I remember one day when I had been scratching about in the middle for an interminable time, he came up to me and said, 'For God's sake, sir, if you must miss – do it in style.'

During that time Eton turned out some really top-class players, including C. H. Gibson, G. O. Allen, W. W. Hill-Wood, R. Aird and Mervyn Hill – later the Worcestershire wicket-keeper. Allen was a very fast and accurate bowler for a schoolboy, and for a summer I fielded to him at first slip. In those years wicket-keepers stood up to the wicket far more often than they do now. Hill used to do so to Allen, so that first slip was like a modern wicket-keeper, except that there were no gloves!

It is of Matt Wright that what I conceive to be the nicest school cricket story was told. Eton were playing some notable visiting side. A young boy struggling for his colours was hit by a dead straight ball, plumb in the middle of his pads which were in front of all three stumps. To a unanimous appeal Matt Wright gave an emphatic 'not out'. When the young boy reached his umpiring end he said, 'Matt, I must have been jolly nearly out that time.' 'My boy,' was the reply, 'you was so jolly nearly out that if you had been one of the visitors you would have been.' Matt Wright was succeeded by another fine Yorkshire character, George Hirst. He was the first professional who took real trouble to teach boys to bowl.

One of my early recollections of the Eton XI was an MCC visiting side in the summer of 1918. P. G. H. Fender came on to the field in pointed black boots, but they did not impair his bowling skill. The quality of our opponents was always a stimulus to a boy to shine.

Our two key school matches were against Winchester and Harrow. In 1921, when the Eton XI was captained by David Brand, the Winchester side contained the most mature batsman of his age in J. L. Guise. It is almost incredible, but confirmed by the records, that, playing on Agar's Plough, the Eton ground, he made 248 in the first innings out of a total of 313. Only one other batsman reached double figures. Guise made the great bulk of his runs with a hook over short leg to the boundary, where there was no fielder. At 248 he played the same old stroke which had been so fruitful, only to be run out by the deep square leg whom he had not seen. David Brand, the Eton captain, when he was asked after the match why he had delayed placing his man there for so long said, 'Oh, I wanted to lull him into a feeling of false security.' As Eton nevertheless won by nine wickets, no post-mortem into the captaincy was held.

Harrow, by contrast, was a gladiatorial contest where the partisans really let themselves go. In 1921 and 1922 when I played for Eton, the crowd was around the twenty thousand mark. No month of the year was free from Eton and Harrow banter, and the wit improved as the day drew near.

When Mr Baldwin (Harrow) was Prime Minister, his Home Secretary was Mr Bridgeman (Eton). One day Baldwin produced some quip in the Eton–Harrow context which Bridgeman did not judge to be up to standard. He bided his time. One morning at Cabinet the Prime Minister congratulated the Home Secretary on the rapid ending to a serious riot in one of HM's prisons. 'How did you do it, Home Secretary?' he asked. 'Oh Prime Minister, it was very easy. I just told the Governor to order the prison band to play "Forty Years On" [the Harrow School song], and the prisoners stood to attention and quietly returned to their cells.'

Fortune smiled on me in those matches in 1921 and 1922, providing runs or wickets or both; so one schoolboy ambition was realized, which was to play at Lord's. In 1922 Harrow were the hottest of favourites. They had in their XI four who won their Blue at Cambridge in the following year, and the remainder were good. The first day was washed out completely by rain, and on the

Saturday we played in a bog. In such conditions the Eton outsiders gained the lead on the only innings played. The Harrovians were disgusted, but who could say that they were the better side? The only satisfaction they took away was a record number of Eton top hats crushed beyond recognition. We bore the loss of our dignity with smug good will.

A few years later, it was at Lord's that I saw the finest stroke played that I have ever seen anywhere. G. O. Allen bowled a really fast ball on the off-stump – little, if anything, short of a length. Leary Constantine lay back and cut it with a flat trajectory straight to the feet of Father Time.

Fives was another game which I played; and Nico Llewellyn-Davies and I were an undefeated First Pair for the School. J. M. Barrie was his guardian and Nico once took me to tea with him. He was charming in his greeting, but thereafter almost totally silent which was rather unnerving for a boy, and I was relieved when Nico told me that he was often like that in the throes of composition. His speech on 'Courage' at St Andrews University I have always thought to be a gem.

He had read to the students extracts from a letter written by Captain Scott in his tent in the Antarctic just before he died and he went on:

Let us get back to that tent with its songs and cheery conversation. Courage. I do not think it is to be got by your becoming solemn-sides before your time. You must have been warned against letting the golden hours slip by. Yes, but some of them are golden only because we let them slip. Diligence – ambition; noble words, but only if 'touched to fine issues'. Prizes may be dross, learning lumber, unless they bring you into the arena with increased understanding. Hanker not too much after worldly prosperity – that corpulent cigar; if you become a millionaire you would probably go swimming around for more like a diseased goldfish. Look to it that what you are doing is not merely toddling to a competency. Perhaps that must be your fate, but fight it and then, though you fail, you may still be among the elect of whom we have spoken.

And then:

Courage is the thing. All goes if courage goes. What says our glorious Johnson of courage: 'Unless a man has that virtue he has no security for preserving any other.' We should thank our Creator three times daily for courage instead of for our bread, which, if we work, is surely the one thing we have a right to claim of Him. This courage is a proof of our immortality, greater even than gardens 'when the eve is cool'. Pray for it. 'Who rises from prayer a better man, his prayer is answered.'

The whole address was a work of art.

What did Eton give to me? An introduction to life in a large and various company; a sniff of the value of independence; tolerance; self-discipline accepted as infinitely superior to orders; responsibility shouldered lightly; to feel, but not to wear one's feelings on one's sleeve; a perception of the fun of living; a recognition that power and authority must be exercised with restraint. All that – while the peace and the beauty and the tradition soothed the soul.

If parents are ready to give that quality of education to their children, who is the 'State' to say that they should not do so? There should be more such schools to meet the demand, not less.

Eton was a good apprenticeship for Oxford, and Christ Church was almost a University on its own. There were, of course, many Etonians there, but not so many as would tempt us to form a clique. Indeed the value of the University was that it provided a circle of friends far wider than those of school.

Christ Church with its size and unfettered processes of selection could supply a greater variety than any other Oxford College. The scope can be illustrated from a cross-section of my own contemporaries.

Roger Makins (later Lord Sherfield) who was able to obtain his First Class degree, and his Fellowship of All Souls, with a judicious mixture of study and fox-hunting.

Harold Acton, who started one of his poems, which had quite a vogue, with the unpromising line of 'Plop, plop, plop into a bucket'. He was a very colourful character and added a lot to the contemporary life of the university in the days when the aesthetic life was scarcely popular.

Evelyn Baring (later Lord Howick) son of Lord Cromer of Egyptian fame, himself every inch a pro-Consul, who became High Commissioner in Kenya, and later Chairman of the Colonial Development Corporation. The great conifer forests on the Swaziland–South African border are only one example of the many imaginative schemes of development which he pioneered in the African continent.

Malcolm McCorquodale (later Lord McCorquodale), a very good and popular Minister under Mr Ernest Bevin in the Ministry of Labour, and a most successful head of the Printing Industry, was at that time the keenest on racing among the undergraduates. For months before the race he had backed Epinard for the Cambridgeshire of 1923 when it was beaten by a short head. He was an enormous young man, and frustration gave him added strength as he bought and tore to shreds every pile of evening papers in the High which reported the bad news. The Town was not pleased, but the Proctors took an understanding and lenient view.

Wilfred Kent-Hughes, who later became Minister of the Interior in the Federal Government of Australia.

Jim Pitman, the pioneer of the vocabulary and dictionary of basic English.

Alan Lennox-Boyd (later Viscount Boyd), the most respected of Colonial Secretaries, who conducted the transfer from Empire to Commonwealth with skill and tact.

My brother Henry, later the 'Birdman' of the BBC who, dancing round a bonfire in the Peck Quadrangle after a college celebration to mark some success on the river, returned to his room to find that his bed had been the fuel for the flames.

Solomon Bandaranaike, later Prime Minister of Ceylon.

I made the most of the opportunity to make friends whom I met again all over the world, and in particular in the Commonwealth, for Oxford was the home also of the Rhodes Scholar. Dean Rusk, with whom I was to work closely in later years as American Secretary of State, was one of these.

With two of my Christ Church friends, I formed a select club, which had but two rules – the first that whenever we met thereafter we should drink the best claret available; the second that we should destroy any aspidistra on sight – and evidence had to be produced to prove it. The founder member was Dick Heathcoat-Amory, and the second member Roger Makins – later our Ambassador in Washington. I used to receive snippets of aspidistra leaves from far and wide, and myself contributed many – not without adventure. Oxford had also helped us to get our values right.

Amongst the Dons there were many characters in their own right.

Dean White ruled with an easy authority.

Dr Carter was erudite in the law and lazy. Above all things he hated his laziness to be interrupted, and then he was rude.

Lindemann – 'the Prof' – the professional cynic. I once said to him in Christ Church Hall that I didn't much care for the portrait of Lord Halifax who was represented with little flesh and no blood, and I said that he must already have been dead and painted at a leave-taking. 'Oh no,' said Lindemann, 'he'd been reading his old dispatches.'

Owen was a benevolent bachelor, and J. C. Masterman tells a story of him which is worth repeating. For years and years he had dined with another bachelor Don, when the latter elected to get married. Rashly he invited Owen to dine at his new home. No word was spoken until at the end Owen said to the new wife, 'I perceive that in North Oxford you have your main meal in the middle of the day.'

One of my regrets in life is that I did not work harder at Oxford. If only I had learned and applied the secret of early-morning working which I adopted later in life, I could have improved upon the Honours degree of a Third which I eventually acquired.

Nevertheless, I was undeservedly in luck, for my history tutors were two most distinguished men – Keith Feiling and J. C. Masterman.

Keith Feiling had founded the History School after the war, and 'J.C.' as he was always called, was his able and willing collaborator. They were hard-pressed in the early post-war years, when Oxford had to absorb many who came back from the services, as well as the output of the schools; but they managed to have time for every pupil, and gave to each one of us much knowledge and understanding. Both of them bore my absences playing games with fortitude, and both taught me much wisdom about life.

J.C. was an extremely good games-player. A hockey and tennis player for England – and an all-rounder at cricket with bat and ball. With the safest of hands at first slip, he was a tower of strength to any team.

His side-line was writing, and his book *To Teach the Senators Wisdom* is still a charming guide to Oxford life. Occasionally, too, he would produce a detective story, and that ingenuity of mind served him well when he helped to run the 'XX System' in the 1939 war. His book on the use of the 'Double Agent' is in its way a classic.

Perhaps J.C. was too tolerant of my passion for cricket – not that I regret for one moment the part which games and sport have played in my life. I am unrepentant in the belief that 'team games' for the young are good for body, mind and soul. 'The Parks' which housed the University cricket ground, were a constant magnet, and I played in the Freshmen's and Seniors' matches at the start of each season when it was often near to snow.

All my senior tutors – Whitworth aged 98 – Masterman 85 – and Feiling 96 – are happily still alive as I write, so I cannot have taken too much out of them.

In 1926, when I went on tour with the University side, a 'Blue' seemed likely, as in the match against the MCC at Lord's, I took the wickets of Challenor (West Indies) and Hendren (England and Middlesex) cheaply; but the final match against Essex at Chelmsford brought about my downfall. Percy Perrin (Essex and England) was in one of his hitting moods, and once his eye was in he made even the good length ball into a half-volley. On this occasion he hit me for three consecutive and towering sixes. This was too much for my captain, and my fellow 'seamer', MacCanlis, was preferred and he played against Cambridge.

I played many matches away from Oxford for the Harlequins and other cricket clubs. Once I went to Nottingham to play for a side raised by Sir Julien Cahn, and on arrival at the wicket found Larwood bowling at one end, and Voce at the other. I somehow survived Larwood's rockets, and then in the second over was hit over the heart by Voce, and went down like a log. My friends told me that my first words on regaining consciousness were, 'Thank God I was not at the other end; I would have been dead!' After leaving Oxford I played the odd game for Middlesex but the pull of the Borders thereafter was too strong.

What did Oxford do for me? It provided understanding of life and more independence of judgement. It was impossible to live one's undergraduate life in Christ Church, the college founded by Cardinal Wolsey, without soaking up the tradition of England; or to dine in Hall in the company of portraits of great men without realizing that it matters what people do. Impossible, too, to rub shoulders with brain and brawn, artists, scientists, classical scholars, historians, mathematicians and churchmen without broadening one's mind. As an undergraduate I was introduced to at least a part of what Kenneth Clark has labelled 'Civilization'. An Honorary Fellowship at Christ Church, and an Honorary Degree at the University later set the seal on a most rewarding part of life.

Before deciding on a career I went on a cricketing tour of South America, captained by 'Plum' Warner, the greatest diplomat of all the cricketers. We were a pretty good side with G. O. Allen and

J. C. White – both England players, and amongst others Maurice Jewell of Worcestershire, Tommy Jamieson from Ireland, and Colonel R. T. Stanyforth, who for years kept wicket for the army in the heyday of its cricketing fame.

Stanyforth told me a nice cricketing story of the 1890s of a match played between two well-known clubs. At the end of the first day Club A had made 340 for 4, and at the end of the second day they had scored 760 for 8. It was a two-day match!

The Argentine was captained by Clem Gibson, who was the most elegant bowler I ever saw. He had bowled magnificently for England against Australia in 1921, and as captain of the Eton XI he had been one of my schoolboy heroes.

I took with me to the Argentine a bat the surface of which I had oiled and cultivated to a point where if one hit the ball in the middle the propulsion was like a jet. One morning before a match 'Plum' found me scraping away at it with a razor blade. He flayed me alive, saying that it was as bad as pouring water into vintage port.

On the tour there was another lesson learned. As we set sail some well-wisher had thoughtfully provided us with an infallible system at roulette. We used to play two or three nights a week at the magnificent casinos, and invariably the system won. We were amassing a small fortune, when one day I was sent to hospital with a rumbling appendix. That evening my companions played the boards, losing all their winnings and mine. One of them timidly came to break the news in the morning. My instant reaction – careless of the appendix – was to leap out of bed in protest; but the deed was done.

Before finally deciding how to conduct the rest of my life I took two sabbatical years, living at The Hirsel and at Douglas Castle, and enjoying the sport which they could provide. My brother Henry was a ready accomplice in shooting, and he and I and some of our young friends used to walk many miles after the varieties of game which Douglas in suitable weather conditions could provide. Henry and I can, I believe, claim a record. One day we hunted snipe. We came home with forty-seven, and had shot at only two more.

Apart from the fact that grouse-shooting takes place when the hills are looking at their best, with the heather in full bloom, it is enjoyable and exciting for the skills which are needed to outwit the birds in their natural element. First the butts have to be laid out on the contours which the grouse are likely to follow in flight, and according to the prevailing winds which will help them over the guns. The skill of the game-keeper and his line of beaters is constantly tested by the direction and strength of the wind which, like much else in life, seldom conforms to the planner's blue-print. The skill of the guns is tested by the infinite variety in the pace and changes of direction which the birds take in flight. At their fastest it may be 50 mph and at the slowest perhaps 5 mph.

Most experienced grouse shooters will, I think, agree that the grouse flying fast and straight down the wind is much easier to shoot than the hoverer into a gale. It is the difference between playing straight fast bowling and the slow bowler with flight and spin.

One day I recall with particular pleasure was with Henry, David Bowes-Lyon and Cosmo Crawley (the Harrow cricketer). The game-book entry ran: 20 grouse, 5 black game, 1 partridge, 1 woodcock, 15 snipe, 5 mallard, 5 teal, 2 gadwall, 4 golden plover, 5 pigeon, 18 hares and 26 rabbits.

Such sport was undiluted fun. On these days we would walk ten miles or more, and were never daunted by any kind of weather. It was genuine 'hunting' in the right sense of the word, and it required an intimate knowledge of the game birds and their ways.

At The Hirsel, the quality of sport was salmon-fishing. We have records going back to 1743 when one of my ancestors caught a salmon on rod and line recorded at 69¾ lbs.

The Tweed has alternated at intervals of about forty years between being a spring and an autumn river. When I began fishing after the First World War it was the most prolific producer of spring salmon of any river in the United Kingdom. Double figures to one rod in a day used to be common, and my aunt Lady Joan Joicey in one short February day landed 28 salmon and 2 sea trout. Now the autumn is once again overtaking the spring.

I suppose that my most exciting day was on 13 November 1926. I had anticipated, from my knowledge of 'which way the wind blew' that the conditions would be ideal for a few hours, and that thereafter the river would rise quickly into a flood. I was therefore on the river by 7 a.m. just as it became light, and by 12 o'clock I had nine salmon averaging just under 20 lb. Sure enough, shortly afterwards, the flood came down, but it could not spoil a memorable day.

But all good things come to an end, and it was time to think of more serious affairs.

III

A beginning
in politics and Parliament

Neither at Ludgrove nor at Eton had I taken much notice of politics. The reason probably was that during most of my time at the former, and for eighteen months at the latter, the country had been at war, and for the duration domestic politics were largely put aside.

In 1914 my father had been mobilized with the Lanarkshire Yeomanry which eventually found itself drafted to Gallipoli to fight the Turks. Just before he sailed he took me down to London from Scotland for the start of the Ludgrove term. He said goodbye that night as the regiment left for Southampton the following day. I shall never forget the long night of agony in the King's Cross Station Hotel which I somehow came through; squeezed of all emotion but fear and rage at the folly to which man could descend. Week after week, as the casualty lists lengthened, it was necessary for young boys to wear a hard shell over their real feelings. Unless we had done that we would have been too vulnerable. Wartime was bad for the young. There can be times, as I have learned, when there is no escape from war, but ever since then, while I revere the patriot, I have detested the jingo tub-thumper, the narrow nationalist and the advocates and practitioners of violence.

Politics were not much in evidence in our home after the war; but I remember well two conversations at The Hirsel which made a lasting impression on me. The first occasion was when Sir Douglas

Haig said to my father, 'Mark my words, Home, the French have been bled white in two wars. They can never again be trusted as a reliable ally.' The second was when Lord Robert Cecil was campaigning on behalf of the League of Nations. With his long legs he used to slide further and further under the dining-room table, until only his hunched shoulders and large head were visible. He was speaking one night in some desperation at the slowness of people to take up the idea of the indivisibility of peace, and to establish an international peace-keeping force. 'Charlie,' he said, 'if we do not succeed in this venture we shall be in for an even more terrible war.' So did the prophets speak.

My father greatly admired Lord Grey of Fallodon, who had been Foreign Secretary in 1914. When he was becoming blind, we used to go and see him taming the birds which he loved. He would sit with infinite patience until they were brave enough to come to him for food. He told me that he could give a wild flock of wigeon from the sea the necessary confidence to nibble the grass at his feet in about twelve days. The last time I visited Fallodon he had lost his sight completely and was bed-ridden. The red squirrels used to come down the chimney to visit him, and their sooty footprints were all over the sheets.

An eccentric visitor to The Hirsel was the author and poet, Maurice Baring. One of his parlour tricks was to get off his chair and crawl round the table with a full glass of port on the top of his bald head, and then resume his seat as though nothing had happened at all.

At Eton, in my last two years, I had joined the Political Society, which staged some rather desultory debates, but invited some distinguished politicians to address it. Both there and at the Oxford Union, which went through a lean time in the years immediately following the war, I was a passive member. Many undergraduates were keenly interested, but even the keenest – although partisan – were never intolerant. Indeed we very often invited speakers to our various clubs just because they held views different from our own.

Plenty of contentious characters came to the Union or the Carlton or Canning Clubs. Lord Birkenhead and Mr Lloyd George and Mr Leo Amery amongst them. Always they were given a good hearing, and always the heckling which followed was lively and intelligent. Our feeling was that if a student could not be tolerant, who could? As the arteries harden prejudices harden too. In this respect some modern students can certainly learn from the past.

When I returned from South America to my home, a tussle started in my own mind as to what I ought to do with my life. The Hirsel and Douglas Estates were ready to hand, and my father was only too anxious to make over the general direction of them to me; indeed that was his expectation and desire. He could raise no enthusiasm about a political career for his eldest son and heir. However, I grew increasingly restive as it seemed to me that life as a farmer and country gentleman was too confined. I decided, if a constituency would select me, to stand in the election of 1929 and in the Conservative cause.

With my father I used rather unfair tactics. He had always plugged into me that it was a duty for one born with the means to be independent to undertake public service, and I argued passionately that politics were just that. He was caught in a dilemma – privately he held that the profession of politics was a dirty business and 'bunk', but he was unconvincing against the contention that, if it was rotten, people should go into it to try and improve the standard.

Anyhow when an opportunity in Coatbridge and Airdrie in Lanarkshire came along, he raised no objection to my name going forward. No doubt he calculated that I should be heavily defeated and that, following his own experience, once would be enough. He was right on the first count, but on the second he was wrong. My mother aided and abetted me, although she always saw too much of my opponent's point of view to be a partisan or even a convinced Conservative.

On the day, I was rejected by a handsome majority of 7,579 by a Mr Welsh, who was known as the 'miners' poet'. My father called him a 'good chap'.

I had gained a lot from the experience of electioneering in an area of heavy industry and high unemployment. Some of the men had been out of work for ten consecutive years, and demoralization was setting in. When the Socialists won the election, confidence evaporated and the prospect for the unemployed became even worse. I felt sure that the Conservative policies were best designed to stem the economic depression, and resolved to continue in politics.

It was then that a real piece of luck intervened, and opportunity was presented right on my Douglas doorstep. The sitting member for South Lanark retired, and I was asked whether I would stand. It was a marginal seat. Colonel Walter Elliot, a brilliant exponent of Conservatism, had held it and lost it alternately in the twenties, and, if a Conservative was to win, he had to attract a proportion of the miners' vote; for the countryside and country towns and villages could not sustain him alone. 1931 was a freak election. An economic slump of crisis proportions had hit Britain, and it was all hands to the pump. Any Conservative who stood on a National Government ticket was virtually certain to reach Westminster. My majority in a 'marginal' was around nine thousand votes. The total of Conservatives, Simonite and Samuelite Liberals and National Labour in Parliament was 552 and out of that 473 were Conservatives.

From the Socialist benches of the 1929 Parliament there came into the coalition of 1931 three figures whose defection was enough to break the Socialist Party as such. They were Ramsay MacDonald, Philip Snowden, and J. H. Thomas.

Ramsay MacDonald had been a Socialist and pacifist and a fine and inspiring fighter for the Socialist cause in the post-war years, but by 1931 he had lost his magnetism. With his height, and fine head of white hair he was still impressive, but the fire had gone out of him. He was lionized by Lady Londonderry and other fashionable London hostesses, and that his party did not like. In the House of Commons he was wont to rise from the Front Bench, and ask permission of Rt. Hon. and Hon. Gentlemen to 'think aloud'. The result was pitiful; and I resolved then and there never to inflict un-prepared or long speeches on any audience. He was in fact carried by Mr Baldwin for the last years of his political life.

Snowden was the very opposite. Small, puritanical, astringent, even acid in speech, he dominated any debate on finance and economics in which he took part; but he was ill and there were other good men in the running for Chancellor of the Exchequer. His influence was short-lived.

J. H. Thomas was a complete contrast to both; racy, ebullient, crude, but with a large heart. He helped greatly to reconcile his Labour colleagues who had crossed the floor to their unusual and as many thought, unnatural position. His language in public was lurid. He was a patriot and King George V and he got on extremely well. He had to leave politics because he was judged to have been guilty of a Budget leak. Years afterwards I met him, looking very sorry for himself on Victoria Station. He hailed me and said, 'Alec, those b—s framed me'. In every way warm-hearted, irrepressible, im-petuous, vivid, he was true to form to the end.

From the Liberal benches came Sir John Simon. Brilliant, with an ice-cold intellect, aloof, although paradoxically wanting above all to be loved. On one matter of supreme importance he served Britain well. In his view, and this was shared by the huge majority, the law as passed by Parliament was sacrosanct, and must always be obeyed unless it was changed by Parliament. In a speech, in the House of Commons, he in effect broke the General Strike of 1926 by stating unequivocally that if it continued, Trades Union Funds could under the law be distrained. In those days the law was strongly up-held by parties and people, and Sir John's word was enough.

But it was Mr Baldwin who took the honours in the 1931 Parlia-ment. He was assiduous, when Prime Minister, in his attendance in the House. Back-benchers like Ministers who stay and listen to them, and they certainly liked 'S.B.' His sympathetic treatment of Mr Lansbury who, in 1931, was left to lead a weak rump of Socialists with a vocal Left wing, forced the Opposition to be constitutional.

Baldwin did it all by kindness. He had an extraordinary habit while sitting on the Bench of making an excruciating grimace, and then planting a smacking kiss on the Order paper. The psychologists must have been hard put to it to find an explanation. A large pipe and thick country tweeds gave the image of a yeoman squire living close to the soil. It was very clever, because in fact he was at his happiest in a room, preferably facing north, with the windows shut, reading Mary Webb.

The 'Clydesiders' – the notorious trio of Maxton, Campbell Stephen, and McGovern, tried everything they knew – and they were a talented and able lot – to drive the fifty or so Labour members to the far left; but with regular stiffeners from Baldwin on the duties of Members of Parliament in a democracy, Lansbury kept control and sustained the conception of the constitutional monarchy and the role of Parliament and the sanctity of the law.

Maxton was a born parliamentarian and an artist in debate. His bark was worse than his bite. Raven-haired, sallow of complexion, with hollow cheeks and dark sombre eyes, and a voice of doom, he was the incarnation of the spirit of revolution; but he was fundamentally lazy and that was his Achilles' heel. I remember that, after a speech which I had made, he said to me in the Lobby, 'Alec, you will be my first candidate for the lamp-post when my revolution comes.' He then paused and said, 'No, I don't think that is right – I think that I would offer you a cup of tea.' He did so there and then, and we talked of cricket which was about his only 'bourgeois' weakness.

In 1931 Lloyd George – I suspect to the relief of the Coalition leaders – stayed on the Opposition benches; for while there were flashes of the old brilliance, he was by then well over the hill. He knew it, and this made him discontented with himself, and at times vitriolic about his opponents. When Sir John Simon had crossed the floor of the House, Lloyd George made a cruel attack, and he spat it out, reinforcing with the long wagging finger which he used to such dramatic effect. He said: 'I do not object in the least to the Right

Hon. and learned Gentleman changing his opinions . . . Greater men than the Right Hon. and learned Gentleman have done it in the past – some of the most honourable men in the political life of this country . . . I do object to this intolerable self-righteousness . . . They, at any rate, did not leave behind the slime of hypocrisy in passing from one side to the other.' I often think that we are squeamish in these days, for then, as far as I remember, no one turned a hair.

There were some really great parliamentarians in the House of 1931. Captain Harry Crookshank, who knew Erskine May from cover to cover. Oliver Stanley, a master of English and of debate, with as pretty and sharp a wit as any politician could command. Duff Cooper, who recited (that is the only word for it) the army estimates for two hours and ten minutes without a single note. Neville Chamberlain, the cool and efficient master of domestic politics; and, on the back benches, Winston Churchill, challenging and provocative with his impish humour always bursting through, speaking from the copious notes which he always held, ever since he had suffered a complete blank in his memory and had been forced to 'ask Mr Speaker's leave' to resume his seat. Lord Winterton who made it his business to puncture pompous political balloons. Lord Hugh Cecil, who had reduced public speaking to a fine art; as brilliant a critic as anyone could find, constantly using the unexpected word and turn of phrase which left his audience alert and asking for more. I walked into the Chamber one day towards the close of one of his speeches in which he referred to some action of Mr Baldwin's of which he disapproved. It went something like this: 'If the Rt. Hon. Gentleman persists in this foolish course, the country will have only one prospect – an endless vista of humble pies.'

My mother-in-law, Mrs Alington, used to tell a story of him out riding with Monsignor Ronald Knox and Father Ted Talbot. His horse was always well behind the others, and would stop and eat the bushes. Irritated, and beating the animal, he was heard to say, 'Why do you not keep up with my companions? Intellectually I am their equal, and socially I am their superior.' Whack – whack – whack!

I suppose that the older generation always seems to be larger than life; but before economics blunted the edges of oratory and wit there were still debating giants.

The most noteworthy performance of that Parliament was without question the piloting of the India Independence Bill through the House of Commons, by the Secretary of State, Sir Samuel Hoare, ably assisted by Mr R. A. Butler (later Lord Butler).

Sir Samuel was a dry, tight-lipped, meticulous character, with little or no sense of humour. He once invited his colleagues in the Cabinet to watch him skating solo in black tights. Against him, in command of a small but able parliamentary band, was Mr Winston Churchill; moved emotionally, because he hated the end of the British Raj; equipped with all the oratorical arts of debate, and able to switch from tears to laughter as he sensed the House's mood.

Victory came to the Government after many weeks of intensive debate, and after every kind of diversionary tactic had been deployed. That the issue was of the first rank there can be no doubt. Once India had become independent of the British Crown, the rest of the Dominions and Colonies were bound to follow. That debate was the first puff of the hurricane 'Wind of change'.

Churchill tried to enlist me and other young Conservatives to support his cause. It was one of his most endearing characteristics that he longed for people to share his enthusiasms and be in on his triumphs. He was once shooting at Blenheim and fired at a hare running wide across his front. A young man standing with him said, 'Mr Churchill, why did you shoot at that hare? – it was too far away.' 'Yes, I know,' said Churchill, 'it was, but I wished that animal to know that it had a part to play in our proceedings.'

But over India I could not 'play a part in his proceedings'. From the start of our administration of our overseas territories we had set out to train the native peoples to play their part in administration and government. From the beginning, therefore, the seeds of independence had been sown.

Like Churchill I would have wished for more time for the colonial and the dependent territories to mature and qualify for responsible government; but the Indian Army had been to Europe in the war, and had seen the 'superior persons' tearing each other apart. The Indians felt after that experience that they preferred their own culture and religion, and that they could manage their affairs at least as well if not better than us.

1917 had brought the Russian revolution. It was one of those horrible quirks of fortune that it came at a time when impatience for the emancipation of colonial territories was in the air. The Communists were thus able to pose as the champions of liberation and that gave a great boost to the militant freedom fighter. Subversion too was right up the Communist street. The pace of change was a dilemma which haunted us for many years, and of which I had a fair dose as Commonwealth Secretary in the fifties. But Africa and Asia were two different cases. The people of the African continent, apart from population in the North and in the Western bulge, were tribal wanderers with no permanent roots in the soil until late in the twentieth century. It was the white man who brought to them agriculture and so a settled life. By contrast, village democracy had worked in India for 1000 years. It had a far better chance to flourish there.

I concluded then, while it was sensible to try to gain some time, and in Africa the more time the better, the cause had to be recognized, and Indian independence had to be conceded. With the benefit of hindsight, and in spite of Mrs Gandhi's lapse into dictatorial rule, which I do not believe that the Indian will tolerate for very long, I think that Churchill was wrong, and we, the majority of the Conservatives, were right.

Under our present electoral system National Governments or Coalitions, however promising their start, have no stamina, and should not be prolonged beyond the duration of the crisis which they are designed to meet. By the time of the next election in 1935, although Mr Malcolm MacDonald, the Prime Minister's son, survived, the visible Socialist contribution to unity was threadbare by reason of natural casualties, and the rest of the 'National' candidates could be numbered on two hands; and although we had all stuck to our labels, coalition no longer carried conviction, nor was it necessary in the national interest, for the economic storm had been calmed. Once more I won South Lanark, with a smaller though decisive majority, and we embarked on a parliament which, though we did not know it, was to last over the lifetime of two normal parliaments until 1945.

We had barely settled in when the country was struck by a very different sort of crisis. It came out of the blue with the declared intention of King Edward VIII, who had lately succeeded his father, to marry Mrs Simpson, an American divorcée, and make her Queen of England. The shock to the system and the Constitution reverberated all over Britain, but went even deeper in Scotland with its strong church-going public. Churchill was a close personal friend of the King, and with his romantic temperament, and his devotion and loyalty, was ready to acquiesce in the King's desire and intention. Baldwin, who saw all the dangers, had therefore to seize the initiative before the 'pros' and 'antis' took sides in public. A 'King's Party' would have meant a divided nation, and would have done grave and perhaps fatal damage to the monarchy. There was not, therefore, much time, and there was always present the knowledge that one false move could precipitate a romantic wave of sympathy for a young man head over heels in love, and impatient of convention.

I had the opportunity to follow Baldwin's handling of the matter day by day, through a close friend who was his Parliamentary Private Secretary – Tommy Dugdale (later Lord Crathorne). It was tempting for Baldwin at his age, and having himself a model marriage, to deal with the matter as an affair of youthful infatuation; particularly as Mrs Simpson was an elegant and glamorous lady for whom anyone might temporarily fall. But to Baldwin's credit he very early recognized the signs of permanent attachment and indomitable will, and thereafter he was able to concentrate his efforts on persuading the King that, if he insisted on his private wish to marry, then he must in public duty act to preserve the throne of Britain. Every possibility was canvassed, including morganatic marriage, and there was little rest for Baldwin night or day. Never once did he put a foot wrong; and at the time I marvelled at his discretion, sensitivity and patience.

Churchill might plead for loyalty; Neville Chamberlain might be restive with what he judged to be fumbling indecision by the Prime Minister; but Baldwin knew his man's deep sense of duty to the nation, and the timing of his appeal was immaculate.

I do not believe that the throne would have survived Mrs Simpson as Queen, and still less the futile alternative of a morganatic marriage. Baldwin was right. When the history of this century is written, and the peacetime Prime Ministers weighed, I believe he will top the list in domestic achievement; and his handling of the Abdication crisis will heavily tip the balance, for he saved our constitutional monarchy. His ear was closer to the ground-roots of the feelings of ordinary men and women than any politician whom I have known.

King George VI and Queen Elizabeth, who also had roots deep in the soil, with great sacrifice and sense of public service, and a winning friendliness, gradually but surely restored confidence which had been shaken to its foundations.

1936 saw the tentative beginnings of rearmament and the preparation for a possible war. Indeed it was then with the 'Spitfire' and the 'Hurricane' on the drawing-board, and the drive of Lord Swinton behind the production programme, that the seeds of ultimate victory were sown. For a man whose energy and foresight were largely responsible for saving Britain from defeat, Lord Swinton has received remarkably little public notice. He did not suffer fools gladly, and was a somewhat irascible politician, but should a Prime Minister in the national interest require the delivery of metals or other sinews of war, he was the man who would find them at the most advantageous price, and in the required time-scale for delivery. The popular politician is not invariably the most useful.

I do not believe that we should put too much blame either on the British public or the Government of the early thirties for the rampant pacifism and dilatory rearmament and lack of realism which was the feature of those years. The demoralization, if that is the right word for it, had begun in the early twenties.

There were at that time a number of misjudgements which contributed to the feeling that after 'the war to end war' the future would be safe and fit for heroes to live in.

When my father and Winston Churchill and others who had fought through those terrible years used to talk in such language I remember feeling a fearful sense of guilt that, although I could understand the idealism, I could not share their confidence in the future. Their trust in the early 1920s was pinned on the League of Nations, but the United States had stood aside from membership, while in Russia bloody and aggressive revolution was rife. I could not escape the feeling that the world was in too imperfect a state and that hate was too rampant for us to dare to put our national security in the hands of the League.

How deeply the statesmen of the day were affected by the overwhelming desire for peace is made sufficiently plain by two facts.

The first was the adoption by the Cabinet of 1924 of what was known as the 'No war for ten years rule'. It was an assumption based no doubt on the advice of the Chiefs of Staff in so far as they could glean accurate information of the intentions of potential enemies. But it was at best an arbitrary judgement, and at worst positively misleading. The Rule was rolled on from year to year and was not abrogated until November 1933. It is impossible not to believe that the wish was father to the thought.

Reliance on the Rule led to the second fact of life in the middle twenties which with hindsight is almost incredible. Winston Churchill, as Chancellor of the Exchequer between 1924 and 1929, cut the armed forces, including his beloved navy, to the bone.

Churchill in the early thirties was the first to recover and rightly battered at governments until they rearmed, but he found it hard going, because people had become lulled into a feeling that all was well in the best of all possible worlds, and that armed strength was no longer necessary. That complacency was the fruit of the seeds of pacifism which had been sown in the early post-war years.

So while it is true that 1936 saw the Peace Ballot with its dangerously loaded questions; while it is true that the undergraduates of Oxford of that generation passed a resolution that they would not fight for King and Country; nevertheless peace at almost any price had taken root ten years earlier, so had disarmament, and so had the feeling that war might be wished away. Winston Churchill read the signs in 1935 correctly, and with the requisite sense of urgency, but if blame for unreadiness is to be apportioned then, the public and governments of the twenties, as well as the early thirties, must bear their share.

In 1936, during the lull before the storm, there had occurred the happiest event of my life when I married Elizabeth, the second daughter of my Head Master at Eton and Mrs Alington. He had left Eton to become Dean of Durham, and it was in that romantic and beautiful cathedral that we had our wedding on 3 October.

We had little recollection of each other during my school-days; but Elizabeth had become a close friend of my sister Rachel, and so we met frequently. We became engaged, having been to the 'Oaks' at Epsom together, backed the winner and won the Tote Double, and gone on to visit the gardens at Dropmore in their full glory of rhododendrons and azaleas. Certainly the conditions were auspicious.

Dr Alington had been Head Master of Shrewsbury School before going to Eton. With his intellectual powers he had a very strong influence on boys. He had a fine presence – tall, with classic features and a head of white hair, all set off in Chapel with the scarlet cassock of a Chaplain to the King. No one who heard them will ever forget his Holy Week sermons, or the Eton Fables given in Chapel at various times at Evensong during the School Year.

Mrs Alington was a truly remarkable person. She was the daughter of the fourth Lord Lyttelton – the youngest of a family of fifteen. A half-brother was Edward Lyttelton. After leaving Eton he became a Canon and he confessed that he could never walk up the nave of his cathedral without speculating whether it would take spin.

I did my best, but it was quite impossible to distinguish between the host of Lytteltons, Talbots, Clives and all the uncles and aunts and cousins who flowed in and out of The Deanery and who, with countless other guests, came away with their worries swept away by their hostess's impetuous hospitality and endless fund of humour. Her way of expressing herself was unique, and often left the listener bereft of speech from sheer incredulity and amusement.

I recall that she said of one woman who was known to be an accomplished liar: 'She has a somewhat open mind as to fact.' She wrote to her shoe-shop, 'I am faintly fussed about the nonarrival of a rather dim pair of shoes which I sent to you for repair.' Of a bad-tempered cook who was always giving notice, she wrote, 'My old thunderstorm is on a somewhat ponderous wing.'

Her sense of the ludicrous could not be kept under. Even at a time of deep personal sorrow she told me of how someone buying mourning clothes in a London store had seen a sign pointing two ways – 'To the left – deeply afflicted.' (There was nothing to be bought there but black.) 'To the right – lightly affected.' (There was to be had grey and mauve.)

When Mr Gandhi came to Eton he brought with him a Miss Slade who was never parted from him. She told my mother-in-law that she must sleep across the Mahatma's door-mat or in the dressing-room next door. 'No, my dear,' said Mrs Alington, 'not while I am a member of the Mothers' Union.' She was incomparable.

Naturally she was loved wherever she went for her warm heart and embracing sympathies. In politics she used to vote Socialist although without much conviction. Every now and then I would make headway in conversion, until one of my more right-wing contemporaries would come along and bring about a relapse. It was an endless game with only one possible result. However, I was a kind of deflector, who diverted the debate from involving the Dean who was an uncompromising Tory.

There was another personality in the household who reigned over the lively family of six with a keen eye and firmly kept everyone in their place. Nanny Shirlaw presided over 'nursery tea' every day with dignity and unquestioned mastery of any and every situation. I was looked upon by her as the authority on the Turf, and she was not above a flutter on the Classics. One Derby Day I only recalled my duty to provide her with a tip on the morning of the race. She always used to call me 'the Lord'; so I sent her a telegram, 'My Love – the Lord'. 'My Love' won at good odds, and a reply arrived at the House of Commons – 'Our love to the Lord'. No Churchman could have quarrelled with that.

Elizabeth, who would not make speeches, but never forgot a face and could always match it to the name, joined me in a political partnership which, except for my own defeat in 1945, and the period of Opposition from 1964–70 was spent almost entirely in office. Our first General Election together was a good example of the hazards of the profession of politics, and the part which each can play. She has always said that she will never marry another politician.

IV

Neville Chamberlain
and the approach of war

In the 1931 Parliament I had to make up my mind on the rôle I should adopt in the House. Curiously enough it was Lloyd George who had stimulated my maiden speech. As a lifelong Liberal he had naturally been a free-trader, but when he saw the number of unemployed approaching the three million mark he concluded that some protection from foreign competition was needed for a time, if any industrial recovery at all was to be staged. I agreed with him that a home-based market was necessary if we were to re-tool our factories for export, and when the Government brought in the 'Safeguarding of Industries Act' I decided to speak in favour of it on the Second Reading. It was doubtless a modest and simple performance, but Lloyd George was kind enough to compliment me on it, and as a beginner I was grateful.

With a very large number of Conservatives in the National Government crowding the back benches and by and large speaking in chorus, the question was how to make the best of the Parliamentary occasion. I decided to improve on my knowledge of the Government machine, and that the way to do it was to attach myself to a Minister as Parliamentary Private Secretary, in those days a fairly low form of political life, but one which took one behind the scenes.

The first to take me on was Noel Skelton, a Parliamentary Under-

Secretary at the Scottish Office. He was a man of ideas and a pioneer of the conception of a 'Property-Owning Democracy' as the basis of Conservative policy; and he wrote an attractive and convincing booklet on it. He would have gone a long way in politics had he not died in his early fifties.

During one month I was lent to the Secretary of State for Scotland – Sir Godfrey Collins (National Liberal). He said to me on one occasion, 'Young man, you are always going to your Constituency.' I replied that I was wont to go about once a fortnight, and enquired how often he visited Greenock. His reply was, 'Oh, about five times in thirty years'. He believed in the scarcity value of the politician!

I next sampled the Ministry of Labour under Colonel Muirhead. Those were exciting days, as the hideous scourge of unemployment was beginning to respond to Conservative treatment, and confidence in the currency was steadily growing. Civil Servants have the reputation of being a race apart, somewhat unfeeling and certainly unemotional. One night Colonel Muirhead entertained about two hundred of his Ministry to dinner. Mr Charles Laughton, the actor, was his guest, and was asked to say Grace. Instead he recited The Lord's Prayer. I have seldom seen any audience so deeply moved.

Finally I arrived with Mr Neville Chamberlain – just as he was moving from the Exchequer to take over as Prime Minister from Mr Baldwin.

What sort of person was this man around whom so much controversy has raged? He was without question a fully-equipped politician, and by any standard a first-rank Minister and administrator. No one could gainsay his success in the fields of Local Government, Health and Finance. Most of his Cabinet colleagues would have admitted that for efficiency, method and intellectual grasp of policy he was head and shoulders above the rest.

He was by no means easy to get to know. One of the tasks of a PPS is to help his Minister to keep in touch with back-benchers in Parliament, and to do this adequately he must be able to give to his chief the feel of the House, which is always a somewhat intangible mixture of conflicting and complementary emotions. Chamberlain had little time to spare for such gossip, and when I used to go in for a general talk to convey impressions of the Party's feelings, he would look up with his pen poised and say, 'What do you want?' – not the most encouraging start to an informal conversation. To lure him into the smoking-room in the House was like catching the wariest bird, and any meetings so arranged stilted and artificial, and he would escape at the first possible excuse. His abrupt manner was not rudeness but shyness. Being less favoured in the family than his half-brother Austen, who was early marked down for success in politics, he had been sent as a young man to manage a plantation in the West Indies, where he was for seven years the sole white man among the natives. Ever afterwards, in spite of Mrs Chamberlain who revelled in the social side of life, and apart from his contacts with a small band of intimate colleagues, he was an essentially solitary man.

When he did unbend he was a fascinating companion, for in the lonely years he had taught himself everything there was to know about birds and butterflies and flowers; and his observations of them were accurate and scientific and his enthusiasm infectious. Music, too, was one of his delights. Fishing and shooting were hobbies which he enjoyed, and he had made himself a good practitioner at both.

But all this attractive and endearing side of his personality was almost deliberately concealed, and the public saw only the forbidding exterior, the dark clothes, the stick-up collar, and the black hat and umbrella of the Whitehall world. The general picture of a grey man was wide of the mark, although admittedly one of the tasks of the PPS and his other secretaries was tactfully to drop his jokes from the text of his speeches. His shyness made him reticent to the point of being secretive – a habit which was soon to bring trouble in his dealings with his Foreign Secretary.

When Mr Baldwin left office there was no question who the successor would be. Chamberlain was the clear heir-apparent, and was welcome to the Conservative Party, as he had proved himself in domestic politics in high office, and in particular his recent conduct of the Exchequer had gained wide approval.

I recall that his attitude in the early days at No. 10 Downing Street was one of confidence. He had become very impatient with Baldwin, and felt that he had in latter years lost grip, in particular of foreign affairs. It was true that Baldwin was not at ease with foreigners. He would even go to considerable lengths not to sit next to one at meals if he could possibly avoid it. Chamberlain meant to change all that; and soon after he took over, he told me how happy he was to have Anthony Eden at the Foreign Office; not only because of his diplomatic skill, but because he was someone with whom he was confident that he could work. Events were to confound that optimism, but at the time he foresaw a fruitful partnership.

He took an early opportunity provided by the traditional luncheon given to the new leader by the 1922 Committee of Conservative back-benchers, to outline his hopes for lessening the tensions in Europe. His theme was positive action for peace, and his analysis was broadly this. In recent years there had been too much drift; it might be too late to arrest the militant attitude of Germany, but he would exploit every means of doing so; with purpose and tact Italy could be detached from the Berlin Axis, for she was an unnatural ally of the German nationalists. The latter achievement in itself would be a contribution to stability, and in any event was a proper strategic objective in the context of either peace or war.

Chamberlain, although he had very little knowledge of the diplomatic machine, had nevertheless a very clear picture in his mind of the aims in the field of foreign and defence policy which he wished to achieve. He proceeded, accordingly, to cultivate and work upon the Duce – Signor Mussolini.

There was no love lost between Italy and Germany. Here, therefore, was an opening which could possibly be played to Britain's advantage.

In view of the criticisms of the policy of 'appeasement' which were later heaped upon Chamberlain, it is worthwhile to recall that Italy did not in fact enter the war until the fall of France was imminent, and Mussolini, if he was to gain any credit or booty, felt that he could no longer remain neutral. The question therefore may properly be asked, 'Would Italy have come into the war at all if France had stayed in the fight?' The answer may easily be 'No', in which case this part of Chamberlain's policy could well have been justified, for the neutrality of Italy would have altered the whole course of the war. Few, if any, foresaw the collapse of France, although Chamberlain himself was apprehensive, having the lowest opinion of the French politicians and the Generals, and of Gamelin, the Commander-in-Chief, in particular. He was, before anyone else became alert, fearful of the morale of the French army. He was right.

There were other calculations present in Chamberlain's mind in his attempt to wean Germany and Italy away from war. He had the liveliest apprehension concerning the expansionist intentions of the Russian Communists. If Germany were to provoke war, and if it was to last for any length of time, he foresaw the weakening of Western Europe to a point where the temptation to Soviet Russia to walk into Central Europe would be irresistible. He saw the Communist doctrine of the inevitability of conflict and ultimate victory for their cause over all the rest as the constant and increasing threat to the free peoples.

Events have proved him to be right. Europe has only survived the post-war years by reason of the collective security alliance of NATO backed by the nuclear power of the United States.

Did Chamberlain, while seeking reconciliation with Italy and Germany, fail to pursue rearmament with sufficient vigour? On the credit side it has to be remembered that he and Lord Swinton saw the absolute importance of air defence in any future war. The fighter planes, which they had authorized, which enabled Britain to survive, were only just in time. They were decisive in victory.

On the debit side of the ledger, I feel that the charge of lack of urgency is valid. No one, for example, who was really apprehensive that war could come in a year or two, would have kept Sir Thomas Inskip to co-ordinate defence at that particular moment. Admirable man as he was in many ways, his appointment had been an anti-climax which none could miss. Chamberlain explained this action as one designed not to provoke; but to Ribbentrop, the German Ambassador in London, and to the German hierarchy, it smacked of lack of determination almost amounting to lack of nerve. I have already written of the disarmament of the twenties which was drastic to the point of reducing our forces below the level of safety; of Churchill's acquiescence in the 'No war for ten years rule'; and of the mood of pacifism which overtook the country, and which culminated as late as 1936 in the Peace Ballot. When Chamberlain inherited the office of Prime Minister, it was not easy to rearm, and to bring the public to the point where they would support the Government in doing so.

Churchill was the first to see the danger and to preach the need for rapid rearmament with eloquence and passion. Almost alone he read the signs in Nazi Germany aright. But, in the early thirties it was his and the country's misfortune that his performance in the field of domestic politics had so often been revealed to be wrong. He had been in error about the re-introduction of the gold standard; he had been wrong in the view of the majority over India's independence; and he had emphatically misjudged the public mood over the abdication of King Edward VIII.

So, tragically, he could not catch the public ear in time. Nor was Chamberlain totally convinced of Churchill's judgement on the time-scale for rearmament until very late in the day. They mistrusted each other for too long, although when the crunch came, they worked together most effectively and with a solid will for victory.

When does an attempt to achieve reconciliation – necessary as it is before a democracy can be brought to fight – become appeasement? My own opinion is that the only time when Hitler could have been stopped was if the Allies had been ready to halt him when he re-occupied the Rhineland in 1936, and that thereafter hope was forlorn. Nevertheless the attempt to divert him from war had to be made. The personal contacts with the Führer at Berchtesgaden and Munich were the last flings of desperation, and, in retrospect, had little chance of success. They were judged in the immediate post-mortem to smack of appeasement. But nowadays in an emergency, statesmen hustle to meet, and in every international crisis such activity is commonplace. I doubt if anyone can seriously argue that Chamberlain's journeys were wrong; for time gained gives to reasonable men the opportunity for reasonable compromise.

But in the Britain of 1938 Chamberlain was acting from weakness and that invites the charge of appeasement.

There was, in fact, nothing on which to build a convincing policy. Co-operation with the French was in disarray; it was France, not Britain, who had run away from an obligation to the Czechs; Russia was playing her own game and keeping the cards close to her chest; America was not ready for intervention; the Commonwealth was not prepared for conflict, and our armed forces were at a low level, while our air defences against invasion were nil.

From Munich therefore I learned the lessons, first, never to go into a negotiation in a state of weakness – it is better to let events take their course; second, never to allow a military alliance to fall into disrepair.

It has often been said that Hitler duped Chamberlain. That is not so. He told me at Munich that Hitler was without question the most detestable and bigoted man with whom it had been his lot to try to do business. Before and since political leaders have had to deal with unpleasant and unscrupulous people; and that is no excuse for throwing in the towel when peace is the prize for which one plays.

Chamberlain's fault, which it must be said was shared by many who were wise after the event, was not to recognize that Hitler was mad – not in the ordinary sense of the word, but in the sense that he was determined to assert his domination by war. There was a reasonable way forward for Germany on any reckoning other than that of her leader being punch-drunk with power.

Germany was strong and sitting pretty. The whole of the Danube basin was economically within her sphere of influence. There was a strong pro-German element in the Ukraine which asked for nothing better than closer association with the Fatherland. All in all, Hitler's ambitions could have been gained without war, and Germany would have been the strongest power in Europe, with her word carrying authority far and wide outside her borders.

Chamberlain's dealings throughout his life had been with men who were capable of being convinced by argument and converted to different policies by persuasion. He got so far as to realize that he was up against a really detestable character, but he failed to recognize that Hitler was possessed by a driving devil whose appetite could only be satisfied by blood.

I did not go with Chamberlain to Berchtesgaden, but I was in my place in the House when, in the last moments of his speech dealing with the critical nature of the situation, the message arrived from Hitler with the invitation to Munich. It was passed to me from the official gallery on the right of the Speaker's Chair. I could not get directly at Chamberlain across the back of the Front Bench, so I handed the note to Sir John Simon. He took a second or two to absorb it and handed it on to the Prime Minister just before he sat down. The scene that followed was one of high drama, and virtually the whole House rose in relief and acclamation. There were a lot of 'appeasers' in Parliament that day.

Chamberlain took me to the last meeting in Munich. On the way out he described his effort as a last throw, but told me that he could not see how it could pay Hitler to push things to the point of war.

The sacrifice of Czechoslovakia in the name of the chance of wider peace was a loathsome business from which none could draw credit and in which none could find satisfaction.

France having failed to honour her engagement to support the Czechs, Britain could scarcely be expected to take the burden on her shoulders alone, but Chamberlain, by his forward policies in the interest of compromise, took the blame very largely on himself and his country.

For those of us at Munich who were not in the Conference Room, the day's proceedings were dull as we kicked our heels in the Delegation Room. I had a short and uninteresting talk with General Keitel, and watched as Goering changed his uniform three times during the day. He was the only one who seemed to be in boisterous good spirits throughout the proceedings.

Mussolini strutted about with his chin in the air – a habit which he exaggerated to conceal an unsightly carbuncle on the top of his head, and was clearly preoccupied and afraid. I noticed that the German rank and file treated the Italians with open contempt.

Chamberlain's actions following the agreement with Hitler and his talk with him the next morning certainly gave currency to the charge of gullibility, but that particular accusation was unjust.

At breakfast on the morning of our return to England Chamberlain produced a bit of paper on which he had drafted a statement declaring that in future disputes Britain and Germany would settle all matters by peaceful means. This action was deliberate, because he intended from the first, if Hitler should put his name to it, to give it the maximum publicity on his return to England. He argued that if Hitler signed it and kept the bargain well and good; alternatively that if he broke it, he would demonstrate to all the world that he was totally cynical and untrustworthy, and that this would have its value in mobilizing public opinion against him, particularly in America.

For what it was worth he took the draft to the meeting. Hitler was in a sullen, unresponsive mood that morning, and I was unsure whether Chamberlain would risk the rebuff which was likely. However he decided to present the paper, and I was watching Hitler closely when he did so. He gave the text one quick reading and almost perfunctorily he signed. It was somewhat reminiscent of the previous attitude of Germany's leaders to scraps of paper.

There is only one further impression of the Führer which I took away. Twice I saw him walking down a passage ahead of me. I noticed that his arms hung low, almost to his knees, and that they swung not alternately but in unison. I do not know whether this was characteristic of his walk when alone and in deep thought, but it gave him a curiously animal appearance.

The 'declaration' was duly given the planned publicity on Chamberlain's return to Northolt Airport. On balance it would probably have been worth while, but for another event which was to take place within the hour.

On our return to London, Downing Street was packed with people waiting to acclaim the Munich achievement. I was with Chamberlain as we approached the foot of the staircase in No. 10, where Cabinet colleagues and others were assembled. Out of the crowd someone said, 'Neville, go up to the window and repeat history by saying "Peace in our time".' I could not identify the voice but Chamberlain turned rather icily towards the speaker, and said, 'No, I do not do that kind of thing.' He was right, because by nature he was the most reticent and the least flamboyant of men. I then lost touch with him on the staircase, and the next thing I knew was that he had spoken the fateful words. Somebody in the last few yards to the window must have overtaken and over-persuaded him. He knew at once that it was a mistake, and that he could not justify the claim. It haunted him for the rest of his life.

Winston Churchill declared in ringing terms that Munich was a national humiliation, and it is hard to gainsay him. But could Chamberlain or indeed any other, have taken Britain united into war in September 1938? I share the view of Lord Balfour of Inchrye who wrote in his book *Wings over Britain*: 'So far as the air is concerned there can be no doubt that the breathing space saved Britain.' In the House of Commons in September 1938 Churchill said, 'England has been offered a choice between war and shame. She has chosen shame and will get war.' True, we got war; but also final victory, whereas war in 1938 would have meant not victory but defeat.

There have been many post-mortems on Munich, and it is too soon to add another; yet there are one or two judgements which can be reached and lessons which can usefully be learnt from the immediate pre-war years to guide us in the conduct of foreign affairs.

The first – the need at all times to keep on intimate terms with the United States. They were no more ready than we were in 1938 or 1939 to enter a war. We ought to have learned the lesson from the 1914–18 war that it would take the United States, Britain and France to win a war against an aggressive Germany. Nothing less would do.

The last-minute offer of President Roosevelt to call a Conference to discuss the situation in Europe was far too late, but nevertheless it should have been accepted.

America was not neglected, but there was not, and had not been for some time, that degree of warmth and intimacy which should always be maintained between the leaders of the greatest of the English-speaking peoples.

There has been a lot of criticism of the handling of our diplomacy in relation to the Russians. Clearly it is a matter of judgement, but I do not believe that if Eden or Chamberlain had at that time visited Moscow that it would have modified their policies by one iota.

It suited the Kremlin's book that the strong capitalist countries of Western Europe should be at each other's throats. Germany would be weakened, and Britain and France would be forced to dissipate a lot of wealth.

The Ribbentrop/Molotov pact with Germany was an insurance policy which bought time for them to see which way to jump. Like everyone else, they underestimated the huge strength of the German war machine.

Now that Germany is in NATO and it is Russia who is the potential aggressor, the closest relation between Western Europe and the United States is still the minimum which is necessary to deter or to defeat aggression.

Even more dangerous on the approach to war was the rift which gradually became a yawning gap between the Foreign Secretary and the Prime Minister, and between the Foreign Office and No. 10 Downing Street.

Chamberlain, as I have recorded, started with a prejudice in favour of Eden, and they ought to have been able to work together, for the one was a professional student of foreign affairs, and a popular and natural diplomat; while the other was a man who had a passionate wish to help to lead the world into the ways of peace.

But Eden was a man of temperament who lived on his nerves; while Chamberlain did not know the meaning of either. Eden – the embodiment of the man of principle; Chamberlain – the pragmatic operator who would break out of conventional diplomacy if he thought that unorthodox methods would gain the end.

Their principal official advisers also were two strongly contrasting characters. Sir Robert Vansittart – the professional diplomat at the head of the Foreign Office; and Sir Horace Wilson – who had been brought into No. 10, and whose career had been spent in the field of industrial conciliation. Sir Robert – acutely aware that villainy was part of the international scene; Sir Horace – accustomed to deal with men who were reasonable.

It is useless to complain when a Prime Minister decides to take an interest in and to play an active part in foreign affairs. He is the First Minister of the Crown, and ultimately responsible for everything from domestic drains to peace and war. It is useless, too, resenting the choice by a Prime Minister of a confidant who acquires a position of intimacy with him. Examples are numerous. Mr Baldwin took to No. 10 Mr Tom Jones. Chamberlain – Sir Horace Wilson. Churchill – Professor Lindemann, and so on. The office of Prime Minister is a solitary tenancy and it is natural to choose someone of trust to be always on call and to ease the burden with advice and company.

Eden was from the start worried by the Prime Minister's personal approaches to Mussolini in pursuit of his policy of detaching Italy from the Berlin Axis. In particular he resented the use of Chamberlain's sister to convey and to receive messages. He suspected (and rightly) that Chamberlain, pursuing his own line of thought and policy of which Eden was known to be suspicious, did not convey all the information which he gleaned to the Foreign Secretary or to the Foreign Office.

Sir Robert Vansittart shared all Eden's doubts and more, believing that only a policy of open denunciation of Hitler, and rapid rearmament and a posture of strength, would halt Nazi Germany in her tracks.

The feud grew, and to make matters worse, partisan groups began to be formed in Parliament which did nothing but fan the flames. There was an 'Eden group' consisting of Leo Amery, Duff Cooper, Lord Wolmer, Harold Macmillan, Ronnie Tree, Sir Edward Spears, Paul Emrys-Evans and others. There was also a 'Churchill group' of which Duncan Sandys, Brendan Bracken, Robert Boothby and a few more were members.

My particular friend in the 'Eden camp' was Mr J. P. L. Thomas, MP, who was then PPS to Eden, and between us we used to try some appeasement on our own. But it became an increasingly fruitless exercise, finally ending with my telling Chamberlain that for the sake of the Government and Party he must make a real effort to reach an understanding with the Foreign Secretary on the direction of the Government's foreign policy in relation to the Axis powers. He agreed, but when Eden came to the talk in Chamberlain's room in the House he had a cold, and looked ill and depressed. Chamberlain interrupted the conversation early on, told Eden that he was not himself, that what he needed was bed with two aspirins and that they could talk more profitably in the morning. That was that.

Herbert van Thal rightly records in his book *The Prime Ministers* that Eden's resignation had in fact nothing to do with Hitler, but with the Conservative Government's attitude to Mussolini. But it is useless to apportion blame. Chamberlain ought to have been more open with Eden over his Italian dealings, but Eden ought to have recognized that they could make sense. Had he done so Chamberlain would not have been so secretive. Chamberlain ought not to have used Sir Horace Wilson on diplomatic missions to the exclusion of some of those in the Foreign Office who were professionally trained to interpret European affairs. But the real truth is that the principals ought never to have allowed themselves to fall out in this critical area of public affairs.

So deep an impression did the tragedy of it make on me that when I was Foreign Secretary I arranged with Mr Macmillan that he and I would meet, apart from sessions of the Cabinet, almost every day to make sure that our thinking on policy was on exactly the same lines. As Prime Minister I made a point of doing the same when Mr R. A. Butler was at the Foreign Office in 1963-4, and again when I returned as Foreign and Commonwealth Secretary with Mr Heath as Prime Minister in 1970.

It is a habit which future occupants of these offices would do well to make a rule; for the consequences of discord are dire.

After Munich there was in reality no chance of preventing war. The demand for a corridor to Danzig was but the last of a series of territorial demands, which had become more and more outrageous, and more and more revealing of Hitler's intention to pick a quarrel and to fight.

In the last week of September 1938 Neville and his wife came to stay with us at The Hirsel. The idea was that it would help him to rest after Munich and to shed some of his cares. He shot some partridges and fished occasionally, but he was off-colour and pre-occupied. Mrs Chamberlain was even more on edge. It was my business to deal with the Prime Minister's letters, but those from his sister always went to him unopened. We were off to shoot pigeons, and I shoved one of her letters into my pocket and forgot all about it. When Mrs Chamberlain later asked me if I had seen a letter from his sister, I pulled it from my pocket – unopened it is true – but by then covered with blood and feathers. She was not pleased, but he was unmoved.

We then returned to another session of Parliament, but the foreboding of disaster was so strong that nobody could behave normally, and tempers showed themselves as badly frayed. Chamberlain and his colleagues were on the defensive. The Socialist Opposition irresponsibly sought to refuse supply for armaments, and even at the last moment voted against conscription. Within the Conservative ranks criticism was rising. Parliament was an unhappy and frustrated place.

The actual declaration of war on 3 September 1939 was received by a House of Commons which had been so saturated with crises, that when the die was cast there was almost relief.

At midnight of that day I stood with Chips Channon on the steps of No. 10 when the thunder roared, the heavens opened, and a deluge of rain came down. I remember that almost simultaneously the words came to us that this was the Gods weeping for the folly of man.

Some time in the early hours of the next morning there was a siren alarm, and we all trooped down to the basement of No. 10, the Prime Minister in half-change, Mrs Chamberlain in a dressing-gown with her hair down her back; and the secretaries and the rest of us in various stages of undress. After half an hour or so the 'all-clear' sounded, but not before Lord Hankey, the late Secretary to the Cabinet who had become Minister without Portfolio, had come into the shelter fully dressed with a rolled-up umbrella and bowler hat! It was the end of peace and the start of the 'phony' war.

In December 1939 Chamberlain visited the troops in their stations on the European Front; and then had a look at the Maginot Line on the way to a meeting in Paris with the French Government and High Command. I went with him.

Our soldiers were anxious about the pace of mobilization and supplies of equipment coming from home, and worried by the obvious lack of air support.

Mr Hore-Belisha, although a clever man, was miscast as Secretary of State for War, and there was little faith in him. But of most concern was the state of morale of the French army. It was judged by our generals to be at rock-bottom.

The Maginot Line was a miracle of mechanical ingenuity. Immune from bombardment from air or land, it was a honeycomb of gunsites bringing to bear heavy crossfire on every possible area of advance. No direct attack on it could have succeeded. But there were two fatal flaws. The mentality which went into its construction had been purely defensive. While so long as there was 100 miles of gap between it and the sea, the fortification could be outflanked. The officers and ordinary ranks manning it seemed to me to be a scruffy lot.

The War Council was in effect a monologue from General Gamelin, to whom Monsieur Paul Reynaud passed the buck. His exposition did nothing to enhance his reputation in Chamberlain's eyes. Monsieur Daladier was more explicit and robust, but was ill at ease, and seemed displeased at the messages which kept flowing in from the ante-room to Reynaud. Later we learned that they were from his mistress Madame des Portes, who at that time seldom let Reynaud out of her sight and control. She was notoriously defeatist.

In 1939 Churchill had returned to the Government. Chamberlain, with the support of the majority of the Conservative Party, felt that he should remain as Prime Minister, and that with Churchill back at the Admiralty the war effort would be efficiently controlled and imaginatively and professionally conducted.

Chamberlain had always been disliked by the Socialist Opposition, for he had a cutting tongue in debate, and never spared them. Nevertheless he persuaded himself that given time they would serve under him and that he was, in the grave national emergency, entitled to the support of all parties. He had underestimated their obstinacy and the parties stayed apart.

It is probable that such a division within Parliament could not have continued very long in any case, but matters were brought to a head by the German invasion of Norway.

On a number of occasions the Cabinet had considered a plan to pre-empt a German invasion of Scandinavia and prevent them gaining possession of the Swedish resources of iron-ore. There were differences of opinion, and the plan was modified and postponed. Everyone was on edge.

Inadvertently Chamberlain at that critical time gave a hostage to fortune. On 4 April he made a speech in which he used the sentence in the context of the 'phony' war – 'Hitler has missed the bus'. Within five days Hitler had struck at Norway, and the Government and Churchill had launched the expedition to seize Trondheim. The tone of that speech was in such stark contrast to the reality that the phrase jarred and when the Expeditionary Force failed in its objective and had to be withdrawn it stuck in the throat. There was bound to be a post-mortem, and on 7 and 8 May a debate was held in the House of Commons which was in a sober and sombre mood.

Churchill's defence of the Norway expedition in Parliament was brilliant. He loyally defended the Government's action and the Prime Minister, but the better he did the more he established his claim as the man best equipped to lead in war.

As the debate proceeded drama began to intrude. Sir Roger Keyes, dressed in the uniform of an Admiral of the Fleet, made an impassioned speech in favour of more urgent conduct of the war. But the most damaging blow to Chamberlain came from Leo Amery – a lifelong friend and colleague of the Prime Minister who in pent-up fury spat out the words with which Cromwell dismissed the Long Parliament, and pointing directly at Chamberlain, shouted 'In the name of God – Go!' That was a dagger in the heart. Faced with the disillusion of many on his own side, and with the Socialists chanting the refrain 'missed the bus' it is not surprising that Chamberlain's final speech for the Government was not one of his best. He appealed for support from his friends in the House, and made the tactical error of adding – 'and I have some'.

Herbert Morrison, a wily parliamentary tactician, forced an adjournment vote. The Government won, but a majority of 80 was not sufficient in the adverse political climate.

On 9 May, Captain Margesson, the Government Chief Whip, felt bound to report to Chamberlain that he could no longer command the support of a majority in the Conservative Party. For a short time Chamberlain felt that he might be able to save the situation at the eleventh hour by persuading the Socialists to serve. By the next day – 10 May – the need for a National Government and a united country had become imperative by reason of Germany's invasion of the Low Countries, and a change in the office of Prime Minister was seen to be unavoidable. On the same day Mr Attlee made it clear that the Socialists would not serve under Chamberlain.

Who then was the Prime Minister and national leader to be? Lord Halifax was favoured by many and the Socialists would have served under him. He was the personal choice of Mr Attlee. But Halifax knew that his qualities were not those of a war leader, and he firmly killed the idea.

So Churchill it was, and his own destiny and that of his country came together as one.

Chamberlain's last act as Prime Minister was a dignified and moving broadcast to the nation, and the theme was national unity. Politics do not spare those who make mistakes or those for whom the luck does not run.

With deep regret that his efforts to save the peace had failed, but without rancour, Chamberlain surrendered the office of Prime Minister, and with all his remaining strength settled down to serve the new Prime Minister and his country in the cause of the defeat of tyranny.

V

A declaration of faith

There comes a moment when one has to confess one's faith, and perhaps this is the right place to do so, for testing trials were ahead.

From my earliest years I had had my mother's and my father's teaching on Christianity on which to rely. It was a good introduction, for she was more concerned with God and individual salvation, while my father applied in his own life Christ's teaching on the duty of man to man.

At Ludgrove religious worship was a routine like any other lesson, and little attempt was made to stimulate a boy's imagination. Every Sunday we went to Church in a crocodile march, and Matins seemed to be made as dull as it could possibly be. Not that routine is necessarily a bad thing in the context of religious observance. I remember a sermon on 'Habit' preached by Archbishop Lang, and his conclusion that it was far better than nothing, because attendance at Church always left the door open, and with it the chance that from presence at communal worship a seed might drop which would ripen into fuller understanding of the message of Christianity. At the very least it was a discipline.

But that did not happen at Ludgrove, and the average boy can only have come away with the impression that the Christian religion was at best lifeless and dull, and at worst fearful and forbidding.

At Eton Dr Alington changed all that in many sermons and lessons especially directed to schoolboys. He talked as an historian with a complete knowledge of the life and times of Christ, and convinced many a doubter by the weight of the historical facts, while at the same time he avoided trying to prove too much, and admitted that to be a Christian was an act of faith. He would recognize that evil was a strong force, but he did not lecture us on sin. The effect of his teaching on boys was the message that Christianity was an exacting but a happy religion. He dispelled the dullness and the sense of hopelessness which inevitably derives from a teaching of the Scriptures which concentrates on little but damnation for the sinful. He was holy without being too doctrinal and dogmatic.

Another who, many years later, influenced my thinking, was Billy Graham, the American evangelist. Like Dr Alington, he spread the joy and hope in Christianity. I cannot say that I was particularly attracted by the spectacular stage-management of his Christian circus, but he got results.

I asked Dr Ramsey, the Archbishop of Canterbury, how he felt about the techniques employed, and he replied that all he could say was that after each of Dr Graham's campaigns in Britain there was a significant number of individuals who joined the Anglican ministry.

At one meeting which he held while I was visiting Rhodesia thousands had collected to hear him. He used words of one or two syllables and the plain simplicity of his message certainly reached the huge audience. It was a brilliant exposition and an unforgettable experience.

I once said to him that the one thing which made me doubt the omniscience of the Almighty was the extraordinary places in which he put oil. (This was before the North Sea strikes.) His answer was, 'How could He have known that the British would be so foolish as to give up their Empire?'

On another occasion when he had literally hacked his way round St Andrew's golf-course, I said, 'I didn't know that you played golf.' 'Oh yes,' he said, 'how else could I swear?' I shall always treasure his friendship and example.

For many years I was content to accept Christianity at second hand, although when I was ill and once or twice looked over the edge into eternity, I began to concentrate my mind. It was then that I finally became convinced that there must be a God, and that if that were so the Christian interpretation of His nature was difficult but not impossible.

I was, and am, impatient of the muddle and confusion and division which the Churches have made of the simple message of Christ, but then man has a habit of creating his own troubles.

In 1946 I was asked to speak at a seminar in Edinburgh with, amongst others, Miss Barbara Ward (now Lady Jackson) and our subject was 'Why I believe in God'. I took the opportunity to clarify my thought. I remember that I opened by asking why, if the conclusion of all our forebears had been that God was incomprehensible, we should continue these rather pathetic enquiries? To that there seems to be only one satisfactory answer. Man is incurably inquisitive, and always trying to discover the origin of things, and the truth of the meaning of life on earth. In his mind ultimate truth and God are inseparable. It seemed to me that if the existence of God was questioned, the onus of proof lay on the challenger, and I said: 'In this matter where so much is speculation, it is fair to take the offensive and to ask "What plausible alternative is there to God as the Creator of the world? Could the earth, and not only the earth but the universe, have arrived by a chance combination of temperatures acting upon inanimate matter? Could a series of chemical reactions have produced the ordered evolution which the scientist and geologists can trace through the ages, and the cause and effect which each of us sees in operation in our daily lives?" It is possible, but even if the sun and its satellites had been the sum total of creation, the probabilities would seem to lie with the presence of a controlling and directing power.'

But the essence of the matter seemed to crystallize in the existence of life and in particular the life of a man who could think for himself, who could modify the work of nature and was indeed in some senses a creator in his own right.

I put the problem of the sowing of the seed of life in the form of a question. 'Is it possible that matter which was formless and inanimate stimulated its own reactions of form and life? – that the earth, so to speak, tired of its passivity, created its own audience? It is possible, although the scientists have established no such theory. But if, having surveyed the whole range of life, I have to choose between some such theory and the existence of a master-mind, then I hold that the probabilities lie with a creator and controller; with a Supreme Being, with a God. Each man can only speak for himself, but of the two theories the last is the lesser strain on my credulity.'

In short I concluded that the complex ordering of nature which included man could not be the work of chance. That proposition seemed to be even harder to believe than a universe the ordering of which was in the hands of a creator conscious of what he was doing.

But the problem of the purpose of life remained, and I went on: 'Of course a world of shapeless matter and even of primitive forms of life with instincts but with no reason could have been the work of either a God or a devil. For if God was responsible for creation we must take the bad with the good. "All things bright and beautiful, all creatures great and small; all things wise and wonderful, the Lord God made them all." On my premise all that is true, but if there is joy in nature, there is sorrow; if pleasure, pain; if trust, treachery; if love, hatred. Perhaps you will tell me that pain came into the world with the fall of man, but the cobra paralysed its victim before man came into the Garden of Eden, before the serpent tempted Eve.'

In my own mind I have never seen a satisfactory explanation of the existence of cruelty in a creation the purpose of which was benevolent.

The animal world before the creation of man was not bothered by a conscience. When man was equipped with a mind it would have been meaningless but for the gift of choice. How else could he exercise free will? If creation had stopped short with the animals it would have been a dead end; for the cow does not know that its milk is the food of man, and the swallow which nests peacefully at The Hirsel does not know that he is to spend the winter with President Amin. 'Poor things,' we say, 'they have no mind.'

It is when I probe the mind of man that I find the first promise of a divine purpose in creation, for the mind brings to man the gift of choice which the animals can never know, and with it original thought and the power of creation, for no shackles can limit his flights of fancy, which may one day become a part of reality. Unlike the lion, man need not eat his neighbour – he can choose between good and evil.

In the Edinburgh seminar I put it like this: 'The existence of a Lord of creation working through the minds of men answers much of the persistent craving in the hearts of the human race, but of course we seek for more.' We look for the whole truth.

I am not sure that, in the absence of the complete truth, I do ask for very much more; for if it is a fact (and Dr Alington convinced me that it is) that Christ was God's personal messenger to man, then the gap which has to be bridged by faith is much less daunting.

It is my mind which will decide whether I take the path of good or evil, the road to heaven or hell, while, as I understand His teaching, His mercy is always there to give me the benefit of any reasonable doubt.

So man has the gifts of mind and choice and I went on: 'If sometimes he chooses to exercise his choice on the side of evil, is his Creator to be blamed? And again, have we not concentrated too much on the existence of evil and too little on the existence of good? Granted that man in time is not far from his animal origin, is it not less surprising that he reverts to animal habits, than that there is in him such abundance of goodness? Love, kindness, sympathy – all these man shows, and they are certainly no part of his animal inheritance. Whence, then, do they come? Truth, beauty, art – all these men seek. Why do they do so, and how do they judge perfection in these things except by a standard laid down by an absolute authority?'

Is it possible that the mind of man will wither and die? I was happy in Miss Barbara Ward's presence, because it showed that intellect (hers) and instinct (mine) could arrive at the same conclusions. She said something of the impact of the first Christian message which I shall not forget. She pointed out that the Romans, even though they were a part of an all-powerful Empire, felt that they were tied to a 'melancholy' wheel. She proceeded: 'Into that society the message of Christianity came like a thunderbolt, but it did not come like a thunderbolt because Christ said "be good and love your neighbour" – everyone had been telling the people to do that for the previous thousand years; the thing about Christianity which gave them this extraordinary sense of relief and power was the news of the Resurrection, that God had become man and had given man the power to break away from the wheel to which sin bound him. They were no longer being told to be good. They were receiving the power to be Sons of God.'

That made good an omission, because I had said little of individual salvation and life in the world to come. I concluded: 'And so, although there are gaps which only faith can bridge, I believe in God the Maker of heaven and earth, and in God the Maker of man, the Giver of man's mind, and I believe in a Christian God Who sent Christ into the world to give man the promise that the purpose of creation was Good.'

I have interspersed these quotations with a modern commentary because I was anxious to see whether an interval of thirty years and a greater maturity of judgement have perceptibly changed my reasoning. I am well aware that a theologian will be appalled by the naïvety of my approach, and the doctrinaire outraged by the lack of interest in the forms of religion as practised by the Churches.

There I am unrepentant, as I believe that men have made unbelievably heavy weather of the message of Christ.

But one emphasis I have changed. Most of my life my weak

witness of Christianity has lain in the belief that if one took the trouble to get to know and be tolerant of one's earthly neighbour that one would more easily know one's God. In an article in a Sunday paper I unwisely expressed this sentiment, only to find that my Bishop came down on me like a ton of bricks. He insisted that I had stood Christianity on its head, and that one could only really love one's neighbour when one had come to know one's God. I felt and feel bound to plead guilty, but I closed the correspondence slightly unfairly by asserting that nevertheless if there was a better code for life on earth than the Christian teaching I did not know it.

At any rate I have in my profession and in my work and play – in fair weather and foul – found myself happier and more relaxed and more confident by reason of faith in God. And a set of positive values is certainly useful when trying to decide in terms of my father's exhortation – what effect my action would have on the other fellow.

If I had to take my discs to a desert island, they would include the 23rd Psalm – 'The Lord's my Shepherd', Scottish version to Crimond's tune – and Hymn 152, Ancient and Modern.

Come down, O Love Divine,
Seek Thou this soul of mine,
And visit it with Thine own ardour glowing;
O Comforter, draw near,
Within my heart appear,
And kindle it, Thy holy flame bestowing.

O let it freely burn,
Till earthly passions turn
To dust and ashes, in its heat consuming;
And let Thy glorious light
Shine ever on my sight,
And clothe me round, the whole my path illuming.

Let holy charity
Mine outward vesture be,
And lowliness become mine inner clothing;
True lowliness of heart,
Which takes the humbler part,
And o'er its own shortcomings weeps with loathing.

And so the yearning strong,
With which the soul will long,
Shall far outpass the power of human telling;
For none can guess its grace,
Till he become the place
Wherein the Holy Spirit makes His dwelling.

That is my Christianity in a nutshell, and the reason why I just
and only just dare to say 'I believe'.

VI

Time for thought

I once said to Winston Churchill, on some issue of policy, that I would like to have time to think. 'My dear young man,' he said, 'thought is the most dangerous process known to man.' I was inclined to agree, for I had learned early in my political life never to accept political office detached from a busy Department of State. Lord Eustace Percy was an extremely able man, and had done very well at the Ministry of Education. At Baldwin's request he became Minister without Portfolio, and was immediately labelled 'Minister for Thought'. That was virtually the end of his political career. The only exception to the rule is leadership of one or other of the Houses of Parliament.

In 1940 however, willy-nilly, I was given more than enough time for reflection.

At the outbreak of war, and before hostilities began in earnest, I had decided, rightly or wrongly, that I ought to see the Prime Minister through to what I foresaw would be an early end to his heavy task. I have often regretted that I did so, because I missed the close companionship of regimental life on mobilization, and the personal sacrifices which are made in war, and which were suffered so gallantly and cheerfully by those on active service – many of whom gave their lives.

All the rest of the family were involved. Henry, whose riding accidents prevented service overseas, went to the Scottish Command. William, who was a genuine conscientious objector, was persuaded to enlist and take a commission. He found himself in trouble for refusing to carry out an order to apply 'unconditional surrender', and ended up in Wormwood Scrubs. The German General at Le Havre had asked if he could evacuate the civilians from the town. His request was disallowed. William then refused to take his troops into the battle. For this he was court-martialled. Three days after Le Havre the German General in Calais made the same request. This time it was granted. Cause and effect? We shall never know.

My younger brothers – Edward and George – who had both been born after the First World War – enlisted; Edward in the Lanarkshire Yeomanry, and George in the Royal Air Force. George was un-happily reported 'Missing, believed killed' in Vancouver, setting out on a bomber-training flight, which, caught in the autumn mists, never returned. He had a charming character, and was already a really talented amateur photographer of birds and animals. Edward was caught by the Japanese, and employed on the notorious railway. The most even-tempered and charitable of persons, he cannot bring himself even now to say a good word for his captors.

The Hirsel was used as a hospital for crippled children, who were evacuated from Edinburgh, and there my sister Bridget worked as a nurse.

When in May 1940 Chamberlain fell, and it was time for me to return to the army, it was too late, for an Army Medical Board turned me down as unfit. Sir Crisp English, the well-known doctor who was in charge of the Board, said that I must have three months' rest before I could be considered for military service, as every nerve in my body was jangling. At the end of this time a second Board said much the same. After a long process of diagnosis, tuberculosis of the spine was revealed which, in the absence of modern drugs, necessitated flaking the shin-bones in order to graft them on to the affected vertebrae. The operation was performed by Sir John Fraser of Edinburgh, who had just returned from America with the latest techniques at his skilful fingertips. After it was all over I was able to tell an audience of nurses that the surgeons had achieved what had hitherto been thought to be impossible – namely to 'put backbone into a politician'; but that was in retrospect, and I cannot pretend that it was even faintly a joke. I often felt that I would be better dead, especially when I was told that absolute immobility for a period of two years was a condition of the cure.

After some weeks in a nursing home in wartime conditions I decided that the only hope for life was to return home. I did so, and the ability to look out on to the Tweed and the Cheviot Hills from my bedroom window began the process of healing. After some time an ingenious ramp on the front steps was constructed down which I could be lowered – bed, plaster shell and all – into a summer-house. I was hot-bottled in the snow, and stripped to the waist in the summer sunshine. The birds and the beasts had no fear of this harmless creature, and they helped me to find perspective and preserve a quiet mind.

It was then that I learned that the human being is infinitely adaptable. It was not possible to move any parts of my body other than my forearms, so that I could do nothing but talk and read. Gradually concentration settled on these two activities to a point where I could scarcely recall that I had ever been physically active. In a curious way too, I almost ceased to worry about the possibility of enjoying normal life again. That, however, was a dangerous mood, as it would have been easy to have slipped into a groove of helpless acceptance of incapacity.

The German bombers droning up the Tweed on their way to Glasgow used to jerk one back into reality.

Until my bed could be tipped at a slight angle, talking for any length of time was exhausting; so I concentrated on reading everything which came my way. I found most of the gadgets for reading when totally flat – such as a periscope on the chest – could not compare with pillows skilfully placed to support the elbows. That achieved, the best system was to keep three different kinds of book going at once. A history, a biography and a novel or detective story were always within reach.

I read the lives of all the famous politicians of the nineteenth century – Melbourne, Peel, Disraeli, Gladstone, and I found a study of their differing characters fascinating. In history I returned always to Macaulay and Trevelyan. I read much of Walter Scott, and all the novels of John Buchan. Of these, if I had to choose, I would place at the top *The Path of the King* and *The Thirty-nine Steps*. Now I suppose the aristocratic and romantic hero is dated, but they were and are fine tales finely told. Among the novelists Charles Morgan, Hugh Walpole and Somerset Maugham. The latter as much for his fastidious English as for the story. And then in detective fiction, Wilkie Collins, Agatha Christie, Marjery Allingham, Dorothy Sayers and Ngaio Marsh. Why are the best writers of detective fiction women? I do not know, but that was my positive finding at that time, and it still holds.

Later I was able to add short bouts of embroidery to my activities, and I managed to complete a set of dining-room chair seats of a simple design. Variety of occupation during the day enormously relieved monotony and increased the will to live. I have never been particularly musical, but music is another boon, so long as it is not allowed to become a mere background of noise. Television, of course, was not yet available.

There were in those days several kinds of refined torture from which I trust those who are afflicted will never have to suffer again. One was that whenever in the nursing home I was moved from my bed for X-ray, four nurses clutched at the sides of the blanket. The grip of one or other would understandably slip. In my plaster shell I was helpless to correct the agonizing rock and roll. I persuaded them eventually to attach leather handles to broad pieces of canvas, and life was transformed. At all times surgical spirit on sore pressure points was as refreshing as iced champagne.

Another trial was that I had to be fed up to the eyes to gain the strength to defeat the bug; and at regular intervals the corrective of castor-oil was applied. It was literally nauseating, and totally unnecessary if not positively dangerous, and if anyone is ever faced with such a situation I strongly advocate a strike. I could see exactly how Mussolini achieved ascendancy over his political prisoners. In orange juice or brandy it is just as revolting. Incidentally it reveals the fallacy in what I am told is the first rule for hospital nurses – never to run.

Just before the two years were up I was allowed to sit; and then, weighing nearly fifteen stone as against the normal eleven, to learn to walk all over again. It took months to unlock the knees, and even then the required result was only achieved by slipping on a rock, when with a crack like a pistol, and a sweating stab of pain the last adhesion went.

My reading had a serious purpose; for I foresaw a deep political division within Europe following a long war; and if the Germans were defeated, an attempt by the Soviet Union to dominate the centre of the Continent. So I read all the books I could find on Communism.

During much of the years 1940 and 1941 the Polish Armoured Division was quartered on us at Douglas, and were billeted round the Borders. Before my illness I had come to know a Count Starzenski, who was then a tank-gunner NCO, and who before the war had been Private Secretary to Colonel Beck, the Foreign Minister of Poland. His modest property in that country had been overrun in the first few days of the war by the Germans, and that of his wife had suffered the same fate shortly afterwards from the Russian invasion.

With extraordinary bravery and much adventure, they had found their way separately into Yugoslavia, Italy and Spain, and when eventually they arrived in England, Starzenski enlisted under that fine man, General Anders.

I never heard Starzenski or any of his colleagues curse their fate, but all of them had the single-minded ambition to destroy the tyrannies of left and right between which they had been sandwiched.

The Poles are gallant and unequalled in stoic acceptance of destiny. But even Starzenski, who had no illusions, quailed at the bloody ruthlessness of Russian occupation, when selected persons above a certain level of education in Poland were shot. The massacre of Katin was in his view unquestionably their crime.

When I was lying on my back Starzenski used to tell me from his own experience in the Polish Foreign Service, of the techniques of subversion which the Russians would use to soften up those whom they wished to destroy. He confirmed my worst fears as to the postwar prospect, and the more that I listened to him and the more that I read, the clearer it became that Communism was for export, and that the purpose of the Soviet leaders was expansion through any chink of weakness which the West might reveal.

No one could object if the Russians wished to adopt a Communist system as their own form of Government, and for their own social order; but clearly there was no such limit to their aims; and Stalin was a convinced exponent of the doctrine of perpetual struggle and of the ultimate victory of Communism over all other social systems and ways of life. He was cruel and ruthless to boot. The new imperialism was real.

As I read I came to be more and more certain that the Soviet alliance, while necessary to defeat the Germans, would turn sour, and that Stalin would keep a Sword of Damocles poised over the European democracies which would be dropped at his whim once the danger from Germany had been removed from Russian and Eastern European soil. I detected in the snippets which reached me from the Tehran Conference of 1942 the first signals of trouble to come.

As the months rolled on the Russian demands upon the Allies became more strident. They wished us to disown the Poles in Britain; they were callously ungrateful for the heroic efforts of the Royal Navy to bring them the sinews of war through the fearful conditions of the North Sea approaches; they wished to open up a Second Front when all military advice insisted that it was premature, and by threats of a separate peace they tried to blackmail Churchill into doing so. All these signs and more foreshadowed active malevolence towards the countries of the West once victory over the Germans had been won.

Churchill was, of course, aware of the menace of Communism; but to hold Russia in the alliance he had been bound in public to praise Stalin and Russia's prodigious war effort to a point where the British people were left in ignorance of the bare-faced indifference of Russian leaders to their allies' sacrifices on her behalf, and of her cold-blooded plans for the take-over of Eastern Europe and more if it came their way.

By the time the Yalta Conference was held in 1944 I had become seriously alarmed at the course which events were taking. The final *casus belli* in 1939 had been the independence of Poland. It might have been rash – the allied guarantee might have been given only because a stand had to be taken against Hitler somewhere – but there was surely an obligation on the allies in victory at least to try to restore Poland to nationhood.

At Yalta it became apparent as the Conference proceeded that, in the face of Stalin's brutal insistence that Poland should be absorbed into the Soviet's sphere of influence, Roosevelt and Churchill had felt bound to capitulate in order to achieve Russia's co-operation in the struggle until victory was sure.

Roosevelt was mortally ill and carried little authority; Churchill had virtually won the war and triumphantly vindicated the trust of the British people in his leadership and it was too much to ask that he should clash and break with the Russians at the eleventh hour. He did try to save Poland and to prevent Stalin from seizing East Germany and Czechoslovakia. He carried the political big guns as the chief architect of victory, but they were as pea-shooters against the adamant rock of Stalin's territorial ambition.

When a debate on Yalta was staged I had returned to the House of Commons. Uncertain as I was whether I could stand the physical strain of speaking on a big parliamentary occasion, I felt that I had to voice a protest at what I deemed to be the over-hasty surrender to Russia's demands; to see if even yet there might be a way to save Poland and to avert the appalling consequences for the rest of Europe which I was convinced were bound to follow the surrender of so much to the Communists.

On 27 February Churchill opened a debate in which feeling in the Conservative Party that Poland had been thrown to the wolves was running high. Being a man of conscience and emotion he was well aware that the Poles had been sacrificed to overwhelming power, but he nevertheless sought to justify the Yalta agreement on the grounds of justice.

When he came to the agreement with Russia that Poland should lose all territory east of the Curzon line, he said, 'I have never concealed from this House that personally I think the Russian claim is just and right.' He went on to talk hopefully about the new Poland which he wished to see, which had been 'liberated' by the Russian armies and on whose independence the Conference had agreed. He added, 'I know of no Government which stands to its obligations even in its own despite more solidly than the Russian Soviet Government. I decline absolutely to embark here on a discussion of Russia's good faith.' The Prime Minister then went on to use words which it seemed to me to suggest that he saw a treaty as a guide and not a rule. He was, of course, in a very unenviable position as, even in 1945, the Russians could have cheated their allies; but a back-bencher was not so inhibited and I spoke as follows:

In 1939, when the people of this country had to make a choice between peace and war they chose war because they were convinced to the point of certainty that so long as appeals to force were the rule in international affairs, there could be no peace, nor progress. Since then, whenever we have had time to lift our eyes for a moment from our self-preservation, we have reaffirmed our intention to rebuild and to restore at least the elementary standards in international behaviour.

A first British interest is peace. A first British desire is to provide over the widest area possible a setting in which the individual may live out his life in liberty and under justice. This is a British concept but we believe it to be a world interest. It is true we must face facts. It would be comfortable to believe that relationships between different communities of men were always governed by reason, but the reality of history reveals that the governing principle is power.

Power has not been destroyed in this war – it has been redistributed. It is still used. It is still the basic element in all human relations. Any settlement at the time must take account of it. I think a valid criticism of the peace of 1919 was that it allowed too much for the triumph of reason and too little for the fact of power.

While all that is true, it is also true to say that the world can never pass from the old order to the new – from the old order of the rule of force to the new order of the rule of law, except by way of a period during which the Great Powers are themselves willing, and are seen to be willing, to exercise restraint in the use of power. The position in post-war Europe will be one of great power and great weakness side by side, and that does not lead to stability.

One reason why there is world concern over the differences between Russia and Poland is because it is the first case – a test case – in the relationship between a Great Power wielding great military might, and her smaller, weaker neighbour.

I went on to speak of Poland's resistance to tyranny.

The British approach to the problem cannot rest upon sentiment, but our hearts would need to be of stone if we were not moved by these considerations. But our relations are generally specific undertakings given in treaty both to Poland and to Russia.

I asked of the Yalta Treaty:

Does the Treaty conform to that section of the Atlantic Charter which reads 'The High Contracting Parties desire to see no territorial changes that do not conform to the wishes of the people concerned?'

I proceeded to question the Yalta settlement by which Poland lost territory:

I believe if you try to force what is an act of power within the framework of the Atlantic Charter you will not whitewash the act, but you will break the Charter.

When the Prime Minister says that he accepts this as an act of justice I must take a fundamentally opposite view. We have dozens of times in our history accepted this kind of arrangement as a fact of power, but I cannot be asked to underwrite it as an act of justice. This is not a quibble of words. I believe most profoundly that it is an essential British interest that we should be seen to preserve our moral standards in international behaviour. When our plenipotentiaries go abroad they go, it is true, in command of great imperial power; but they also go as representatives of a great Christian people.

I turn therefore to the second instrument which regulates our relations with Russia – the Anglo-Russian Treaty of 1942. If I might interpret the word 'treaty' to the Prime Minister it would be that a treaty is 'a rule and not a guide'. Perhaps the House will allow me to read Article 5.

'The High Contracting Parties agree to act according to the principles of not seeking territorial aggrandisement for themselves, and of non-interference in the internal affairs of other States.'

I asked how it was that such a clause had not been included in the de Gaulle–Stalin Treaty in 1944. It seemed to me to be an ostentatious and sinister omission.

We could never be a party to a process under which a whole range of the smaller countries of Europe was drawn by a mixture of military pressure from without and political disruption from within into the orbit of another and a greater power.

I concluded with three questions:

Did Russia adhere to the clauses of the Treaty signed with us in 1942? and would she make her actions correspond to her pledged word?

Did Russia hold approximately the same ideas and conceptions of the structure of Europe as we did? On the answer to these three questions very much depends. Unless you have sanctity of treaties, unless nations are going to keep their pledged word there is not even the minimum condition present for the coherence of international society.

It was indeed a case of troubles casting their shadows before.

The speech was, of course, a feeble gesture, because Poland's fate was already sealed. But perhaps it helped my friend Starzenski and his brave companions to know that some of us understood their agony and were prepared to speak up for their country.

Some Conservatives voted against the Government on the issue. Strongly as I had spoken I did not do that; for I felt that it was not right in wartime to vote against Churchill unless one was ready to see the Government fall. For that I was emphatically not prepared.

The eclipse of Poland was only one of the dire consequences of Yalta; for the Russians were also allowed to advance deep into pre-war Germany and to seize Berlin. Again I am sure that when the records are open to detailed inspection they will reveal that Churchill tried hard to avert such a result, but that the impotence of Roosevelt and the rampaging mood of Stalin brought his efforts to nought. I have always had a nagging feeling that with a different political directive to the allied armies Berlin could have been saved.

Curious to discover if this might have been so, I went, shortly before he died, to see General Eisenhower at his home in Palm Springs. He had been greatly annoyed by a German author whom he felt had written a false account of the last twenty days of the war. Eisenhower was in a talkative mood, and began to give me an account of the allied dispositions before the final crossing of the Rhine. Given the opening I asked him why more attention had not been paid to the strategic importance of Berlin in the context of a post-war European peace; and whether the prize could not have been gained for the allies? His answers were interesting. First, he said that the Russians were so close to Berlin and the allies comparatively so far, that it was assumed that the Russians could and would get there first. Secondly he said that the political directive of the politicians was explicit. Wherever the German armies went they were to be followed and destroyed. They went south and south-west of Berlin. There were second thoughts, but they were too late to gain this political strategic goal. The result of the Russian occupation of Berlin was a packet of trouble for the allies.

Mr Khrushchev built the Berlin Wall in 1961 to keep the East Germans in. A mass exodus could have resulted in war and he did not want that. Berlin is still a potential trouble-maker, even under the four-power direction of Britain, France, America and Russia which was the only arrangement to which the Soviet leaders would agree.

The actual danger I was able later to measure when the Soviet leaders tried to block the allied air routes into the city by dropping 'metal chaff' from their bombers in front of the approaching allied aircraft, carrying soldiers and civilians into the city. All the instruments on which the pilots relied for safe approach and landing went hay-wire and hundreds of lives were put in jeopardy.

It so happened that Mr Dean Rusk, the skilful and staunch American Secretary of State, Mr Gromyko, the Soviet Foreign Minister, and I were together in Geneva on other business. Rusk and I tackled Gromyko on the matter and told him that this dangerous breach of the Berlin agreement must stop or we could not answer for the consequences, which would be serious in the extreme, and could lead to war. He denied any knowledge of any such action by the Soviet Air Force and dismissed our representations as intolerable and insulting to the Russian nation. It was clearly a case for blunt talking. We told him what we knew about the Russian planes, and that was a great deal.

On one critical evening we gave him until midnight to contact Moscow, and insist that the orders to the bombers be rescinded. He blustered, but agreed to do so. We must have carried conviction; for in the early hours he returned to us, declared that our accusations were outrageous, that there had been no such excursions into allied air-space in the past, and that it followed therefore that in future there would likewise be none. We had double whiskies and went to bed tired but content.

Dean Rusk was a splendid man with whom to do business. He was, of course, fully equipped intellectually for his high office. But it was his clear recognition of Russia's real aims which forced their leaders to take notice of the United States; and his calm authority with Congress which kept the United States as a full-blooded ally in NATO.

At the start he had a bit of trouble with the whizz-kids who circled like minor planets round the President, as his messages used to bounce off them before they reached their destination, but he soon got through their shield and became indispensable to Kennedy.

One never quite knows how far the Soviet Foreign Ministry is aware of a particular activity of the military or of the KGB, for their policies run in parallel up to the Politbureau and the Foreign Minister is not necessarily a member of that body. On the occasion of the bombers I think Mr Gromyko must have known, but he never batted an eyelid at any time, least of all when he brought his message of tacit agreement to our demands.

Since then there have been no serious attempts to isolate Berlin from the West; but the iniquitous Wall is still there with its sentries and its machine-guns constantly trained on an arid area on each side, on which a beetle could not crawl without being seen. It is a dreadful reminder in the middle of the most advanced and cultured continent in the world that the veneer of civilization is paper-thin.

How different the story of post-war Europe would have been if Berlin could have been designated by the Allied High Command as a military target of supreme political importance, and had been occupied by the allies. Whether capture by the allied armies would have been physically possible if the political directive to the army command had been more flexible cannot yet be judged with certainty, but the city has been for thirty years a festering sore; and it still has a potential for infinite trouble; for with Russian pressure constantly upon it, Berlin has to be subsidized to keep it alive, and clearly the Communists intend that it should die.

When peace came in 1945 Britain resumed the business of democracy, and party politics came to the front of the stage once more. Many would have preferred the wartime Coalition Government to continue in order to launch a programme of national reconstruction, but the Socialists who had preserved their party organization intact throughout the war years, while the Conservatives had let theirs go, scented a chance of outright victory, so the scene was set for a General Election on party lines.

Winston Churchill had generously offered me the post of Parliamentary Under-Secretary at the Foreign Office while the preparations were set in hand for the hustings, and there for a short time I had the opportunity to watch the professional handling of our foreign relations by Sir Anthony Eden. He spoke and acted with the authority of a leading member of a team victorious in war, and with power at his elbow; and he was certainly a master of the situation and of all the diplomatic arts.

Churchill naturally expected to follow up his victory in war with a decisive win at the election. But there is no such thing as gratitude in politics. The Labour Party played upon the impatience in the forces for demobilization; and the British public, being shrewder judges ot character than the politician is apt to allow, did not place Churchill on a pinnacle as a peacetime leader, as they had unanimously done in war. They came back to him later, but for the time being the majority wanted other men.

Mr Attlee, whom Churchill once playfully described as a 'sheep in sheep's clothing' succeeded him. He had already proved, as second-in-command in the War Cabinet, that this jesting description was wide of the mark; and as Prime Minister he enhanced his personal reputation and authority. The doctrine of Socialism brought the country deeper and deeper into trouble; but, never wasting a word, never suffering fools, always terse and abrupt with his colleagues, and even at time contemptuous, Attlee kept discipline in his party. Even the senior members of his Government were afraid of his tongue.

With many others I was defeated in 1945, which may well have been a blessing in disguise, enabling me to continue my education in foreign affairs, to nurse myself back to complete health, and, over the next five years, to coax the Lanark Constituency back to the Conservative cause.

On the flush of victory in 1945, Mr Tom Steele, my Socialist opponent, had done a foolish thing. His win went to his head and he wrote and published in the *Daily Worker* – the Communist newspaper – a letter of thanks to the Communists for the support which they had generously given him. I was tolerant of most of my opponents' actions, but this I could not stomach. Too many Socialists were ready to denounce Communists from the platform and to accept their help at the polls and in other ways, so I resolved to teach him and them a lesson. When the next election came in 1950 I had his letter of 1945 distributed at all Socialist meetings about two days before the vote, as a reminder of his willingness to use Communists to help him into Parliament. Tom Steele puffed and huffed and threatened to sue me; but he had set the trap and caught himself. I won by 685 votes. Never again did he flirt with the Communists. There is a moral here, for he became a pillar of Socialist orthodoxy and sat for West Dunbartonshire as MP for many years, so the story had a happy ending for both of us.

Electioneering is an art at which one improves with practice. Before I started in 1929 Sir John Stirling-Maxwell had given me a priceless tip. He said that when an aggressive heckler asks a question which seems likely to stump one that it is good tactics to say ever so politely, 'I am very sorry, sir, but I did not hear. Would you please repeat the question?' I can testify that the formula works like a charm. Almost always the questioner, having made his effort, will not be able to repeat the question, or if he tries will fumble it. In either case he has lost the attention and sympathy of the audience. If, in the rare case, he does get it right, the candidate has had time to think.

Amusing incidents are too numerous to record. One night in December I was shown by my host into a room in a remote wing of an old and rambling house. He was the only other person in residence, and was in a distant part of the building. My bedroom had clearly not been occupied for many years. In desperation to get some fresh air I climbed on a chair to pull down the top of a six-foot-high window. At the first tug the whole window frame fell inwards on top of me, and I fell backwards through a full-length mirror. Snow, backed by a gale, blew in. It took several towels to mop up the bleeding. In the morning when the lady who called me saw the mixture of blood and snow, she ran shrieking down the passage, 'There's been murder in the night!'

In the thirties there were some violent meetings. At one, when the platform was stormed, I was commissioned to push my chairman's sister head-first out of a window at the back of the platform. I fumbled badly as she had so many petticoats on that I could not find her legs. Once outside, as I drove away, the door of the car swung open and hit a woman on the head who was screeching abuse. She went down like a log. I bent over her, and a really ugly crowd collected. Suddenly she jumped up and loosed at me such a stream of blasphemous invective that not only I but the crowd were stunned.

Intensely relieved that she was not dead I jumped into the car and drove off.

In Lanark I had a woman agent who drove a small car. One night very late I offered to swap cars with her as she had further to go. She accepted, but had only gone a mile or so when the car began zigzagging across the road, narrowly missing a bus queue. It transpired that during my meeting youths had loosened all four of the wheels. The thirties were rough times for the politician in industrial Scotland.

During one meeting Elizabeth sat outside to guard the car. As the audience came out she heard one old woman say to another, 'Aye, yon was a guid enough speech, but I'm still going to vote for Mr Churchill.'

Perhaps the best vote of thanks I ever had was given at the end of a meeting where the audience were almost one hundred per cent Conservative. The lady who gave it said: 'I have only one request to make of this audience – Vote as you've *never* voted before.'

At the end of the first week of each election I always felt that I would not live to see the end, but by polling day one had acquired such a horrid competence and facility and stamina that one almost wished the campaign would go on.

I sat on the back benches with the Conservatives still in Opposition, although the Socialist majority was much reduced. During these months there was one event which threw a shadow before. Mossadeq – the Iranian leader – broke the contractual agreement which governed the administration of Abadan and seized the oil-fields.

In a short debate in the House I gave a warning that this sort of piracy should be stopped, for there were others watching and all too ready to try their hands at the game of snatch and grab. We were to pay dearly for failing to stop Mossadeq at once.

Not long afterwards my father died suddenly, and I was transferred automatically to the House of Lords. We were at dinner in the House of Commons when I received the news. I had left some notes in the Chamber, and unthinkingly went in to fetch them. I learned later that someone had reported me to the authorities for breaking a rule, which of course I had done, for I was already a peer.

Had anyone suggested then that I might once again be a member of the House of Commons, I should have told him to go away and be certified as insane. I was resigned to the ending of my political career.

VII

Scottish prelude
to the Commonwealth

A politician, unless he can reconcile himself to defeat which may be final, is peculiarly vulnerable, and one in those days who succeeded to a peerage had few chances of reaching the upper branches, let alone the top of the political tree. So I turned to the life which seemed to offer to a countryman the next best prospect – that of farming and managing the Hirsel and Douglas Estates; but I had scarcely become accustomed to the idea when a political summons came out of the blue.

Scottish nationalism had begun to rear its head. Its platform was discontent with the lack of understanding of Scottish problems shown by Whitehall, and a desire for matters which were demonstrably Scotland's affairs to be processed in Edinburgh.

James Stuart, who was Secretary of State for Scotland, told the Prime Minister that he felt that the situation would best be met, and many of the grievances allayed, if a Minister was appointed who would be largely resident in Scotland, but who could also speak in Parliament on occasions from first-hand and up-to-date knowledge of contemporary events in Scotland. He asked for me to fill the post. Churchill agreed and said, 'All right – have your Home sweet Home,' and so I became the first Minister of State for Scotland, with a political platform in the House of Lords.

The Prime Minister's personal directive to me was characteristic and terse: 'Go and quell those turbulent Scots, and don't come back until you've done it.'

I had a good deal of sympathy with Scotland's aspirations; for long-distance correspondence is no substitute for personal contact, and Whitehall was large and impersonal.

Stuart and I devised a plan whereby I travelled far and wide in Scotland – visiting the local authorities and the firms and farms who were contributing to the Scottish economy, listening all the time to their points of view, and, where possible, incorporating their sensible findings in legislation, or in administrative changes. At any rate the recipe worked, and the activities of the nationalists sensibly diminished until they no longer represented a political challenge.

James Stuart was a character in his own right. Born with the distinctive good looks of the 'Bonnie Earls of Moray', he was apparently detached, work-shy, and bored with life. Nothing could have been more misleading; for his nonchalance was carefully cultivated to disarm.

Once on a political platform his wife passed him a note. There were jeers and catcalls to the effect that he could not answer his questions without prompting. Innocently he asked, 'Would you like to know what was in the note?' To a chorus of exhortation he said: 'The note asks, "must you really look so bored?"'

On another occasion, when speaking in the House, someone from the Opposition bank-benches shouted 'Speak up'. 'Certainly,' said James, 'but I thought no one was listening.'

The Socialist Opposition never had a clue as to how to get to grips with him, and they could scarcely be blamed, for he would just slide away from the attack like quicksilver.

A man of strong likes and dislikes – I once followed him out of the Chamber of the House of Commons when one of his *bêtes noires* had just finished speaking. He said, 'That man is a – – –' The man concerned had followed close behind us, and said, 'Captain Stuart, you have no right to use such disgraceful language about a colleague, even in the privacy of the Lobby, and I must ask for an instant apology.' The apology which he got was, 'Yes, I am sorry, I should not have said it, I apologize. Have you anything better to suggest?'

Outward appearances were never more deceptive. Behind the façade of withdrawal there was a clear mind, intense application and a keen political sense. As Chief Whip he learned one day from Winston Churchill that he meant to give office to a Member of Parliament of whom James had a low opinion. He turned to the door. 'Where are you going, Chief Whip?' the Prime Minister asked. 'To be sick,' came the answer. No more was heard of that particular appointment.

The Scottish Office in Edinburgh was in fact a miniature Whitehall, and the resident Minister of State could see the working of Agriculture, Education, Housing and Health, Police and Industrial Development.

During the years that I was Minister we were heavily engaged in trying to diversify industry as the traditional business of Scotland – coal, shipbuilding and steel – inevitably declined. Hill-farming, too, always presented problems because, unless the end-price for the beast was right, in the English market the breeding cows and ewes would be slaughtered and the stores would not come from the hills and the glens, and the whole of British agriculture would decline.

The level of grant for Scotland which should come from the United Kingdom Exchequer was a subject of unending discussion. For some time after I had left St Andrew's House the formula of 11/80ths of the UK gross national product, fixed by Goschen when he was Chancellor of the Exchequer in 1888, was still in operation for the simple reason that, despite all the talk over forty years, no one had been able to prove that it was not a fair division of revenue.

As a result of my years at the Scottish Office, when Mr Heath asked me in 1969 to examine the question of devolution from Westminster to Edinburgh, and to make proposals, I needed but a short refresher.

I will return later, in more detail, to the recommendations which that distinguished Committee put forward under the title of

left A last minute conference at Heathrow with Sir Denis Greenhill, head of the Foreign Office, before leaving for New York.

centre A consultation with James Stuart at the Scottish Unionist Association conference in 1952.

below Croquet at Hatfield with Bob Menzies and Dame Pattie during the Suez crisis.

Bearing the Sword of State at a service in St Giles Cathedral, Edinburgh on June 24th 1953 to mark the Queen's coronation.

left above with Harold Macmillan, then Prime Minister, at Douglas in 1960.

left below Reading telegrams with my then Private Secretary, Antony Acland, on a picnic.

Electioneering in Kinross and West Perthshire, November 1963

'Scotland's Government'. We suggested an Assembly in Edinburgh, including the power to legislate on purely Scottish Bills. Not, I think, before time, since the first suggestions for devolution had come from Mr Gladstone in the 1890s. All our proposals were subject to the overriding economic and political interest of Scotland that the United Kingdom should remain intact. That is the *sine qua non* of any sensible plan of devolved powers; and any Scotsman who ignores that has forgotten which way his bread is buttered.

When Sir Anthony Eden took over the office of Prime Minister from Mr Churchill, he asked me to be Secretary of State for Commonwealth Relations, with a seat in the Cabinet. Some surprise was occasioned by the appointment, but in fact it was a natural graduation from the Scottish Office, for both essentially involve an exercise in public relations, although the Commonwealth, of course, was on an infinitely grander scale.

I had studied my great-great-grandfather (Lord Durham)'s Constitution for the Dominion of Canada, which had become the pattern for independence in the old Commonwealth, and by the time I took over I was able to read the signs of evolutionary change. Empire was finished; the modern Commonwealth could not be a military alliance nor an economic bloc; if it was to remain a recognizable entity it would have to be a political association, the members of which had decided that on balance it was better to face the problems of the complex modern world together rather than separately.

To keep such a body cohesive would not be an easy task; for when the same problems are looked at from such different angles as Asia, Africa, the Antipodes and North America, there are bound to be divergencies and sometimes clashes of views. That was the more likely when the people examining the problems were at very different levels of political education and experience.

In 1955 Britain was expected to take a lead; and Britain's word counted in the Commonwealth for more than that of any other member, more indeed than that of all of them together, although if a British Prime Minister was wise he would give weight to the contributions to the discussions made by able and experienced statesmen. They were, after all, following the terms of the Statute of Westminster deemed to be of equal status one with the other.

Soon after I had digested the information to be found in the Commonwealth Relations Office – then a separate Department from the Foreign Office – I set off to see for myself the special Commonwealth relationship and to judge how best to steer the political and economic development of a modern multi-racial association of nations which geographically spanned the world. There were no outstanding differences between the members at that time so it was a good opportunity to review the future in an atmosphere which was calm and friendly.

New Zealand was furthest in distance; but in every other respect the nearest thing to Britain which could be found. Politics did not at that time very seriously intrude into the country life of farming and working in a land which to a Scottish eye was a veritable Garden of Eden.

The country ran on milk and lamb, and with Britain's economy at last picking up after the war, the future to a New Zealander seemed reasonably assured. They were beginning, too, to cultivate trees in the lava soil which had hitherto been assumed to be barren, and the foundation of a prospering wood-pulp and paper industry was being laid.

Mr Walter Nash was Prime Minister. A short, square dynamic man who was a Socialist with his feet on the ground. His only disconcerting habit was that at breakfast he would mix a raw egg, orange juice and hot water and drink the horrible concoction with obvious relish.

Mr Sidney Holland succeeded him before long. A competent Conservative Prime Minister who greatly enjoyed telling stories against himself. He told me that on one royal visit to Wellington his car with flag flying was stuck in a queue and the spectators assumed that one of the Royal family was in it. An individual dashed through the police cordon and, having opened the car door, turned to the crowd in disgust and said, 'Ach, it's only poor bloody little Sid!'

Some years later when he and Mr Nehru were both receiving the Freedom of the City of London, Mr Holland did everyone present a public service. Mr Nehru had in the morning made an appropriate speech in reply to the Lord Mayor, but in answering to the toast of 'The Guests' after luncheon he ignored the convention that a Freeman's second speech of the day should be short. After one and a half hours, the Prime Minister of India was still going strong. He was accustomed to speaking to millions who had come from far and wide and wanted their money's worth. I passed a note to Mr Holland by one of the waiters saying 'If you get up and say that there is no more left to be said, and second the Toast formally, you will be the most popular man in London.' He did exactly that, and sat down to ringing applause.

New Zealand's unwavering loyalty was a good launching pad for my Commonwealth tour.

Australia was a very different country with a brashness and an unbounded youthful energy which was infectious. Huge fortunes had been made in wool; and in 1955 the country's well-being was still broadly carried on the backs of the merino sheep. There were signs of mineral wealth in the north-west, and the Snowy River Power and Water scheme was opening up new industrial prospects; but agriculture was still the foundation of Australia's economy.

There Mr Robert Menzies was in charge of Federal affairs, and I very soon found myself on his wave-length. I had first been attracted to him by his style, by his fastidious choice of words and the clarity of his exposition which went like an arrow to the target. There were big men and good politicians in Australia like Mr Dick Casey (later Lord Casey), Sir Philip McBride and Mr John McEwen, but they would have been the first to agree that Menzies towered above them all in political stature. He was a statesman who had *gravitas* and an orator who carried conviction both when he was expounding Australia's traditional ties with the Monarchy and with Britain, and expressing her new aspirations and hopes as a young nation.

He was helped through his years of office by a sectarian division between the Roman Catholics and the others in the Australian Labour Party; but faced with the difficulty of moulding a Federation out of a collection of very independent-minded States, he made a masterly job of it and firmly put Australia on the international map.

He had a ready wit and gift of repartee which Mr Evatt – for many years Leader of the Opposition – endured with resigned fortitude. Soon after I arrived both were present at a dinner given by the Governor-General, Sir William Slim, and Evatt spent the larger part of it quoting cricket statistics to Sir William's ADC – Colonel Martin Gilliat. After dinner I said to Menzies, 'I can't think why you dislike that old man so much; there is nothing that he does not know about cricket.' 'Just cold statistics,' was the Prime Minister's reply. He made no concessions to a political opponent.

Menzies had a passion for and a deep knowledge of the game of cricket. While he was in authority in Australia and I was Commonwealth Secretary, for over five years the meetings of Commonwealth Prime Ministers were wont to take place at the same time as the Test Match at Lord's. If Mr Macmillan and the others noticed the coincidence neither they nor we ever let on.

During my first week in Australia the Governor-General gave me some very wise advice. He said that if at Press conferences and interviews I wanted the Australian Press to report accurately what I had said, and not what they thought I had said, I would be wise to proceed at slower than dictation speed. Then and ever after in matters of importance I have carried out his instructions to the letter – and not only in Australia. It has always paid a handsome dividend.

The affair of the Soviet spy Petrov had lately shaken the complacency of the Australians who had previously thought that they were invulnerable to such activities as subversion. Menzies, who knew as well as anyone the recoil of 'reds under the bed' speeches, realized that the Communist finger was in every pot where trouble might be brewed, and was not displeased by the clumsy display of the Russians when, as they sometimes do, they played all their cards wrong in full view of the Australian public.

Menzies was a strong protagonist of collective security, and although well aware of the weakness of SEATO held it was surely worth while to engage the United States and Britain in keeping open Australian communications through the Indonesian seas, the Indian Ocean and the Pacific, should the need arise. I felt the same way; for I could not and cannot imagine that Britain could ever allow Australia and New Zealand to be isolated, not only because of the sacrifices which they had made for us, but as a matter of self-interest in preserving the right of English-speaking peoples to live the life of their choice.

Menzies and I therefore found ourselves in accord over the whole range of Anglo-Australian and Commonwealth relations. I was to seek his counsel many times in the years to come.

One of our SEATO Conferences in Australia produced an amusing incident. Mr Foster Dulles, with the rest of us, was a guest of the Prime Minister at dinner. Menzies, who was a connoisseur of food and wine, had taken much trouble with the menu. On reading it through Dulles's first reaction was to put in front of his plate five bottles of pills to neutralize acidity. Menzies held his peace until proposing our health, when he speculated on the effect of each of the bottles on American foreign policy. Dulles, who could be a dry stick was, to his credit, highly amused.

Dulles had the reputation of being a good lawyer, and I have no doubt that was true. But he was legalistic in his approach to problems, and gave the impression of inflexibility and lack of imagination. During that Conference, however, I came to appreciate his single-minded opposition to the advance of Communism. He was, however, a difficult man in whom to have confidence, because he seemed to place so little reliance in anyone but himself. He was the personification of austerity and it seemed that his only relaxation was to swim.

Australians are not very tolerant of a loser in politics (or cricket) and, although we had won the war, they were impatient at the signs of economic weakness in Britain, and apt to try and take it out of British visitors, who often reacted defensively. I decided early on to take a risk and be bullish on Britain's recovery. I was fortunate, for before long came the years when we 'never had it so good'.

The Australians were glad to hear good news. I gave it as far as I thought it to be justified in every capital of every State. I left the country convinced that Australia, under good management, would be a great country in her own right; while they were reassured that Britain still had a part to play on the side of law and order and peace, and that in trouble we would be at their side.

The State Premiers were jealous of their right of direct approach through the Commonwealth Secretary to the British Government and to the Sovereign. There were some great individualists among them.

Once when I was inspecting a uranium mine with Mr Tom Playford of South Australia, who held the office of Premier for over twenty years, I happened to say that I had never seen an emu at close quarters in the wild. He seized the wheel of a miners' bus which could hold twenty, and we bobbed across country like corks on a rough sea. Before the end I never wanted to see an emu again even in a zoo. On that trip I saw a duck-billed platypus in the river near Canberra, and learned that it can kill a man, so poisonous are its claws.

Menzies and I had discussed with some apprehension whether the pace of advance in the emancipation of colonial territories would find them able to carry the structure of democracy which Westminster was handing down to them, so I set out to the Republic of India with an enquiring mind, taking in Ceylon *en route*, which, under the guidance of Sir John Kotelawala – a staunch Conservative loyalist – had maintained for the time being that country's direct allegiance to the Crown.

The bounty of heaven had been given to Ceylon, and with a minimum of competence a government ought to have been able to make of the country more than a going concern. But that minimum was not there and even in 1955 there were signs of decline, and lax administration and corruption were much in evidence.

One day I was so much alarmed by the antics of a chauffeur, that I asked my Ceylon friend if it was easy to get a driving-licence in Colombo. 'Oh,' he said, 'it's £25 if you can drive well – £50 if you drive badly, and £100 if you can't drive at all!' It was sadly too near the truth for comfort.

Elizabeth had joined me in Colombo, and she and I greatly enjoyed a beautiful island and contact with such a happy-go-lucky people. The relics and the statues of Buddha at Kandy and Polonnaruwa are a never-to-be-forgotten sight.

I have only one literally distasteful recollection – the milk of the King Coconut, which was served at 11 o'clock in the morning as a great delicacy and refresher. Elizabeth recorded in her diary that it was like 'warm barley-water laced with castor oil'.

And so to India. Directing the affairs of that vast land were persons of powerful intellect, all of whom had been 'freedom fighters'. Their views were coloured by Socialism which they were convinced was the only political system appropriate to the circumstances of their poor country, but the Congress Party was in 1955 monolithic, and Socialism was practised rather less than it was preached.

Mr Radhakrishnan, the Vice-President, was a philosopher, and very proud of his Honorary Fellowship of All Souls. I asked him why I found it so difficult to fathom the mind of the Hindu, whereas, comparatively, that of the Muslim was an open book. His reply was, 'Oh, it's easy; it's our religion. Our Hindu Gods have many arms and whenever we feel inclined we add another so that we can embrace and justify any theory and practice which at any time we prefer.' He was a fascinating companion.

Mr Pant, the Home Minister, and Mr Moraji Desai, the Minister of Finance, were heroic in stature, and would have adorned any Cabinet; but the one above all whom I was impatient to meet was Mr Nehru who presided over all with an authority which was absolute. I knew that he could be moody and indulge in long silences or moralize to a point where a visitor began to feel irritated or ill at ease. I was therefore anxious, but I need not have worried; for from the moment he saw me fumbling the opening of a mango and performed the rite for me with his own hands and much to his own aesthetic pleasure, everything went with a swing.

He talked of his anxiety for his people and, in particular, his desire that they should meet their own needs in basic foods, improve their health and curb their birth-rate. He felt that in the early days of independence too much emphasis had been placed on a kind of copy-cat industrialization which had set the sights too high. Too many had been given a non-technical University education and their aspirations could not be met. The result was disillusion and discontent.

He sent me, with one of his District Officers, to a village meeting under the auspices of the Community Council movement, which was designed to teach to the village people husbandry and hygiene.

The performance took one back to stories of Biblical days. The officer and I sat on chairs in the centre of the village population. Some three hundred of them were gathered round, and he began to teach them, accompanied by a one-string banjo. The refrain was something like this:

The great Mahatma Gandhi said that if the family did not keep the cow in the house health would greatly improve.
The great Gandhi said that if a fence was put round the head of the well the water would not be polluted and fewer would die.
The great Nehru said that if the sower of grain did not pour all the packet of seeds into one hole, but distributed them in many holes, the result would be more rice and bread.

and so on, repeated over and over again.

It was totally primitive, and quite clearly from the passive and fatalistic faces any impact would be in the long term. The District Officer however was certain that the results would be seen over the years; and certainly now that twenty years have passed, India is more nearly self-sufficient in food. Mr Nehru had, on second thoughts, got the priorities right. Even so population and food still race neck and neck.

On one issue I was impatient with the Prime Minister and with the leaders of the Congress Party. They were wont to be very high-minded about other people's affairs and were ready at the drop of a hat to tell the Western democracies that we did not understand Russian Communism and that pacts of collective security were immoral. I thought that I should put the record right, and I did so tactfully but explicitly in a talk to the Council of Foreign Affairs in New Delhi.

I said:

It is possible to state with truth that the objectives of the foreign policy of the United Kingdom and India are identical. But it is right to admit that our differing experiences in Europe have sometimes compelled us to adopt different methods by which we hope to reach the same goal. Three times in half a century we held out the olive branch of conciliation to the Kaiser, to Hitler and to Stalin, and the lessons we and our friends in Europe have learned in a bitter school, is that weakness invites aggression and that neutrality has no meaning in the context of totalitarian ambition.

To match strength with strength has been a policy of risk which to you in Asia might seem unnecessary and dangerous but the North Atlantic Treaty corresponds to an instructive and genuine need for self-preservation which is felt in Western Europe.

I then talked of signs of lessening tension and continued:

I would not ascribe it all to NATO but the knowledge that an attack on the free world would bring instantaneous and annihilating retribution has, I believe, helped to bring us nearer the point where we can seek a constructive peace agreement.

The Indian Press, doubtless encouraged from on high, did not like the speech, but thereafter they were apt to allow that we might know our own business best.

Although I was doing no more than to claim that the Western Europeans should be allowed to judge the pattern of defence which was most likely to serve them well, the Indian newspapers were critical. Mr Nehru was never able to understand that Communism was essentially international, and that pink bourgeois Socialism was just as much a target as blue Conservatism. A year or two afterwards he staked a lot on the observance by the Chinese of the 'Five principles of co-existence' and when he was let down with a bang by Mao Tse-tung he was badly hurt. Although shaken by the fate of Czechoslovakia he still continued to sup with the Russian Communist Government with a shorter and shorter spoon.

For two reasons I was not too much alarmed that Mr Nehru should thus play with fire. I doubted whether any outside power could for long dominate the Hindu, and I noted that over the years, while the moralizing to others still went on, the Indian leaders refused to sign the international convention surrendering the right to make the nuclear bomb. Mrs Gandhi, with her hard-headed realism, still keeps the option open. She has always had a streak of iron in her make-up which was absent from her father's character. But in putting many of her political opponents in prison she may have miscalculated. Indian society is matriarchal, but they do not like a dictator whether man or woman.

From India we went to Pakistan where we were the guests of the President Iskander Mirza. He had been educated at Sandhurst and had kept the North-West Frontier quiet during the war, and understood the British ways. He was a wise statesman and tried hard to improve Pakistan's relations both with Afghanistan and India. Having visited the Khyber Pass I could not imagine a successful attack from that quarter against modern guns and planes, and calculated that there would be no open war with Afghanistan.

But the same could not be said of the quarrel with India over Kashmir. War between these two Commonwealth countries was a constant possibility. Sir Owen Dixon, the persuasive Chief Justice of Australia, came the nearest to bringing about a reconciliation, but he failed at the last throw. Subsequently every mediator has had his fingers burned.

Mr Nehru and Iskander Mirza's successor, Ayub Khan, had the necessary authority and status to settle the matter over the heads of their peoples, but they missed their chances. War finally came, and Pakistan was defeated and dismembered and lost to the Commonwealth.

The worst ordeals of overseas tours are usually faced at meals. In the Officers' Mess of the Frontier regiment we were faced with eight sheep's eyes on a skewer. I was overcome with revulsion against tapioca at my private school ('frogs' eyes' as we christened it), but at least that did not look at one with reproach!

In subsequent years I was to expand my knowledge and acquaintance of the countries of the Commonwealth and its leaders.

In Malaysia, where Malays and Chinese lived side by side, danger lurked, for the easy-going and happy-go-lucky Malay was always afraid that the more intelligent and more active Chinese would gradually destroy his culture and oust him from the best jobs. The temptation was to place restrictions and conditions on the education of Chinese children, and that was much resented. That this crisis was averted was in the greatest part due to the instinct for fair play and open government practised by the Tunku Abdul Rahman. He had a sense of the limitations of power, and a flair for the possibilities of politics possessed by very few. A prince of the Royal blood, a religious leader and a keen sportsman, he radiated a confidence and gaiety which was infectious. He taught me – or rather tried to teach me – the ronggeng, the Malaysian dance in which the male, as far as I could see, plays a subordinate role to the female with hilarious results. Like Winston Churchill, the Tunku liked others to share his enthusiasms.

The Finance Minister – Mr Tan Siew Sin – was an extremely able man whose father owned a wonderful house in Malacca. The front door was in one street, and the back door in another, and in between the two were corridors and rooms of priceless Chinese treasures. His taste was impeccable. The combination of the Tunku, a Malayan, and Tan Siew Sin from an ancient Chinese family, held the country together through some testing and vital years.

Singapore always had in it the promise of boom as a great entrepreneur port and city, but it was not until the advent of Mr Lee Kuan Yew that the place began to hum. Equipped with the keenest of intellects – he was a Double-First at Cambridge, a Socialist, (although I would not have known it), the most articulate of speakers and a born administrator. He had to take the key decision as to whether or not to enlist the aid of foreign capital, and a great deal of it, in order to create a modern port and to establish indigenous industries.

He went out to attract capital with his eyes open, and it has paid his people a handsome dividend. His relations with the Tunku were passably good, and this prevented trouble between the city and the hinterland, as the Malaysians have always feared that the rich and expanding city would steal their trade and take them over. Wisdom has prevailed and there is enough for all.

The Commonwealth was proving to me every day that politics is essentially about people.

I found Canada to be perhaps the most interesting of all the Commonwealth countries at that time, because her leaders seemed to understand more clearly than others that if the modern Commonwealth was to achieve anything, there must be a cross-fertilization achieved by the different Commonwealth countries in communication with each other.

As Commonwealth Secretary I had been very conscious in Whitehall that the contact was almost solely one way – that was between London and the individual Commonwealth country concerned – and I had taken the opportunity in Canada, in 1956, to speak as follows:

> The new relationship is not only between the United Kingdom and the new partners, but between each old Commonwealth country and the others, for this is nothing less than the launching of a multi-racial Commonwealth with no formal bond of union.

In Montreal in 1957, at the Commonwealth Economic Conference, I took the chance to talk over the problems with some of Canada's leaders.

Canada, during the long Premiership of Mr Mackenzie King, and later under Mr St Laurent, had established a reputation for a liberal interpretation of democracy, and for a wide tolerance in her overseas relations, and so had the ear of the new members.

The Montreal Conference was significant in this context. It started with the expressed desire of the old members to provide the means for development for the most backward countries, so that at least an infrastructure on communications, agriculture and power would be there, on which industry could be built, and thus create a gradually rising standard of living for their peoples.

When we had proceeded as far as we could with that matter, Sir David Eccles (later Viscount Eccles) the Minister of Education and I, under the supervision of the Chancellor of the Exchequer, Mr Derick Heathcoat-Amory (later Viscount Amory), launched a plan to assist education throughout the Commonwealth. It was received with acclamation, and has proved itself of very considerable value.

Two very different personalities showed their enthusiasm. Mr John Diefenbaker, Conservative Prime Minister, and Mr Lester Pearson, later to fill the same office as a Liberal. Two people more different and antipathetic it would be difficult to imagine. Diefenbaker, lay-preacher, carrying the out-back with his fiery salesmanship of Canada for the Canadians, and Parliament with his droll debunking of political opponents; impetuous, illogical and at times terrifyingly simplistic, nevertheless he held his political public for many years. Pearson, quiet, persuasive, full of fun, seeing – for a party politician – almost too much of both sides of the question; international in his thinking, held in high esteem by all thoughtful Canadians, and by a great public further afield. He would have been in his element as Secretary-General of the United Nations, but unluckily the opportunity never came his way.

Canada has played a telling rôle in holding the new Commonwealth reasonably steady throughout some difficult years; in sharing some of the burdens of leadership with Britain, and setting the pace in direct communication with Asian and African Commonwealth countries. It is to be hoped that the example will tell, for sufficient time has passed for the ex-colonial countries to take their eyes off the grievances of colonialism and of neo-colonialism. They should now settle down to make of the Commonwealth a Council of Nations, which can meet without a veto, and in good temper and comradeship try to take an objective view of the many problems that beset mankind, and find peaceful solutions to them.

The process of cross-fertilization of ideas has still to be taken a lot further, if the Commonwealth is to carry conviction in the rest of the world that it has a constructive part to play in international affairs.

There is in the world too little friendship – too little trust – too little co-operation; and if the Commonwealth countries can demonstrate these values in their working relationship with each other, then the association will be an asset. But it must do no less than that, for a smaller and paler version of the United Nations could not survive.

VIII

Africa

After India had become independent and declared eligible for Commonwealth membership in spite of the fact that she had become a republic, the wind of change had become a gale. In African countries like Ghana and Nigeria where there was no question of a white minority of settlers wielding political power, the problem of the transfer to independence was comparatively easy. For centuries the coastal belt of the West African bulge had been in contact with traders, as first the Phoenicians, then the Arabs and then the Europeans found their way round the coast.

The success or failure of independence depended very largely on the quality of African leadership available in the early days and years, and in the West there was a substantial range of choice.

Dr Nkrumah of Ghana was a naturally flamboyant figure who ran a campaign for freedom highly charged with emotion. He was a curious mixture of sophistication and paganism. On one occasion, climbing the stairs to his room, I saw a large cage of white doves. I asked his private secretary whether the Prime Minister was fond of birds. 'Oh no,' he said, 'these are for a different purpose. They are sacrificed, and their entrails consulted for the omens whenever His Excellency travels by air.' Sure enough, a week or so later, the Prime Minister had set off for Ashanti with some High Commissioners, when his aeroplane had developed a fault and had to return to the

airport. Ministers and their wives, who were there to see Dr
Nkrumah leave, clamoured for more doves, and the order was sent
to fetch them from Accra. However the engine-trouble was mended
quickly, and the extra delay in sending for doves was too much for
one of the High Commissioners. He took Dr Nkrumah by the arm,
and said, 'Prime Minister, I've had enough of your bloody doves.
You come with me.' And he ran him up the gangway to the plane.

This man Nkrumah sat as an equal with the Prime Ministers of
the old Commonwealth and each in turn tried to steer him into
responsible ways; but power had gone to his head and Ghana was
given the worst possible introduction to the international family.
Power for those unused to it is heady wine.

Nigeria's leadership was a complete contrast. I shall always
remember the statesmanship shown by Sir Abubakar Tafawa Balewa
in his reply to my introduction of Nigeria into the United Nations
Assembly as a nation in its own right.

Here are some extracts from it:

Now to deal with the more general problems of Africa, problems
which are bound to arise when the Powers which colonized
Africa in the last century are now relinquishing their control and
granting independence to their former colonies. The most serious
problem in those cases seems to me to be that in itself political
independence is totally inadequate if it is not accompanied by
stability and economic security and if there is no genuine personal
liberty, with freedom to express one's views and to profess
whatever faith one desires.

Economic weakness lays a new country open to every kind of
pressure and results in other countries depriving its people of the
freedom to choose a form of government which they feel suits
them best. Spreading political propaganda or more insidious
infiltration through technical assistance can virtually rob any
under-developed country of its freedom. I therefore feel that if
the advanced nations of the other continents are really desirous

of seeing the new African States stand on their own feet, and make their own particular contribution to the peace of the world and to the happiness of mankind, they should make a real effort to desist from fomenting trouble in any of the African countries. The best way for them to assist us in reaching maturity is not by spreading ideological propaganda, in whatever form it may be disguised, but by helping us genuinely with really good will, to develop our resources and to educate our human material up to those standards which are necessary for proper development.

Many of the new African States are, indeed, potentially rich and should contribute to improving the world but for the fact that they lack the technological knowledge and the financial capital necessary to develop their resources. It is especially in this field that I commend the many schemes which the United Nations has sponsored for assisting the under-developed countries. Indeed, I wish that there were many more of them. I would not necessarily limit technical assistance to the United Nations, but I do seriously suggest that it is in the best interests of world peace for assistance from elsewhere to be given only to those countries which, although still under-developed, are politically stable and have a properly constituted government which is capable of understanding the risks of accepting aid from another country. I certainly deprecate direct assistance being given by individual Powers to countries which are not yet able to stand on their own feet and are politically unstable, because such aid would only give rise to suspicion and, in the end, the receiving country may find itself involved in the ideological war, a thing which, as I have already said, we in Africa must do everything in our power to prevent.

I wish to make our position plain beyond any measure of doubt with regard to the African continent. We in Nigeria appreciate the advantages which the size of our country and its population give us, but we have absolutely no aggressive intentions. We shall never impose ourselves on any other country and shall treat every African territory, big or small, as our equal because we honestly feel that it is only on that basis of equality that peace can be maintained in our continent.

We in Nigeria honestly believe in the principles of the United Nations, and we believe that with a change of heart among the Members, and especially among the more powerful nations, there is no reason why there should not be peace and happiness. I think that all will agree that the present tension in the world is due to mutual suspicion and the efforts made by groups of countries to impose ideological notions of one kind or another on their neighbours. I am speaking frankly to you, Mr President, because this is the first occasion on which my country has been able to speak out in the councils of the world. One great advantage which we new nations have is that the accession to independence makes a clear cut with our past and presents us with the opportunity to enter the field of international relations untrammelled by prior commitments. It is probably the one occasion in the life of a nation when it is possible to choose the policies with the inherent qualities of goodness. And so, as we gratefully take the place to which you have invited us, we feel an immense responsibility to the world which you represent. We see nation wrangling with nation, and we wonder how we can help.

Just one week ago the clocks were striking midnight and Nigeria was on the threshold of independence. There was a brief ceremony at which the leaders of three different faiths each said a brief prayer. We then realized, all of us, that however much we might imagine ourselves to be responsible for the happy accession to independence, we realize that, above all, there is a divine Providence, and I do honestly believe that one primary essential for international friendship and co-operation is for each man to be true to his religious beliefs and to reaffirm the basic principles of his particular creed. It may be that then, when we hear the world crying out for peace, we may receive the inspiration to deal with these intractable problems and be able really to devote all our resources to the advancement of mankind by applying those eternal truths which will inevitably persist long after we ourselves are utterly forgotten.

Tragically he was murdered, a shocking loss to the cause of moderation in Africa.

Unhappily too, his hopes for Nigeria were to have a serious set-back during the Civil War which followed the Ibo revolt against the Federal Government; but after much anguish General Gowon was able to pick up the pieces, and his policy of reconciliation with the Ibos which sprang from his Christian upbringing and character brought renewed confidence. But military governments are not trained in the arts of social, economic and political reconstruction, and nine years later his administration was overturned. African society is still essentially tribal and the Nigerian Federation could fragment. But provided it is not seduced by Communism it still represents the best opportunity to establish a black state in Africa which is politically and economically stable and fairly governed.

The problem of constitutional advance was very different in the countries of Africa which formed the Federation of Southern Rhodesia, Northern Rhodesia and Nyasaland; for there the Europeans controlled in one way or another virtually all the land, having taken possession of it before the African had any system of land tenure.

Before the arrival of the white man many of the African tribes had wandered from area to area with no roots in any particular place. The Europeans introduced fixed land tenure and good husbandry, and were intent on improving the fertility of the soil, so that their children and grandchildren could inherit it. They considered themselves to be 'Africans' by right of possession. They intended to rule the country and to maintain their superiority even though they might be outnumbered by the black African by more than thirteen to one.

Mr Macmillan had sensed the danger involved in a small white minority refusing to prepare the majority for partnership in government and he chose South Africa, already an independent member of the Commonwealth, a country where the European minority was about one to four, and correspondingly assertive of their superiority, to describe how the wind of change was blowing. His message was that the whites should accommodate and adapt themselves to it before it became a tempest and swept them away.

Whether the timing was right is a matter of opinion, but Macmillan's diagnosis was correct. He hoped that the South African Government would accept the need to modify the practice of 'apartheid'; that the leaders of the Rhodesian Federation would begin to practise what they preached, which was the intention to train Africans in administration and government. If both these things were done he thought that there was a chance that the white man could share power with responsible African persons capable of appreciating the advantages of a non-racial society.

When I arrived on the scene the Federation was composed of three very disparate units. The first, Southern Rhodesia, was a beautiful country, already comparatively rich, well-fitted to grow tobacco and other crops, and clearly capable of very considerable development, provided water could be harnessed to produce power for medium-sized industries. The ratio of European to African in Southern Rhodesia was 150,000 to 2,000,000. The territory had been virtually self-governing since 1923, and Britain had never seriously intervened in her internal affairs. Her leaders could therefore make a good case for Dominion status (i.e. complete independence within the Commonwealth) on the country's record and prospects.

I found in charge of Southern Rhodesian politics Mr Garfield Todd, an immigrant from New Zealand. He had been a missionary; had turned politician and was favourable in theory to African advance; but when at regular intervals I used to press him to take more Africans into his Government and administration, his answer was invariably evasive. He argued that the pace had to be very slow because otherwise he would be repudiated by the white electorate who commanded the huge majority of the votes. In that respect, in spite of his later protestations he was exactly the same as his predecessors and successors.

The second and third of the trinity – Northern Rhodesia and Nyasaland – were still under the control of the Colonial Office in Whitehall, and therefore my only status in relation to their governors and politicians was the Federal link.

In Northern Rhodesia the ratio of Europeans to Africans was 40,000 to 2,000,000 so that the slant of the people's thinking was strongly towards the Africans' rights and instinctively antagonistic towards the European-dominated set-up in the South. I was much less happy about the attitude of white to black and vice versa in Northern Rhodesia than I had been in Southern Rhodesia. The copper-belt population consisted largely of recent immigrants from Britain of the artisan class. Fresh from wartime austerity at home, they suddenly found themselves possessed of servants and cars and comfort beyond their dreams. Whereas the white settlers who had pioneered in Southern Rhodesia had grown up through times of hardship during the pioneering years of exploration and development, and were therefore friends of the Africans who respected their dedication and skills, the newcomer into the North tended to parade his new-found affluence. Whereas the worst accusation against a Southern white which could be made was that he was paternal, there was at least a grain of truth in the accusation that the Northern Rhodesian white was in the first place looking after himself.

Nyasaland was quite different – the poor relation of the other two – a country in which the Church of Scotland in particular had planted many missions, and had preached assiduously, but with little political sense, the Christian idea of equality. Many from Nyasaland were so poor that they needed to supplement their family's income by going to work in Southern Rhodesia or South Africa. There, although they earned good money, they became aware of their inferiority and returned colour-conscious.

The Colonial Secretary in the Conservative Government of 1955 – Colonel Oliver Lyttelton (later Lord Chandos) who was a successful industrialist, had seen much attraction in the idea of an economic union of the three countries, perhaps to be extended eventually further afield in East Africa. But before the economic union could show results his successors – Alan Lennox-Boyd (later Viscount Boyd) and I – inherited a Federation where all the emphasis was on politics, and where each unit eyed the other with dark suspicion. Federation, difficult enough to establish and sustain in Australia and Canada with all their sophistication, was infinitely more hazardous in Central Africa, where the majority of inhabitants were illiterate and with only the minimum of experience of community living, let alone political organization.

Almost from the beginning Southern Rhodesia had been piloted in its politics by Dr Godfrey Huggins (later Lord Malvern). He was a practising doctor who had delivered almost every baby in Salisbury and its neighbourhood, and·tended the population black and white through their illnesses and ailments. He was universally popular; he was pungent in all his comments, and his word was virtually law by reason of its earthy common sense. Such an impression had he made on British and other Empire politicians that by general consent he represented Southern Rhodesia and later the Federation in person at meetings of Commonwealth Prime Ministers, even though his country was not independent. He once told Elizabeth that, while he would fly from Salisbury to London, he would not return that way because he did not like flying uphill!

Stone-deaf in his later years, he would, in the House of Lords, use his hearing-aid to emphasize the points in his speech which he wanted his colleagues to hear, and then when they replied would leave the instrument clearly visible on the Bench beside him.

When Federation came, the office of Prime Minister of Southern Rhodesia was put in the shadow by the Federal Government which, when I first arrived, was led by Sir Roy Welensky, a muscular forthright politician who had been a heavy-weight boxing champion, and was apt to think and talk in terms of 'knock-outs'. He told me that as a young man he used to hire young African sparring partners for 1d each, and that he would get through fifty before exhaustion set in!

Welensky was a personality in his own right, being the son of a Northern Rhodesian of Polish origin, who, after producing a large family, died and left Roy to be head of the household as an adolescent boy. He was determined not only to fulfil that family trust, but to educate himself for higher things. He became a railwayman and engine driver, and used to teach himself the classics on the footplate at night, by the light of the full moon. Such qualities of physical strength and of mind were bound to bring him to the front.

If there had to be a Federation, the first mistake was to put its government in Salisbury. It was a natural site but it was regarded by Africans elsewhere as the seat of white privilege. Added to that was the 'desertion' of Sir Roy himself from Northern Rhodesia his native country, to the land of European rule, in which he was seen to be more at ease with the whites than the blacks, and was suspected of using the European vote to postpone into infinity any effective African influence or constitutional advance.

Sir Roy always insisted that, while power should be shared, it could only be given to 'responsible' Africans, but the trouble was that, because of lack of education and training, there were in fact very few Africans at that time who, by Western standards, could take the strains involved in a democratic society. That one or two were tried in the lower ranks of government and failed, was seized upon by most of the politicians of the right as an excuse to go even slower in educating the rest to a point where they could conceivably be a political challenge. It was always too little too late.

However, Southern Rhodesia in the late fifties was not an unhappy place, and there was not then and there is not now the gulf between the races which had so divided society in South Africa. But in the Federation as a whole trouble was brewing.

Alan Lennox-Boyd, who was an extremely able and sympathetic Colonial Secretary, and had to conduct the emancipation from British rule of many colonies, was faced with a situation in Northern Rhodesia and Nyasaland which would have tested the patience of Job and the wisdom of Solomon. He saw all the advantages which would flow from economic and political co-operation of the three territories; but his officers on the spot in Northern Rhodesia and Nyasaland could not conceal their distrust and dislike of the Federal experiment. When things were difficult for Welensky they made it more so. They were not disloyal to the British Government policy, but when distaste for the tie-up with Southern Rhodesia was written all over their faces, it was easy for the Africans of the two countries to see in which direction their sympathies lay. It is a strange thing that when anyone enters the continent of Africa he becomes caught up in its emotions and personally involved in its problems. It is almost impossible to avoid taking sides, and after a time no one tries very hard.

Lennox-Boyd and I strove to preserve our objectivity and to find ways forward which would give to the three territories a Federal structure from which each and all races would derive benefit. But divided responsibility always leads to trouble in politics and many of our schemes were frustrated.

Central to the transfer of power in all cases was the design of a political pattern where the majority elected on a qualified franchise would eventually rule, but would accept an obligation to protect the rights of minorities.

In Africa risks could be taken in countries where the European minorities were tiny, and where most of them were tenants rather than owners of the land; but in the Rhodesias and Nyasaland the Europeans were the landlords of virtually all the good land. They had created the agricultural wealth of the country, and they were simply not ready and willing to see their work wasted and their children denied the heritage to which by the right of peaceful occupation they felt they had the moral and legal title.

Our problem was to try and discover the constitutional processes fitting to the peculiar social make-up of the territories which could lead to eventual majority rule, which was consistent with our policy for the new Commonwealth, and which would at the same time guarantee the future of the Europeans as full citizens of the new state. There was our dilemma.

In 1961 I was in correspondence with a Church of England curate working in the copper-belt, who had written: 'Since England will have to deal with Welensky some time, why not now?' His 'deal with' was framed in the context of the dissolution of the Federation which to him and many others in Northern Rhodesia seemed to be desirable. I replied, and I give some extracts because they reveal the state of my thinking at the time.

Anyone can give a country independence without worrying about the result; but if the aim is to launch a nation in which there will be law and order, tolerance and justice, a nation which is capable of surviving economically and will conduct its foreign relations according to the code of the good neighbour, then it all becomes much more complicated. I confess that I am not satisfied that freedom is everything and the rest nothing. If, therefore, we are to fulfil our trust to these people we must try to give them an independence where they have at any rate a chance of making it work to their profit and credit.

I went on to describe the danger of reversion to tribal rivalry and said: 'Unless we are very careful we could get a belt of chaos from Angola, through the Congo, Ruanda Burundi to Kenya. That would be a dreadful prospect.' In respect of the three territories I wrote: 'I have no doubt what would be best for Nyasaland and Northern Rhodesia. They should be in a tight economic and a loose political Federation.'

There were many comings and goings and long discussions in the Commonwealth Relations Office and the Colonial Office to try and find the formula for improved Federation; and, while we pondered, the temperature of the Africans in Northern Rhodesia and Nyasaland slowly but surely rose to boiling point.

Apart from the British Government's conviction that Federation was worth preserving, we were under an obligation to Sir Roy Welensky to persevere in our efforts to make it acceptable to the three component parts, and thus to bring about Commonwealth status and independence.

Another adverse factor had meanwhile intervened. Ghana had received her independence from the British Government, but the flashy President and Prime Minister, Dr Nkrumah, had created a bad impression everywhere, and made the worst possible impact on the white Rhodesian leaders. He stirred up feelings also in the United Nations against the Federal experiment, and so confirmed the belief of many Europeans in the territory that African politicians were feckless and totally unfit to rule.

The coincidence of one of these ill-tempered debates in New York upset the chances for Sir Edgar Whitehead, who had become Premier of Southern Rhodesia, and was a forward-looking man, who might well have found an acceptable compromise for constitutional advance in that key territory. It was largely the news flowing in from New York on the extremism of the African speeches in the Assembly which lost Sir Edgar the election of 1962. Very blind, very deaf and monosyllabic, he was nevertheless trusted by the Africans.

He was in many ways a man of singular capacity. He once arrived to talk with me at Dorneywood, and between 8 p.m. and midnight consumed thirteen bottles of beer. When, before driving back to London, I had asked him if he would like to retire, his reply was 'Certainly not'.

It was in this exceptionally unfavourable climate for statesmanship that the British Government had to act.

There were two problems – the first to impose Federation on the two dissenting territories by force of arms; the second to find some way of popularizing it in the eyes of the Africans to a point where they would find a version of it to be acceptable.

On my early visit to Rhodesia I had been distressed to discover how bad the Federal politicians had been at selling their achievements in development to the citizens of the Federation and to the world outside. In a meeting with Federal Ministers, chaired by Sir Roy Welensky, I advanced the proposition that the success story might carry conviction if it was told with objectivity by some body which had examined the record of four years of activity. I said that it seemed that as Rhodesians they were unwilling or unable to influence public opinion in their favour; that unless it was done for them it would go by default, and the cause of Federation would be lost in the tumult of noisy and ill-informed Opposition.

I had conceived the idea of an all-Party Commission from Britain. I had thought that there was a chance that, after the first-hand evidence collected by a visiting Mission, the Africans could be convinced that the Federal structure would serve the peoples of the three countries better than any other, and that the testimony of experienced and respected persons might carry the day with the British Parliament. I could see no other hope.

The Federal Government were very reluctant to agree to any such proposal. However, after a lead from Sir Roy Welensky, and after positive assurance from the British Government that the break-up of the Federation would not be in the terms of reference of such a body, it was agreed that I might test the feelings of my British Cabinet colleagues.

Macmillan was not particularly keen on the proposal, but he and the others agreed that if the situation was to be saved, this could be a way of doing it. It was a very long shot, but worth trying; and it would keep the topic away from the British hustings during the General Election campaign which was due. The Prime Minister persuaded Sir Walter Monckton (later Viscount Monckton) to be the chairman. He was a born conciliator.

I was really keen to enlist the help of Mr Gaitskell to form an all-

Party Commission. It was a gamble; but with men and women of substance of Conservative, Socialist and Liberal persuasion on it, with a capacity to study the facts of Federal achievement, such a Commission might carry conviction in a way which nothing else could do.

I had a high opinion of Hugh Gaitskell's patriotism and ability; but though I pleaded with him, I could not bring him to agree that members of his party should serve, unless the terms of reference could include the right to recommend the break-up of the Federation. To that I could not agree.

Curiously enough, the only sharp differences which I had with Gaitskell were over African matters. The first had been his insistence that it was unsafe to send Seretse Khama back to rule over Botswana. He had, I think, been over-influenced by Seretse Khama's uncle, Tshekedi Khama, who felt that Seretse's marriage to a white wife would be likely to ferment trouble among prejudiced African tribesmen. I felt that exile on £10,000 a year in Brighton, which was the fate to which the Socialist Government had condemned him, was for Seretse Khama worse than death, and that the colour complex in reverse was nonsense. I therefore returned him to his country soon after I came to the Commonwealth Relations Office. The 'gamble' was a complete success; he and his wife have lived happily ever after. He has presided over his people with their complete approval.

The second occasion on which I felt Gaitskell was guilty of lack of imagination was this refusal to allow his followers to take part in the Monckton Commission. He failed to see that the issue would plague all parties and all governments unless it was settled by inter-party agreement. Anyhow I believe that a unique chance was lost.

Even with the official Socialists absent we were able to gather a Commission consisting of persons who commanded wide respect. Before Sir Walter left, we talked about the difficult problems with which the Commission would be faced by reason of the political situation on the ground, and the terms of reference which did not allow them to recommend the break-up of the Federal structure. He said that obviously there would be a lot of talk to which they would have to listen. I agreed, and told him that I was fairly sure that a case could be made for the Federation which would commend it on the merits of its performance since its inception, and that, if this were to be the Commission's finding, it would help the Governments concerned to decide how best it could continue. Positive support by the Commission pointing the way forward could possibly restore flagging confidence.

When the Report eventually emerged the Commission was condemned by European opinion in Rhodesia which held that the terms of reference had been breached. I could not agree with that interpretation. What they had done was to express their view that the Federal structure had served Rhodesia reasonably well, and that in their opinion it could still do so – if certain adjustments were made to the franchise and the composition of the parliament.

I believe that the final opportunity of preserving the Federation was lost when Sir Roy Welensky, in instant reaction, refused to accept the Commission's findings as a basis for discussion with Her Majesty's Government; but one is bound to add that it was by then a very outside chance. When this opportunity was gone, and as the use of force was judged by all of us to be out of the question, the break-up of the Federation was sure to come.

In that situation, ought the British Government to have faced the Governments of Northern Rhodesia and Nyasaland with the independence of all three parts or none?

It would have been possible, and perhaps in terms of real politics we could have done so with a reasonably clear conscience but hitherto, when handing over power to another government, we had always done so to a majority; and if there was to be an exception, and we were to pass the authority to a minority, we felt that we must take scrupulous care to ensure that the majority would be helped along the road of shared political authority, and eventually of majority rule.

R. A. Butler, who, as a last throw, had been asked by Macmillan to assume special responsibility for a settlement with Rhodesia, has written in detail of his last-minute attempt to salvage an economic link between the three countries. But it was all in vain for tempers were too hot for compromise. The Federal experiment was right on paper, but the units were too different to fit into any mould, and the actors too young in political experience.

The next move of substance in the unfolding drama was the 1961 Constitution for Southern Rhodesia, introduced by Mr Duncan Sandys (later Lord Duncan-Sandys) – my successor in the Commonwealth Office. With great patience and perseverance he obtained the assent to it of the Southern Rhodesian Government and the African representatives at a London Conference.

The blunder this time – and it was the gravest of all – was the responsibility of an African – Mr Joshua Nkomo – the well-educated and influential leader of the Africans. He accepted the Constitution in London; but when he returned home he was persuaded to go back on his word. The double tragedy of that recantation was first that it enabled the Europeans to say that, as they had always told us, the African leaders were neither responsible nor trustworthy; and secondly that, had the terms of the settlement been put into practice, the Africans would have been able to look forward with confidence to taking charge in a reasonable time-scale of a genuinely multi-racial state. Mr Nkomo's action was more culpably short-sighted than anything which had gone before. Doubtless he sees that very clearly today.

This condensed story has been taken far enough to indicate the near certainty of deep trouble far ahead for Rhodesia with the alternatives already posed – evolutionary progress or bloody violence. The chief actor in the next instalment was to be Mr Ian Smith.

South Africa's case was different. The early European settlers as they pushed north, had been attacked by hostile tribes with a ferocity which bit deep into the minds of the Dutch pioneers. They

saw the nomadic African tribes as barbaric persons unfit for contact
with civilized people; and the Boers equated them with the hewers
of wood and drawers of water of Biblical times – indeed as inferior
beings who were less than human. For the Afrikaaner social contact
was unthinkable, and 'apartheid' was part of the natural law.

Over the years to one mistake they added another. They alienated
the coloured population whose expressed desire was to be put on
an equal footing with the white Europeans, and who, admitted to
equality, would have been their strong supporters.

It is strange that with all its indignities the system of 'apartheid'
did not attract adverse criticism from the outside world long before
it actually happened. A most respected statesman, General Smuts,
had presided over South Africa while 'apartheid' was practised
although not yet rigidly defined, and he was credited with a wide
and liberal outlook on human affairs. He kept his counsel and outside
critics were mute. It was not in fact until Dr Malan and later and
more boastfully Dr Verwoerd, began to advertise the 'virtues of
apartheid' and to thrust racialism down people's throats, that the
world began to take notice and to condemn.

Gradually the place of South Africa in a Commonwealth, the
members of which were pledged to the promotion of human rights,
began to be questioned; and matters came to a head at the Commonwealth Prime Ministers' Conference in London in 1961.

On the whole the mood of the Ministers attending was to give
South Africa another chance. Even Dr Nkrumah was on his best
behaviour and did not want to see South Africa expelled. But Dr
Verwoerd, who was a grey-haired, fine-looking, father-figure of a
man, and could be moderate and disarming in discussion was definitely not at his most conciliatory. He was in fact so stubborn that
even his friends began to slip away. He gratuitously offended
President Ayub Khan of Pakistan; and Mr Nehru, who had from
the start been uneasy, began to show visible signs of annoyance.

Mr Diefenbaker of Canada had for long had a conscience which
we thought had been temporarily laid. But at lunchtime on the

third day he became so exasperated that he let himself go to the Canadian papers and the headlines quickly returned to London.

So a Conference which started with a good chance that South Africa's case would be accepted, and that it should be given one more chance, was thrown away by Dr Verwoerd.

Macmillan with foresight and tact arranged a formula so that Dr Verwoerd could withdraw. That was duly done but in truth South Africa had expelled themselves.

'Apartheid' is wrong, but it was a sad and lamentable day for those who believed that South Africa had a contribution to make to the economic prosperity and above all to the physical security of the continent of which she is a part and of the Western world.

The British Empire had come to us almost by accident, through the operations of British merchants who in the course of trade built up obligations to the peoples with whom they did their business.

It was only when the responsibilities grew beyond the capacity of the traders that British governments with great reluctance assumed the responsibility for the security, and then increasingly for the well-being of the people and the territories which went with them.

From the start the British began to train the native population in the arts of politics and administration. Once that process had begun the ultimate goals of self-government and independence were sure.

The progress was naturally uneven. It was much easier to graft the British political system on to those countries where the population was largely composed of British stock than where the people were in the majority African or Asian. India's basis of village democracy was strong, but in the case of Africa there was no such firm foundation on which institutions could be raised. Looking back it seems that we were almost crazily quixotic to persuade ourselves that such political refinements as tolerance of parliamentary opposition, and restraint in the use of political power which it had taken us six hundred years to design, could take root in one or two generations. In the result – particularly in Africa – the Westminster pattern of democracy has placed too great a strain on the communities and it has had to be abandoned.

Nevertheless in countries like Tanzania and Zambia and Kenya the process of consensus by which the community arrives at its decisions will eventually, if given security and peace, flower into a more elaborate democracy. The caveat of security and peace is necessary because the risk of a reversion to tribalism is real.

In Rhodesia the question was posed whether it was possible to create a genuine multi-racial society with Europeans, Africans and Asians all taking their share in government. It is possible that we might have succeeded if the wasted years of two world wars had not intruded, and if militant Communism had not taken a hand in the campaign for freedom. Possible, too, that with a little more foresight and political skill European and African leaders in Rhodesia might have laid the foundations of racial partnership.

Now that ambition is not to be realized.

The hope must be that the Africans, who are in the overwhelming majority, will recognize that the European capital and skill and experience is needed to secure for the country the prosperity and well-being which is its due.

IX

The diplomacy of Suez

Another part of the African continent was now to present the British Government and the Commonwealth Relations Office with a critical situation.

The rights and wrongs of the British military intervention at Suez have been argued so often that I will not add to the defence of the Government's action which I gave in the House of Lords on 12 December 1956. (Appendix A)

But I was a close observer of the diplomatic activities which preceded and followed Colonel Nasser's seizure of the Suez Canal Company's assets, and they had great significance for the Commonwealth.

The first thing which struck me during the negotiations which concerned the financing of the Aswan Dam, was Nasser's readiness to play off the West against Russia. He had more than enough time to accept the offers which were made by both America and Britain, but he clearly enjoyed prevarication, and got a kick out of playing with power.

He certainly had no legal grounds for the seizure of the Canal, and I recall that Hugh Gaitskell was so outraged that he described the deed as 'exactly what we had experienced from Hitler and Mussolini'.

The action of Mr Foster Dulles when he had finally announced that the United States would not subscribe to the Dam was abrupt and ill-considered, but Nasser had no valid excuse for the violent response which he made.

In the weeks of negotiation to try and find a settlement it is impossible to exonerate the Americans from being ham-handed.

Eden, in the early days, had warned President Eisenhower that, while the intention was to use every art of diplomacy to reach a settlement, if all else failed force would have to be used. The American administration was therefore plainly put on notice, and Dulles was also told the same thing by Macmillan in the last week of August.

If, therefore, the United States felt that force must be avoided, one might reasonably have expected that they would have taken care to see that their diplomacy matched the stake which they were trying to win.

The first opportunity which they missed came when a committee was sent to Cairo to see Nasser and try and persuade him that a settlement was possible which would combine continuing Egyptian sovereignty with the legal rights of the canal users. Dulles ought to have led the Committee, or been a member of it, because it was America who had the influence and the power and the authority. He failed to take the chance.

In the absence of Dulles the statesman who led was Mr Robert Menzies of Australia. He was an excellent choice and he took with him representatives of Ethiopia, Sweden, Iran and the United States. There was nothing colonialist or neo-colonialist to offend Nasser in that lot.

The start of the meeting was as successful as anyone could have dared to hope. Menzies was so pleased with it that he played up his luck and told Nasser that in his view a settlement fair to Egypt was possible, but that it would be deadly dangerous if he were to dismiss British and French military preparations as bluff. This advice was well taken, and in his own account of the matter Menzies wrote that he thought the odds against it had fallen from 1000 to 1 to 100 to 1. So far so good.

The President of the United States and Dulles were of course kept abreast of every move. Nevertheless, just at the moment when all was in the balance, Eisenhower wrecked the chances of the mission when in an off-the-cuff answer at a Press conference he ruled out the possible use of force.

In his book *Afternoon Light* Menzies has written: 'If force was unconditionally excluded what had Nasser to do except sit tight, reject the Dulles proposals, reject any watered-down proposals that might be made, and continue the process until he had in the homely phrase "written his own ticket".' I recall vividly the near despair which hit us when the news came of the breakdown of the talks. There can seldom have been a more inept piece of diplomacy.

But Dulles was to produce a second barrel which was almost as bad. In the second week of September a Suez Canal Users Association was formed in yet another attempt peacefully to assert the users' rights. The idea was that the dues should be paid into an account by the users, and that an arrangement would be worked out by which Egyptian sovereignty of the canal would be recognized.

America, with the full blessing of Dulles, became a member of the SCUA. Asked what America's reaction would be if her ships were fired on in the canal, he replied that they would not push through but 'go round the Cape'. Once again the pressure was taken off Nasser at a critical time, and so the SCUA went the same way as the earlier committee and diplomacy had conspicuously failed.

My special area of responsibility during this traumatic time was to hold the Commonwealth together.

Mr Nehru, in particular, although he recognized the importance to India of passage for ships through the canal, was at all times sensitive of anything which he could interpret as a revival of colonialism; while his Foreign Minister, Krishna Menon, took a positively malicious delight in egging on anyone who showed signs of twisting the tail of the West.

I am not sure that we could have held India in the Commonwealth, but for the influence on her brother of Mrs Pandit, the

Indian High Commissioner in London. She did not hesitate, when it seemed that the tensions must snap, to go to Nehru direct and to by-pass her Foreign Minister.

Pakistan was upset for a different reason – that of sympathy for their Muslim brethren. Muslim unity was always a highly political emotion in Pakistan. Now it looked like boiling over.

I was lucky that their High Commissioner in London – Mr Ikramullah – was a highly-skilled diplomat. He exerted all his talents to calm his leaders down and a break was avoided.

In the end it was another Commonwealth statesman who pulled the chestnuts out of the fire.

Mr Lester Pearson of Canada had always been aware of the danger to the concept of international law which would follow if the exponents of snatch and grab were allowed to get away with their spoils. He was a born conciliator, and when diplomacy failed and force resulted he began to try and find a way by which some advantage for the world could be snatched from failure.

For some time before we decided that force was inevitable we had sought to get the Security Council of the United Nations to carry the responsibility for insisting that Nasser should return to the rule of law. Our efforts were thwarted. When finally we called off our action in the Canal Zone the way was open for the troops from the United Nations to place themselves between the Israelis and the Egyptians. That this was done with expedition was due in large measure to Pearson's activities.

Whatever the final verdict of the historians on the British occupation of the Canal Zone, they will be bound to record that had it not been for a sad lapse on the part of American diplomacy, peaceful persuasion had a good chance of gaining the day.

X

Foreign Secretary under Macmillan

In the summer of 1960 Derick Heathcoat-Amory began to feel that he would like a rest from the Exchequer and from politics after a very successful period in that office. Macmillan therefore was faced with a reshuffling of the Cabinet. In Selwyn Lloyd he had a Minister of wide experience, who had stood the strain of Suez with remarkable fortitude, and was undoubtedly capable of handling the economic problems which faced the country, and accordingly he was moved to the Exchequer. That appointment left a vacancy in the Foreign Office; and there was much interest in the field of possible runners for the succession.

When the rumour began to spread that it might go to me the newspapers expressed incredulity. A fair example of the reaction was the comment of the *Daily Mail* that the Prime Minister still had time 'to stop making a fool of himself'.

There is nothing so annoying as to have backed every horse in a race except the winner. The media had done just that, and when the rumour became fact all hell broke loose.

The *Daily Herald* asked, 'What have we done to deserve this?' One enterprising journalist said that 'never since Caligula appointed his horse a Consul had a political office been so abused'.

All the excruciating puns on 'Hume' and 'Home' blared out from the headlines. Mr Gaitskell moved a vote of censure in the House of

Commons, saying that, while he had no objection to me personally, to place the Foreign Secretary in the Lords was a political scandal; and so it went on.

I was asked by Lord Stansgate from the Opposition Front Bench how I reacted to this adverse reception, and I replied, 'I don't deny that the last few days have not been easy to face. Occasionally some of the criticisms have tended to get me down; but at those moments my Scottish blood has come to my rescue, and reminded me that all the publicity is free.'

Macmillan characteristically refused to flap. The vote of censure failed to shake our Parliamentary Party, the House of Lords appreciated the added prestige of having the Secretary of State on their benches, and gradually the hubbub subsided.

There was of course some method in the Prime Minister's madness. A thorough knowledge of the Commonwealth was the best possible training for the wider stage; a Foreign Secretary in the Upper House has more time to travel and to become acquainted with and gain the confidence of his opposite numbers in other countries. Having served in the same capacity in both Houses there is no doubt in my mind that one of the most exacting posts in government is more easily carried in the House of Lords than it is in the 'other place'.

One of the journalists who had shortly but vividly expressed his sense of outrage was Randolph Churchill. He wrote to tell me that my selection was intolerable, and that he intended to denounce it with suitable invective in that Sunday's *News of the World*. He invited me to luncheon in the Ritz Hotel so that he could confirm his impressions and improve his copy; and he told me that he had to hand in his script by 5 p.m. on the Friday afternoon – the day which he had chosen for our meal. Knowing his lazy habits and his liking for food and wine, I strongly suspected that he would not have written anything by lunchtime, and would be hard pressed to meet his editor's dead-line. I therefore wrote out, in the form of question and answer, my own appreciation of myself, and described the main lines of my approach to British foreign policy. I took it to the luncheon and when we rose at 3.30 I said, 'Randolph, I have made a few notes on how I see my task ahead in the next two or three years, and something of my philosophy which will underpin foreign policy. In case it is of any use as an *aide-mémoire* put it in your pocket.' The result was better than I had hoped, for the document came out virtually verbatim, and until his untimely death I had a committed ally.

The main principles which underlie British foreign policy are dictated by geography. Throughout our history when any one power has tried to dominate the centre of the continent of Europe, there has been an automatic muscular reaction. The reason why we have been alternately enemies and allies of Spain, France and Germany is that at one time or other each of them has tried to establish supremacy over a large part of the continent. The main business of British diplomacy for almost three centuries has been to form alliances with continental friends who have a similar interest in curbing overbearing power.

Nor could we tolerate any naval threat to our communications by sea. Uninterrupted passage through the Atlantic was literally vital to us. During the whole of the reign of Queen Victoria we were able to rely on our own resources and those of the Empire. The *Pax Britannica* was real. Britain's foreign policy stemmed from strength.

But in the reign of Edward VII the shadow of German expansion began to appear, and the King in person decided to visit France and to establish an *entente cordiale*. It was a diplomatic act of state which was prudent and timely for when the Kaiser broke the peace, neither France nor Britain could have weathered the storm alone. In fact when war came, victory was only won when the United States added her power to that of the European allies. They were needed not only to keep the Atlantic free, but to fight alongside Europe's armies.

We did not, however, learn the lesson at that time. Following the war reliance was placed on the League of Nations to provide collective security, but the one country which had been able to prevent the domination of mainland Europe, and to ensure the freedom of navigation in the Atlantic Ocean, was not included in the organization. Nor was any sustained effort made to secure from the United States a pledge that she would enter the lists against an aggressor at the start, should the peace again be challenged. It took yet another war before Britain and her allies understood that a powerful aggressor could only be deterred, or a war won, if the United States was tied firmly into an alliance for collective security.

Mr Bevin, the Foreign Secretary in the early days of the Socialist Government of 1945, saw that point very clearly and so NATO was formed.

It was a recognition by the Western Europeans and the United States that, if the free democracies were to survive, notice had to be given to any potential aggressor that he would be met by a military response which was automatic and united.

I was out of the 1945 Parliament, but I was greatly relieved when Attlee and Bevin carried their Socialist colleagues in support of the policy. For it was not a case of Europe or America; Europe and America was the minimum guarantee of security.

There was only one possible aggressor on the horizon and that was the Soviet Union. The conclusion of the alliance meant that a majority of the Socialist Parliamentary Party no longer saw everything Russian through the rosy spectacles of previous years. It also meant that we could anticipate, in respect of the defence of Europe and the Atlantic Ocean, a broadly bi-partisan foreign and defence policy between Socialists and Conservatives.

From then on the first duty of any Foreign Secretary was to keep the NATO alliance intact, and its defensive armament sufficient to meet any Soviet military adventure, and to do so until the Russian leaders gave unmistakable evidence that their policy had changed to one of real *détente*.

It was my belief that we could and should retain some military presence further afield, and that the political dividend which we should earn would far outweigh the financial outlay.

Singapore, in particular, was a very important centre of communication, and the fact of a British naval presence in that busy port was a reminder to all that Britain was still a power which had worldwide interests; while it helped to reassure Australia and New Zealand that our membership of the SEATO alliance had some meaning in relation to their security.

There were, too, our bases in Aden and Gan, and the naval facilities given to us by the South African Government in Simonstown. There were even then signs of a strong Soviet interest in the Indian Ocean, and our oil supplies ran through it and round the Cape of Good Hope. It was clearly important that the Russians should not be allowed a monopoly of power and presence in those areas; not because they might be expected to sink our tankers, for that would be an act of war, and risk the nuclear response, but because it gave them opportunities for political and economic blackmail in a wide arc of countries from Iran through the Gulf States to East Africa.

So the priorities for British diplomacy were – first the containment of the United States of America in NATO – secondly, the maximum cohesion between the European countries who were members of it; thirdly, the ability to man and use the minimum of bases overseas – Cyprus, Gan, Singapore, Hong Kong and Simonstown, which could be identified as serving a distinctly British interest. Fourthly, to foster trade. And lastly, to take trouble about the Commonwealth and to gain for Britain the greatest possible number of understanding friends. Such a programme, even though our power had shrunk, was within our diplomatic and economic capacity.

I was also anxious to retain a sufficient number of units of the services which would be ready to go overseas at short notice if a British interest was threatened, or if one of our friends needed help. Such situations are not easily foreseen, but several occurred while I was Foreign Secretary. One such involved sending a military expedition to save Mr Nyerere's government in Tanzania from rebels who sought to overthrow it. Other expeditions had to go to Kenya, Uganda and Kuwait to deal with critical situations. I once asked Lord Mountbatten how often we had sent expeditionary forces from Britain since the end of the war, and in how many cases the situation had been foreseen. His reply was, 'Forty-eight, and none.'

We managed to retain at reasonable cost the necessary bases and forces sufficient to deal with unexpected needs.

The challenge in the international situation was that thrown down and constantly restated by the leaders of the Soviet Union, namely the overthrow of every economic and political system which did not conform to Communism. The two instruments which they were prepared to use were subversion and a growing level of forces and armament, which would give them the option to use force if it was necessary to achieve their end.

Their attitude was well expressed by the industrial organizer of the International Socialists, when he said: 'Whilst we do not seek a Socialist State through the means of violence, we are certainly not going to be intimidated and defeated solely by our refusal to use it.'

The main strategy of the Russian hierarchy was clear. To sustain a programme of rearmament so massive that it would place the maximum strain on the economies of the Western democracies. And parallel with that to use subversion to exploit any weakness in the body politic of any country which might get in the way of their plans. In the background always was military strength.

It is one of the amiable characteristics of the British people that they cannot believe that others can fall below the standards of neighbourliness which they practise themselves.

Hitler wrote down his intentions – so did Nasser – so did Castro, and very few took much notice. The young are apt to think that Communists cannot differ very much from themselves. They do, for they are indoctrinated to believe in perpetual struggle as soon as they can talk and read.

After their atrocious behaviour to their allies in the war, I cannot pretend that I approved of or liked the Russian hierarchy, but I had no innate hostility to revolutionary Russia so long as the Communist leaders did not try to thrust the virtues of their dogma down other people's throats. But in fact Communist doctrine was for export and its apostles had the zeal of crusaders.

At a Conservative meeting in 1960 I put the problem like this: 'I have no doubt that the Russian as a man is a patriot, but as a Communist he is a conspirator who must undermine patriotism in others. What we have to do is to frustrate the conspirator and negotiate with the patriot.'

For many years I did just that and it is an art of which I shall have more to say.

In 1960 I was alarmed. Western Europe, exhausted and weakened by the German war, was an obvious target for the Communists, but public opinion scarcely seemed to recognize the threat or the effort which would be needed to avert it.

NATO was clearly a top priority in all our security plans and must be seen to be so. I was already convinced that a common economic and political association of the countries of Western Europe was necessary as a buttress to the alliance; while I felt strongly that to complete the picture Britain should possess a nuclear weapon which would be under her own control.

The United Nations might one distant day be the ultimate guarantor of peace; but so far had been unable to provide security for anyone, nor was it likely to do so in the foreseeable future.

We had therefore to rely on our own will and our own arms within a military alliance in order to find safety.

At the Conservative Party Conference of 1960 I said that we must try our hardest to substitute a balance of reason for the balance of terror. But I warned that the Communists could not be appeased, and that we must be on constant alert, and then added: 'Although we may be a nation of shopkeepers, on the national counter freedom never has been and never will be for sale.' Some of the newspapers talked of jingoism, but public opinion began to turn my way.

The British public had in some degree been hypnotized by the stream of adverse propaganda which was directed against us as a capitalist state, and a colonial power, by the Russian leaders, and it had given people an uneasy guilt complex. It was necessary that they should snap out of it; that they should desire to defend the essential freedoms and feel that Britain could stand up successfully for its chosen way of life. Conservative policy could help a lot by being clear and direct, and by being seen to be geared to serving Britain's interest.

The climate was favourable for British diplomacy, for one event had occurred in Western Europe which was of overwhelming importance in terms of economic expansion and of collective security. It was the *rapprochement* between Germany and France. The two architects of it were Dr Konrad Adenauer of Germany and General de Gaulle, assisted by Robert Schumann for France. Neither was an easy or conventional character, but they both had a vision which looked out over and beyond the prejudices of history. Each could claim that he had led his country out of the valley of despair, and restored to his people self-respect and hope. They had their differences about the destiny of Europe. Adenauer was convinced that nothing short of complete American involvement in NATO could guarantee West Germany's future. De Gaulle felt that to raise the morale of defeated France, he must establish complete self-reliance and that in any way to be beholden to the United States was to dilute the spirit of France of which he was the symbol.

I enjoyed my work with both of these distinguished men, leaning rather towards Adenauer's thesis than that of de Gaulle, as having more validity in terms of the physical security of the Western world.

That Germany should have confidence in NATO was essential from many points of view, not least because, if Germany felt that the NATO alliance could not guarantee her security, a school of thought would be sure to develop which would look for insurance with the East.

A Germany, too, which was thoroughly embraced in the Western alliance, removed any excuse for the Russians to label her as aggressive.

Adenauer seemed instinctively to sense all this, and we established a rapid *rapport*. Whether or not he was injected with monkey glands as rumour had it I do not know. But he was possessed of exceptional vitality and a clear and incisive mind. His face looked like a brown nut, and his jaws like nut-crackers. At the age of 85 he was still in full possession of all his faculties.

I was to carry on the understanding with Herr Willy Brandt, and his able Foreign Minister, Herr Walter Scheel (now President of the Federal Republic of Germany) – one of the few Foreign Ministers who can have written and sung a song which was top of his country's 'Pops'.

So long as Germany is in NATO, and American troops are in Germany, the danger of Russian aggression against Western Europe is reduced to the minimum.

General de Gaulle would not admit this, and his insistence on France first at all times and at all costs, and that America should take a back seat, was much more difficult to reconcile with British interests. I found him at all times courteous, charming and disarming, but obstinate.

I remember one occasion in connection with preparations for a Summit with the Russians, in which he proposed that we should take an initiative and that France would stand aside while we did so. I thought this outrageous, and said to him: 'But, General, if you limit yourself to floating the idea and then leave the negotiations entirely to us, France will get a lot of credit if we succeed, and avoid the criticisms if we fail.' 'Yes, my boy,' he said, 'and what is wrong with that?'

I recall the occasion in 1960 when he came to London on a State visit. As always he had memorized his speech and held his manuscript throughout at the level of his left knee. I noted from the translation that he omitted a sentence which referred to 'over-ambitious lawyers'. I asked his ADC whether he had done so through sensibility, because both the Lord Chancellor and the Speaker were eminent lawyers. 'Oh no,' he said, 'he remembered that he owed money to a lawyer in Paris, and thought he might be annoyed.' That was real presence of mind.

His own colleagues hesitated a long time before they crossed his path. On one occasion we had been stuck in a NATO communiqué for hours over one word; and I knew that it must have been chosen by the General himself, for Couve de Murville was adamant. I said across the table to him, 'Oh, for God's sake, Couve, telephone to the General and tell him that the alternative word will do just as well.' All Couve de Murville said was, 'One does not telephone to General de Gaulle.' I apologized for a very foolish suggestion.

There can be no doubt that de Gaulle was made of different clay to most men. He could be extraordinarily angular and difficult and was cordially disliked by such different men as Churchill, Chamberlain, Eden and Eisenhower. But is it possible to imagine any situation more humiliating than that in which he found himself on the defeat of France?

A patriot and a proud soldier, he had seen his country surrender and the French army beaten into abject defeat. Pride and shame must have fought a battle inside him; pride won, and if it left him outwardly arrogant that could be understood. It took supreme courage to stand up for France alone.

Towards the end of his life the General became careless about outraging the feelings of others; as in the case of the studied gaffe in Canada – '*Vive le Quebec*'. But no one else could have extracted France from Algeria with dignity, or breathed the spirit of life into Frenchmen following their total defeat. I was happy to receive a copy of his book signed by his own hand on the morning of the day on which he died.

Couve was the coolest of all the Foreign Ministers; seldom allowing his expression to register any emotion. He was, in spite of his public reputation, an anglophile, and how, with his acute political sense and high intelligence, he so consistently carried out de Gaulle's instructions to the letter I shall never understand. Never was loyalty so blind, so complete or so exasperatingly efficient.

There was one misunderstanding between de Gaulle and Britain which could have had even more serious consequences than in fact it did.

When the Americans decided to scrap the 'Skybolt' missile, the possession and continuation of which was of enormous consequence to us, the question arose as to whether we should try and hold them to the contract which they had made for that piece of mechanism for the conveyance of the nuclear missile, or try and persuade them to make a similar arrangement in respect of its successor and much better alternative – the 'Polaris' submarine. The latter had the over-whelming advantage of being virtually undetectable by the enemy as it lay on the bed of the sea, so that as a second-strike weapon it was a real deterrent. There were indications, although there was no certainty, that President Kennedy would give us all the technical knowledge as well as the hardware on favourable terms, although the Pentagon and State Department were said to be strongly opposed to his doing so.

Before going to Washington to talk about all this, Macmillan met with General de Gaulle in France, and some of the time was spent by the two men walking and talking with no one else present and no record taken. They parted, with the General, from his subsequent account, apparently believing that Britain would co-operate with France, and that Macmillan would refuse 'Polaris' at any rate until there had been further discussion between the two heads of Government about the possibility of co-operation with France on an Anglo-French deterrent. Misunderstanding is always possible when speaking in somebody else's language, but Macmillan's French was very good, and I do not believe that the General was in any doubt that we would accept 'Polaris' if the terms were favour-able enough. Macmillan was very well aware of the importance of a nuclear weapon for Britain which was credible.

From his own account of the facts he told de Gaulle plainly that

Contacts with the Communist world

In Moscow for the signing of the Test Ban Treaty, August 1963. (l. to r.)
Adlai Stevenson, Ted Heath, Mr Gromyko, Dean Rusk, Krushchev, the
author, U Thant and Hubert Humphrey.

With Chou En Lai in Peking,
1972.

overleaf Dean Rusk, Harold
Macmillan, JFK and the
author. This photograph in-
scribed by the President was
taken outside the White House.

With Willy Brandt on the
Berlin Wall, January 1962.

For Lord Home —
with appreciation for his
most useful efforts to
budge the ATlantic — and
with every good wish
John F. Kennedy

Africa, Southern, North & West

With Ian Smith signing the settlement of 24 November 1971.

left With President Sadat in Cairo, September 1971.

With Sir Abubakar

we would either have to accept 'Polaris', or build a conveyor of our own.

The question of 'Skybolt' was acutely political, for at home the insinuation was that the Conservative Government had been gullible, and that we were going to be left with no effective nuclear deterrent at all. The Prime Minister was conscious of all that, and of the parliamentary urgency of the matter; and he could not have given any pledge which would have left us naked for an indefinite time. France could not on any count, or in any given time-scale, have joined us to provide an alternative credible in terms of security.

At the Nassau Conference which followed it became clear that there was no future in 'Skybolt'. It was obviously useless to acquire a system which the Americans were putting out of production. It was apparent, too, that President Kennedy was prepared to let us have the 'Polaris' with the necessary equipment on extremely generous financial terms, and with a clause in the agreement which enabled us to operate without American consent, if the Prime Minister of Britain judged that 'our supreme national interests' were at stake. There was no doubt whatever in my mind that we had been offered a first-class bargain, and that the national interest required that we should accept it. We were in a way only receiving back our own idea, processed and perfected, for we had given to the Americans the original nuclear knowledge which had enabled them to win the Pacific war against Japan.

Macmillan kept General de Gaulle informed by daily telegrams in the hope that he might see the advantage of the weapon to France, and be able to share with us the favourable conditions which President Kennedy was willing to give. The General's final refusal was curt. He also let it be known that he felt that Macmillan had gone back on a personal understanding, and had accepted a position subservient to the United States.

I do not believe that this was anything other than a situation created by the General to achieve the diplomatic effect of chastising the 'Anglo-Saxons' and to boost French self-reliance and national morale. He would never have accepted an American offer however favourable, because he was pledged by every word and action to the total recovery of France, unbeholden to anyone else.

He was quite entitled to his decision to have nothing to do with America, as that was part of the image which he wished to establish for reasons of internal politics; but it was short-sighted and wrong to implicate the British Prime Minister.

Still more wrong to allow the rumour to gain currency in France that his veto on British entry into the EEC was a riposte for a breach of faith at Nassau.

It took quite a long time to re-establish cordiality, and for as long as he lived the General was always scathing on the subject of Britain's 'special relationship' with America.

But in spite of differences the partnership between Germany, France and Britain was close. Over Berlin we saw eye to eye, and that being so, the regular meetings held by Germany, France, Britain and the United States on our relations with Russia in the management of the city, were held against the much wider canvas of the security of the allies. The defection of France from NATO planning did not in these circumstances matter so much. That does not excuse de Gaulle's insistence that detailed planning against instant aggression was not necessary. On that he was obstinately wrong.

At any rate Adenauer and de Gaulle had taken the first steps towards the conception of a Europe economically and politically united, and from the ashes of their three wars the small flame of hope for a continent at peace with itself began to flicker into life.

As I started with the premise that we had to engage America's sympathy and allegiance to a point where a President would take the supreme decision to drop the nuclear bomb to save Europe, and as I shared Adenauer's conviction that the physical presence of the American services on German soil gave the Germans the confidence necessary to rely on NATO, I was more than ready to take trouble to establish intimate relations with the American Secretary of State and President Kennedy.

The President had, in the enthusiasm of his early months in office, made a decision to go and see Mr Khrushchev in Vienna. It was a mistake, for, in the encounter, the Russian leader – tough, cynical and ruthless – made rings round the young man inexperienced in international affairs. Kennedy was quick to recognize his error, and partly for that reason was all the more grateful when the older Macmillan was so willing to place his wisdom and experience at his disposal.

The relationship blossomed, and paid a high dividend in terms of Anglo-American relations. The Presidency of the United States is perhaps the most lonely job in the world, and Kennedy clearly appreciated the trust which Macmillan placed in him.

It was reciprocated in tangible response because it was Kennedy who, on the British Prime Minister's advice, reversed the wishes of the Pentagon and the State Department, and gave the all-clear when the time came to go ahead with the Nuclear Test Ban Treaty.

Kennedy was a natural leader. His exhortation in his Inaugural Address 'Ask not what your country can do for you – ask what you can do for your country' struck a chord in America's youth who were looking for moral leadership. It was heard further afield. The assassin's bullet removed from the front rank of the world's statesmen a young man who had the vision of which the strain of two world wars had almost drained his elders dry.

So with Kennedy and Macmillan, Adenauer and de Gaulle, and such men as Henri Spaak and Joseph Luns, the security of Europe and the North Atlantic was in good hands. That was as well, for Russia was a formidable opponent, and Khrushchev an erratic leader.

XI

The Soviet Union and the United Nations

Khrushchev was a meteoric character. He was also the first of the Russian leaders to move around the world. He revelled in the limelight. On the occasion of his famous speech to the United Nations Assembly, during which he used his shoe to demonstrate his contempt for the Americans, one of our delegation was sitting with a side-on view of the rostrum. He could not understand why, during the Secretary-General's introduction, Khrushchev was quietly undoing the laces of his shoe. The effect was carefully prepared.

He was a bully, and during Mr Macmillan's speech to the Assembly he interrupted with rude and crude noises. When Macmillan said mildly, and much to the delight of the audience, 'I would like a translation of that', Khrushchev was not amused.

He would switch from the coarse and unmannerly to bonhomie in a flash. At one moment at a luncheon he was denouncing me as one who would grind the faces of the poor in the dust, and at the next comparing notes about our grandchildren.

Once, when I was seeing him off from the Waldorf Astoria Hotel we descended in separate elevators. Mine was delayed for a few moments, and when I arrived at the street door, there he was addressing a large crowd, and saying, 'But how can I leave without my Lord?'

He also had luck. To the dinner following the Test Ban Treaty

Mr Dean Rusk had brought twelve Senators and Congressmen – six Democrats and six Republicans. In one of the endless toasts Mr Khrushchev said, 'Mr Rusk, you won't mind me saying that I find your bodyguard half clean and half unclean.' He then turned to me and said, 'Lord Home, you have no bodyguard – which are you? clean or unclean?' I said, 'I think U Thant had better answer that, as he is arbiter of all things.' U Thant said, 'I don't know about Lord Home, Mr Chairman, but do you know what U Thant means in Burmese? – Mr Clean.' What had promised to be a sticky dinner party went with a swing.

I came to understand his mixed-up personality and to like him for his humanity. It had come to him late in life, but it was there.

It suited him from time to time to respond to his contacts by a show of flexibility, but the underlying purpose of Russia's foreign policy did not change, and it was militant. They had stymied any worthwhile initiatives for peace-keeping in the United Nations by their prolific use of the veto; they had taken every opportunity to encourage the newly-independent countries to turn against the West; they were forcing the pace in rearmament, and were always ready to hot it up to put an extra strain on the economies of the NATO countries; they constantly tried to find holes in the Four-Power plan for the administration of Berlin; while in Asia they were using a combination of subversion and force to overthrow the existing governments of South Vietnam, Laos and Cambodia, and to replace them with 'sympathetic' régimes.

I had made up my mind that the only way to deal with the leaders of the Soviet Union was to be strictly pragmatic. They clearly had the general objective of overturning the capitalist and free societies. In that they would not relent, but it was doubtful whether they had worked out a hard and fast plan, and anyhow their tactics allowed them to be flexible as long as a temporary concession did not prejudice their ultimate goal.

The post-war story had shown that it was useless to look for spectacular gains from negotiation, but it was possible that here and there a compromise suitable to both sides might be reached on a narrow front.

Mr Gromyko was the man with whom in the main I had to deal. He was in reality a Civil Servant, and at that time was not even a member of the Politbureau. I discovered early in our dealings that the only way to get down to business and to gain any respect was to show him that we knew exactly what his masters were up to, and that it was useless to try and pull the wool over our eyes.

At our first meeting in New York he was pretty rough, and as he moved to the door he made an aggressive remark on the possibility of nuclear war. I halted him, and said that there was one thing which I wished to make clear. I told him that twice in my lifetime my country had been subjected to bombing, and if Russia was to attempt to bully us in the same way into submission we would stand up to it even though the bombs were nuclear. We knew very well the devastation which we should suffer, but he should be clear on one thing. That should Russia bombard us every nuclear bomb we possessed would be dropped on Russian cities. He asked if I meant that, to which I replied 'Yes'. After that we sat down and talked business.

It was laborious at best, for it meant long hours of entirely negative and sterile conversation, in which Gromyko would recite the communist formulae *ad nauseam*, and I would repeat my piece much more shortly, but it had the advantage that we both knew the basis on which business could be done. When he said something unusual I could recognize the cue.

Once when the Chairmanship of the Conservative Party happened to be vacant while he was visiting London, I offered it to him, and he enquired what he had done to earn such an honour. I said that he had repeated to me that morning the same refrain concerning Berlin which he had used fifteen years before, and in identical words. That made him the best Conservative that I knew. True to form he said, 'I do not think it would be appropriate.'

Sometimes the tedium of repetition – particularly when it was aggressive – became unendurable, and something had to be done to stop it. There was an occasion in Geneva when I was subjected to hours of specious argument about the iniquity of any suggestion that inspection was necessary to verify whether any explosive noise inside the Soviet Union would have been an earthquake or an explosion as the result of a nuclear experiment. Others were willing to be inspected, but the Russians were totally stubborn. The conversation took place at a time when Mr Molotov was being discredited with a lot of propaganda and clatter. Endlessly I had to listen to Mr Gromyko repeating, 'You will know that the noise which is recorded is an earthquake, because I will tell you so, and you will believe.' In the end I could stand it no longer, and said, 'But Mr Gromyko, might not there be another explanation of the noise I heard? Could it not be Mr Molotov being kicked downstairs?' The Russian delegates looked grim, and I thought for a moment that the lot were about to walk out. Then one of them laughed (I doubt if that was wise) and the marathon on inspection was not repeated – at any rate not with me.

Mr Gromyko, over the years, was a wonderful servant to his masters, and all of us who dealt with him had a considerable affection for him. Mrs Gromyko, too, whose approach to life was completely non-political, was always full of vitality and humour.

On the last official visit when I was his host in London, I took him rather daringly to lunch at the Carlton Club which I explained was the hot-bed of Toryism. During the fish he turned to me and said, 'Do I not feel myself moving perceptibly to the Right?'

Once when Gromyko was in London he talked about buying guns for himself and his son. Mrs Gromyko's comment was, 'When you buy a gun for my son, buy a better gun than you buy for my husband, because my son allows the ducks to rise off the water.'

Dealing with the Russians was clearly going to be a hard chore, but there was one other speech which I was anxious to make early in my tenure of office, in order that the public should think straight on the subjects of foreign policy and security.

Having watched two sessions of the United Nations, I had come to the conclusion that it was in real danger of lapsing into futility. My anxiety went further. Britain was getting the rawest of raw deals, since the Soviet Union used the cry of neo-colonialism to poison the minds of the newly-independent countries against us; and innocently they opened their mouths wide and asked for more. I did not wish to see a repetition of the experience of the twenties when the British people had put their trust in the League of Nations which was in reality a broken reed.

Even President Kennedy was not above a dig at British colonialism. In his speech to the Assembly in September 1961, he said that the United States had been a colony, and had suffered the exploitation associated with that status. I followed, and said that as I listened to him 'I couldn't help thinking that America looked pretty well on it. If, in the course of time all our colonies are as happy and prosperous as the United States there will surely be a rush of others queuing up to be exploited a little further.'

But the performance of the United Nations was beyond a joke, and I decided to give a public warning, and to make a considered protest against the abuse of a fine idea.

I chose a quiet season, and on an evening shortly after Christmas, I delivered a speech on the subject to a small and frozen audience in Berwick-upon-Tweed.

The United Nations' 'double standard' hit the world's headlines with a vengeance, and there was in the left-wing quarter a blaze of angry reaction that anyone should have dared to accuse so saintly a body of falling short of the ideal.

No one, of course, had bothered to read the balanced summing-up at the end of the speech; but I was completely unrepentant as I knew that unless the faults were brought out into the open, the organization in terms of reconciliation and peace-keeping would be worse than useless to the nations of the world.

I quote some extracts, so that the readers of today may judge for themselves. The speech was made in the aftermath of the Indian Government's seizure of Goa by force.

Why then, if there is such a universal urge for peace and the machinery to achieve it is ready to hand, is there a crisis of confidence in the United Nations?

The answer is that for the first time since its foundation a number of countries have voted publicly and without shame in favour of the use of force to achieve national ends.

Four countries which were members of the Security Council supported a Resolution condoning the use of force by India against Goa. Had the debate been in the Assembly many more countries, perhaps even a majority – would have voted the same way.

The significance of such action is this. Whatever the provocations suffered by India or the excuses made by her or for her, there is no doubt at all that her actions were a direct breach of the Charter and of international law.

When the United Nations approves that, it could be as Mr Adlai Stevenson said, 'The beginning of the end'.

Many of us had foreseen this crisis of confidence. For years the Russians had been frustrating the proper working of the United Nations, but lately a new and dangerous practice had begun to prevail.

I went on to draw attention to the reckless Resolutions which were an everyday feature of the United Nations' agenda, which were calculated to force Britain, France and other countries to give constitutions to colonial territories for which they were not ready. I quoted from one such Resolution:

'Inadequacy of political, economic, social or educational preparedness should never serve as a pretext for delaying independence.'

Such a Resolution and others like it reveal an almost total lack of responsibility and certainly pay no heed to the main purpose of the United Nations, which is to ensure order and security and peace.

When, therefore, we have reached a stage when a large part of the Organization which is dedicated to peace openly condones aggression; when an Organization which was founded to sustain law and order encourages policies which must endanger it, or when a refusal by many to carry their share of the cost brings a prospect of power without responsibility, it is an understatement to say that there is cause for anxiety.

I then turned to the problem presented by the 'Double Standard'.

The founder members laid the whole emphasis on the organization of peace through collective security. They set up a Security Council to bear the primary responsibility for maintaining the peace. They named the Great Powers as permanent members, in the expectation that they would agree on how to keep international order, and would deal together with any breach of the peace by the Smaller Powers by united decision and co-ordinated action.

In the event of disagreement between the Great Powers each was armed with a veto on action by the others.

The best there could be was collective security collectively imposed – the worst (so it was supposed) stalemate and the *status quo*.

The supposition was wrong, for almost immediately the Russians showed themselves determined to use their veto to further the international objectives of Communism. Russia's decision to subordinate the main purposes of the Charter to her own national ends was the first breach in the spirit of the Charter, and the first threat to the life of the United Nations.

For years the Russians have used the platform of the United Nations to prosecute the cold war. Now another breach is beginning to appear and the origin of it is somewhat similar. A large number of new countries are putting their campaign for acceleration of independence for colonial territories before the main purpose of the Charter which is to provide peace and security. They are more concerned to impose their views of 'colonialism' on others than to fulfil their primary duty which is to 'harmonize the action of nations'.

I would not equate their motives with those of the Communists, although far too often they find themselves bedfellows, but the effect of their actions is to weaken the Charter and to call in question the good faith of the United Nations. Unwittingly they play the Communists' game.

This leads me to illustrate how this concentration on colonialism leads to the adoption of a double standard of behaviour by many of the newly-elected countries.

Russia's Empire is occupied by military force and ruled by fear. No one who has witnessed what has happened in Hungary and East Germany can have any doubt that Russia's colonialism is the most cruel and ruthless in history. In the United Nations her technique is undisguised – it is that of the bully.

By contrast the British record is one which has freed 600 million people in 15 years, and transferred them from colonial dependence, to complete independence within the Commonwealth, where they are equal partners and in no way subordinate. We are moving fast – perhaps faster than in prudence we ought – in the direction in which the new countries want to go. The United Nations' members know that to be true, but they seldom condemn the Russians, and constantly harass us. It seems as if pushing at an open door is not good enough for them. To co-operate with the metropolitan power in completing the process of independence in an orderly way; to ensure that new nations get a good start in international life is apparently emotionally unsatisfying and politically unrewarding.

Since we in Britain are agreed on independence anyway, the only way to pick a quarrel is over timing. Self-government today regardless of whether there is anyone capable of governing –

independence tomorrow even though it would mean other Congos.

The double standard as applied to Europeans and Russians and Europeans and Afro-Asians had become so blatant that I proceeded:

The United Nations, and in particular this Assembly, must show itself to be impartial. I'm only going to ask this question; I'm not sure of the answer. Is there growing up, almost imperceptibly, a code of behaviour where there is one rule for the Communist countries and another for the democracies? One rule for the bully who deals in fear, and another for the democracy because their stock-in-trade is reason and compromise? But if the United Nations is to be the body which we wish to see, which guards the weak and is jealous of the independence of small nations, then they must not yield to the temptation to put public pressure always upon the reasonable nations because they feel that in the last resort those nations will be decent, and therefore will give way. That would be to deny justice to others which they themselves wish to enjoy.

This evidence of a serious falling away from the principles of the Charter places Britain in an appalling dilemma.

Peace – for ours is a most vulnerable island – is the first of British interests. We practise the rule of law and if it is important for us at home it is equally so abroad where we have to earn our living. We want above all to co-operate with all nations without exception. Our safety lies in making and keeping friends and the more the better.

All our instincts and interests therefore combine to urge support for the kind of United Nations for which the founders drew up the Charter. The question which many sober and responsible observers of its practice are asking is whether we can continue to do so, and whether the United Nations of the authors of the Charter has had its day?

I then went on to state the credit side of the balance sheet, and asked the support of the audience for a realistic course for the United Nations 'neither sailing off into the blue of Utopia, nor foundering on the reefs of cynicism'.

For Britain there was therefore no alternative until the United Nations mended its ways to collective security through alliances of like-minded countries.

It is not without interest that Dr Henry Kissinger returned to this theme in 1975, when he went so far as to threaten that the United States could be driven to a point where they would leave the organization. The warnings should be heeded for the substance of them is fair.

For all these matters concerning Scotland or the Commonwealth or Foreign Affairs my platform during these years was the House of Lords. It was an agreeable place from which to operate and made the more so for, until I took over the Leadership in 1967 I was for much of the time understudy to Lord Salisbury. He was the most courteous, civilized and accomplished of politicians, with the ability, like all the Cecils, to turn a phrase, so that it caught and held his audience. He had been one of the architects of the Charter of the United Nations; but he clung to no illusions when the Communists began to veto every peace-making endeavour, and was a strong supporter of NATO. He believed too that the House of Lords had an important role to play in the British constitution in spite of the pruning of its powers.

We hatched between us a scheme for the reform of the House which would have consisted of two hundred hereditary peers elected by themselves, and two hundred life peers who would be appointed. That would have been the active voting House, while others could have come and spoken in debate. It came to nothing because Lord Alexander of Hillsborough – the leader of the Socialist opposition – felt that he could not endorse anything which prolonged the hereditary principle.

We were, however, successful in launching and carrying

through the Life Peerage Bill. The original conception was that these would be working Peers, but that has been diluted in recent years. But it was and is a good idea. The hereditary system does provide able young men who willingly undertake the donkey work involved in the various and detailed parliamentary stages of legislation. If they were not there, young men would I suppose have to be found from party lists; for I recall Lord Montgomery of Alamein saying on one occasion, 'If you think that retired Field Marshals and Admirals are going to sit on the Committee Stage of Bills you're wrong.' He was right.

I had largely missed him and Lord Alexander of Tunis owing to my absence from military service during the war, but membership of the House of Lords enabled me to get to know them well. They were a complete contrast – Alexander quiet and loath to catch the public eye – Monty extrovert and confident. He once asked me to send him some red willows for his garden. The first consignment all died, and I received the following note: 'Pray send me another two dozen willows with exact instructions as to how they should be planted – and British Foreign Policy *in five lines – no more.*'

The nicest and most typical story of Alex is of his response when Winston Churchill went round the Cabinet table asking each individual for his point of view on a certain course of action. Alex's reply was, 'Well, Prime Minister, if it is right we should do it.' Politics were not his element.

I do not know if any future government will seek to reform the House short of a complete restructuring of our system of government. Most of the senates which I have seen overseas are hoary with age.

It may be indefensible and illogical in its present form, but it works, and obstinately the British public seems to like a Lord.

XII

The strategic scene

By 1960 with the advent of a more realistic appreciation of the rôle of the United Nations in relation to British security; with the broad strategy settled in favour of support of NATO plus retention of such bases overseas as could be seen to serve our interests; with the acceptance of the proposition that the Soviet Union must never be allowed to calculate that the alliance would not respond to a conventional attack with nuclear weapons delivered to the heart of Russia, the foundations were laid for planning. First the minimum deployment of forces, which would deter; and secondly, the best ground from which to make progress on *détente*.

There was no doubt at all about the most effective deterrent – it was the 'Polaris' submarine; which, because it was virtually undetectable, was a genuine second-strike weapon which robbed the pre-emptive attack of all its former attraction.

There was, however, a running argument among the professionals as to whether the line between the Warsaw Pact and the NATO forces should be thinly held (by a trip-wire) or more strongly manned, so that a Russian attack could be contained for a number of days or weeks to allow diplomacy a chance to restore peace.

The balance of argument through the years moved towards a substantial conventional force, but it was gradually rendered somewhat academic by the introduction of the tactical nuclear weapon.

Held by both sides in substantial numbers, it is now certain that, unless conventional forces and arms are greatly increased by the West, in the event of an attempt by Russia to change the territorial *status quo*, these weapons would be used.

An imbalance of conventional strength therefore which led to the temptation to probe weakness would at once bring about a dangerous and critical situation. Today's superiority of the Warsaw Pact is in personnel roughly 3–1, and Russia's lead in numbers of tanks and aircraft is such that the allies are on the margin of safety.

To some extent the advantage is neutralized by the introduction of new defensive weapons, some of which were proved in the Israel–Egypt war, but the truth still holds that it is the existence of the intercontinental nuclear missile and the uncertainty of the Russians as to the nature of NATO's response to attack, which keeps the peace.

Between 1961 and 1964 we were diverted from seriously pursuing constructive and long-term plans for organizing *détente* by Russia's actions in Berlin and in Vietnam.

The latter experience is worth recounting at some length because it is a classic example of how the Soviet Communist leaders are prepared to compromise, provided that it does not affect their medium or long-term aims. It is also a vivid illustration of how far they are prepared to go to get their way.

America, it is true, had become involved in assisting South Vietnam to achieve the independence from the Communist North which she desired, and to which the Russians objected. That Soviet opposition was understandable, although 'self-determination' was a slogan to which the Soviet leaders paid lip-service.

But that was not the point. The point was that the dispute could be solved either by peaceful means or by war. Which would the Russians choose?

1954 had seen the first flare-up and the first International Conference. After months of negotiation in which Mr Anthony Eden took a leading part, the Russians and Chinese became parties to a

Treaty, the stated objects of which were to end outside intervention in the affairs of Laos, Vietnam and Cambodia; to organize the withdrawal of troops; to limit arms to those necessary for policing; and to provide for the political machinery necessary for the reunification of the two Vietnams.

An International Commission was set up to supervise the carrying-out of the terms; and there was a real chance that these three countries could become non-aligned and removed from the arena of a political conflict involving the great powers.

The Russians signed, but no sooner was the ink dry on the document than they ratted on the terms of the Treaty. The Commission was totally frustrated, and the promising initiative ran into the sand. The only slender anchor which just held was that the British and Russian Foreign Ministers had been designated co-Chairmen of the Conference which was deemed to be continuing.

When I took up the tale in 1960 the war-clouds were gathering ominously yet again, and I began to pester Mr Gromyko to re-assemble the Conference.

When a Russian does not wish to act he will use any device to stall; and the only hope is to have the letter of the law on your side. This the signatories to the Treaty had; and after a lot of argument, Mr Gromyko agreed that the Conference should be re-convened in Geneva. For months no measurable progress was made, and it seemed that we were deadlocked; but I had made a useful friend in Mr Cheng-yi, the Foreign Minister of China, who had no love for the Russians.

He was, of course, a Communist, and one night, after we had dined well, I tackled him about Chinese penetration into Africa, and asked him why the Chinese Communists couldn't leave others alone, and get on with their stupendous task of internal reconstruction and development. He interrupted me and said, 'Oh, please, do not go on talking like that. The trouble with you Westerners is that you always think in terms of a lifetime. Now we consider that to be fussy!'

This time, however, Mr Cheng-yi adapted himself to the urgency of the agenda.

Geneva was a place for confessions, for it was there that Prince Sihanouk told me that, faced with the choice, he would rather be red than dead.

I doubt if the Conference would have succeeded but for two men possessed of unlimited patience. I had asked President Kennedy if he would raise the level of his delegation, and he readily sent Mr Averell Harriman, and as his opposite number I brought in Mr Malcolm MacDonald. They settled down to make the time which an Asian requires to come to a conclusion. Both rank high amongst conciliators.

When Mr Gromyko was there he used to greet me in the morning with, 'Well, what have you been plotting against me during the night?' Eventually he was persuaded. The Pathet Lao, the Vietminh and the Viet-Cong, the Laotians and the Vietnamese North and South, were brought into line, and we signed the second Treaty, embodying the same objectives as the first. We set up, on the precedent of 1954, the second Commission of Control, and yet again the Foreign Ministers of Britain and Russia were Chairmen of a continuing Conference.

But once more the techniques and the mechanics of opposition were repeated. The Russians proceeded to make a mockery of the Commission's activities. The whole area began to seethe, and once more there was war in Vietnam, with America in it up to the neck, and the Soviet pouring in arms to the other side.

It is not my intention to retrace that story. The Americans had become involved at the start from the highest motives of ensuring that the South Vietnamese could choose their future, but they found, as the French had discovered before them, that there are no prizes to be won for anyone in a war on the mainland of Asia.

But I must recall the sequel to 1954 and 1962; for in 1973 yet another Conference was arranged in Paris which once again included the Soviet Union, Britain, America and China, and those in the area who were involved in the fighting. This time the Secretary-General of the United Nations, Dr Waldheim, was present to lend it extra prestige. After talk and argument a communiqué was signed – known as the Treaty of Paris. It was a solemn agreement. But yet again the farce was repeated. A fresh Commission was installed; but at once its work was stultified. The Americans withdrew from Vietnam; but the Russians continued to send arms, and the Chinese to reinforce North Vietnam's industry with manpower, so that South Vietnam and Cambodia were overrun. The Communists had cheated for the third time. To borrow a phrase from Winston Churchill – 'Three times is a lot'.

When the democracies are genuinely seeking peace, and believe in self-determination and human rights, and hold that treaties are signed to be kept, it is difficult not to despair when faced with such a record of duplicity by the Communists. Yet we have to live on the same small globe, and rapid communications are bringing all of us closer and closer together. There is nothing for it but to try and negotiate a more positive coexistence. Provided that we recognize that there is safety in numbers, and in the friendship of those who feel like us; provided we realize that the Communists' business is to undermine; provided that we keep our nuclear second-strike weapon, we can live our own lives. But we should never make a concession without achieving a concrete *quid pro quo*. Let up for one moment on vigilance, and everything which we value could be lost in the twinkling of an eye. It is infinitely frustrating, but these are the only rules consistent with safety and freedom.

Although the most powerful members of the NATO alliance have remained solid, their flanks have been eroded. Portugal has been severely weakened by internal strife.

Spain ought clearly to have been a member of NATO from the start. The dislike of the Franco régime by the Scandinavians, and in particular by Denmark, and the deep feelings of British Socialist Governments prevented this happening, but the security of Western Europe is not complete without Spain's reinforcement.

Even more threatening to the cohesion of the alliance is the open difference between Greece and Turkey over the future shape of the constitution and government of Cyprus. From the moment when Archbishop Makarios decided to champion Enosis (Union with Greece) and General Grivas took up arms to harass the forces of order on the island, the fat was in the fire; because the Turks would not tolerate a system of government in which the Turkish Cypriots would come under Greek domination.

The Archbishop, recognizing the error which he had made, switched to a demand for self-government leading to rapid independence and membership of the Commonwealth, but the damage had been done, and the Turks continued to see in every political move a cover for the ultimate end of Enosis.

There were endless meetings of the United Nations, and Britain held long talks and put forward many varying proposals aimed at a fair distribution of powers within the island as between Greek and Turkish Cypriots; but the same fundamental objections were raised by the Turks; namely that there would always be local discrimination against their minority, and that the real, if concealed, aim of Makarios was Union with Greece.

Eventually, with the help of U Thant, a settlement was reached which included all the adjustments and refinements which were necessary to induce Greek and Turkish Cypriots grudgingly to cooperate. It could have worked, but it did not really do so because the mistrust of the Archbishop was never laid.

An uneasy truce lasted until 1975, but there were increasing outbreaks of violence, and more and more talk of partition, until at last the Turks lost patience, invaded the island and asserted their authority in the Turkish area. From the British point of view there had been two real anxieties from the start. The first concerned our bases and communications centre, and the second the weakening of NATO's flank in the Eastern Mediterranean, by reason of a quarrel between the two allies.

During the years from 1964–75 both the Archbishop and the

Turks gave definite pledges that the bases should remain under British sovereignty. So far that is so, and it is important that the facility should be kept intact. Greece has withdrawn co-operation from NATO, but the Turks, who have a clearer perception of Russia's intentions, remain.

In a different order of concern was the situation of Iceland. There is something about the Law of the Sea which brings out the worst in everyone.

In 1962 Iceland denounced the fishing agreement which she had with us, and proceeded to talk and act as though she intended to launch a 'cod war'. After several incidents which involved force on both sides, the situation was tense and there seemed to be no end in sight to the quarrel. The NATO members were anxious about a dispute between two allies on the northern flank of the alliance, particularly as, if the irritation of the Icelanders mounted, the future of the important American base at Keflavik could be involved.

Luckily the Icelandic Foreign Minister and I found ourselves together late one evening, following a session of the NATO Council. The building was locked up and everyone had apparently gone home; but we found an upper room with a bare wooden trestle table on which we sat and agreed that the quarrel must stop. We each undertook to see to it that it did. Negotiations followed and although there were some ticklish moments, the Foreign Minister, Mr Gudmundsson, was as good as his word and all was quiet for another ten years.

In all these situations and difficulties Britain was expected to play an active part in finding solutions.

It was during those years at the Foreign and Commonwealth Office that I became aware of two errors which were commonly made about Britain's conduct of foreign policy. The first was a failure to recognize that our rôle in the world had changed as our relative power had diminished, and that the change was permanent. Again and again when some tragic, disturbing or dramatic event took place, people would ask me why the British Government was not taking steps to put things right. They did not like it when I said that we had shed the power which would have enabled us to do so. Secondly, I learned that strong declarations of intent without the backing of real power achieve nothing.

When Mr George Brown (later Lord George-Brown) succeeded me as Foreign Secretary, he removed the picture of King George III which faced the Foreign Secretary's desk, saying that he could not bear to look at the fellow who gave away the British colonies. He substituted Palmerston, the gun-boat diplomatist. It was a typical and defiant gesture – the only trouble being that the gun-boats were not there.

But the opposite error to nostalgia was just as bad, which was to conclude that, because we had less power, we therefore had no influence at all. For example, the Socialist Government had withdrawn (prematurely in my opinion) from the Gulf, but the fact that in the past we had looked after the security of the Gulf States, and that our diplomatic advisers had won the confidence of the Rulers gave us a considerable say in the shape of things to come.

Our ex-colonies too might denounce us in the United Nations and elsewhere as aggressors, but when they ran into trouble it was Britain to whom they turned. It is a great mistake to underestimate the influence which our experience of international affairs and our skill in diplomacy can bring to bear. It is my experience that even when our advice is not taken it is weighed carefully in the scales.

So a modern Foreign Secretary has to accept that Britain cannot match the military performance of America or of Russia, or China to come; nor, unless they defeat themselves by internal dissension, can we equal the economic thrust of Japan. We are a medium-sized power, but it is useless to cry over spilt milk, particularly when in the creation of a Commonwealth of nations, totally independent of us, we did much of the spilling ourselves.

A little knowledge of our past can put our frustrations into perspective, for in truth, out of the total span of our recorded history, the period during which we were a dominant power was scarcely a hundred years.

Our sense of humour too can help. A pompous man, who was to propose a toast at a public dinner, was ushered on arrival into a room which he considered to be beneath his dignity. He said to the hotel attendant, 'But, don't you know who I am?' to be met with the reply, 'No, sir, I am afraid I do not. I will go and make some enquiries and let you know.' In Britain we have made the mental adjustment. We now know who we are, and in which room we ought to be.

We have, in fact, reverted to our previous state – that of a middle-sized European power which can exercise some influence, but which can wield real authority on world affairs only in so far as we are prepared to go into economic and political partnership with our European friends, and always to retain a close friendship with the United States of America.

A Europe which is supplemented by the North Atlantic Alliance is the only combination which can guarantee security to ourselves and our friends.

If we pull our economic weight so that we are not always the poor relation, and so get down to the task of ensuring that the European Community and NATO work, then no one power will dominate the centre of the continent of Europe – and no aggressor will try to cut our communications by sea or air, and we shall live at peace. If also we give a lead in the Commonwealth councils we can do quite a lot to guide the Third World into sensible ways.

XIII

The succession to the Premiership

In 1961 I had concluded on the evidence before me that the United Kingdom could not afford to stay out of the European Community, and I made a speech to that effect in the House of Lords.

My experience as Commonwealth Secretary had convinced me that the erosions of our economic preferences which had begun in Australia and which were depriving us of our share of Commonwealth trade, were bound to continue, and that we must act to find alternatives to protect our national income.

There could be no complaint about the reduction of the preferences which we had in Commonwealth markets. Australia, for example, wished to establish her own manufacturing capacity and to broaden her economic contacts with South-East Asia and with Japan. Having brought up our once dependent territories to be nations in their own right, it was not for us to insist that they should stay tied to our apron strings. It seemed to me therefore that membership of the European Community, with its 200 million consumers, was a market on our doorstep which we could not ignore.

The politics of the matter weighed with me even more. NATO it is true was an effective military shield of Western Europe, but the Communist threat to the free area of the continent was as much political as military; and anyhow the youth of Europe, if war was to be averted, would need to be inspired by a philosophy of freedom at least as dynamic as that of the Communists.

Harold Macmillan had always been a keen European, so we embarked on a long negotiation with the six Common Market countries, with the objective of achieving entry on reasonable terms within the rules of the Treaty of Rome. They were conducted with great skill by Mr Edward Heath, only at the last lap to be vetoed by General de Gaulle on the specious grounds that Britain was not yet ready to assume the responsibilities of partnership.

To be rebuffed in open diplomacy was an unhappy and frustrating experience for the British public and for the Conservative Party; and some of the blame for the failure, however unjustly, rubbed off on the Government. The electors began to be critical and Members of Parliament restive.

In politics misfortunes seldom come singly, and in 1961 and 1962 there was a series of incidents concerning security which, to say the least, were unsettling.

The first concerned the unmasking of the spy George Blake. Little notice was taken of the success of the security services in catching him, and the media were much more concerned with the fact that he could have existed at all.

The second arose from the arrest of a young Civil Servant in the Admiralty called Vassall, who came under suspicion for breaches of security. This would normally not have excited much comment had not disgraceful stories been bandied about that Mr T. G. D. Galbraith, who was a Junior Minister, and Lord Carrington, who was First Lord of the Admiralty, had associated with him in a way which was prejudicial to the safety of the realm.

It was necessary that their names should be publicly cleared and as the Civil Service was involved a judicial enquiry had to be held and it had to be enabled to take evidence on oath. In the event the Ministers were completely exonerated, but two other consequences were far from happy.

The enquiry revealed that Communist pressures were being brought to bear on Civil Servants which caused unease among the public; while during the enquiry two journalists who refused to reveal the sources of the stories which they had circulated were sent to prison. Neither they nor the newspapers as a whole forgave Macmillan.

Thirdly, and close on the heels of these events, came the confession of Philby who declared that he had tipped the wink to Burgess and Maclean, which enabled them to give the security officers the slip.

Then on top of all that came the accusation against Mr Jack Profumo, the Secretary of State for War, alleging that he had formed an undesirable association with a girl who was simultaneously living with a member of the Russian Embassy staff. The wretched story need not be repeated, and since then Jack Profumo has more than redeemed himself. But there is no doubt that Macmillan's apparent hesitation in facing Profumo with the need at any personal cost to tell the truth was due to his experience of the Vassall incident. Two Ministers of the Crown had been accused in that case and had been proved to be guiltless. Who was he, when another of his Ministers was faced with a similar charge and had publicly denied it to the Attorney-General and to Parliament, to call his honour in question? He hesitated and hesitated again and was lost.

All of us knew that Jack Profumo was incapable of giving away official secrets, but a Minister of the Crown had deliberately deceived the House of Commons, and the Prime Minister, for however understandable a reason, had failed to act in time to secure his resignation, and the penalties had to be paid.

There was a widespread feeling that Macmillan had lost his grip and that the Party was heading for electoral disaster. Conservative and public morale sank to zero. As a Government we badly needed a success. We were able properly to claim it in August in the Treaty which we signed with the Soviet Union and the United States, banning nuclear tests in the atmosphere.

It was, in fact, very largely Macmillan's advocacy and perseverance which brought it about. Over the years the Russians had stood out firmly against any system of inspection of armaments, while the Americans had been equally obdurate, and said that unless inspection was allowed they would sign nothing.

Macmillan decided to go over the heads of the Pentagon and the State Department direct to President Kennedy. He had by then established an easy and natural relationship with the President, and the various meetings which were held had been intimate affairs with a spicing of fun.

On one occasion when the President arrived in Bermuda, he flew a 'Stars and Stripes' flag on Government House, beside which our Union Jack looked like a postage stamp. The Governor, Sir Julian Gascoigne, decided that this would not do, and sent people into the town to buy up as many Union Jacks as could be found. They were then sewn together, and by the next morning our demonstration was as impressive as theirs. Garter King of Arms would have had something to say, but honour had been saved, and Kennedy was highly amused.

To another meeting we took with us Sir William Penney as scientific adviser on weaponry. The President turned to him and asked how many atomic bombs it would take to destroy the City and State of New York. Sir William, in his broad Australian accent, without pause or punctuation said, 'Ow, Mr President, give me two or three and throw in another for luck and I'd mike a good job of it – m'y I 'ave another gin and tonic please?' The President's rocking-chair rocked well into the evening, as the flavour of it kept coming back to him.

On this occasion the Prime Minister, knowing his man, limited his request for action to tests in the atmosphere, where inspection was clearly less important, and argued that to end nuclear fall-out was something universally desired, which would make people a lot less jittery, and would begin to restore confidence that human life would go on.

President Kennedy was gifted with imagination. He overruled the departmental objections and so we were free to proceed.

During the weeks preceding signature, Mr Macmillan sent Lord

Hailsham to Moscow to carry forward negotiations. His house in England had developed dry rot, and Lady Hailsham sent him several telegrams describing the steps necessary for a cure. The Russians could not believe that anything *en clair* could possibly mean what it said, and spent profitless weeks trying to crack the code.

On one of my visits to Moscow I was told that I must leave my keys behind, because the Russian housemaids in the Embassy would undoubtedly take impressions of them. I then asked if I could not be supplied with a dozen keys which opened nothing, which the Russian ladies would press into the soap, only to confuse the KGB. A bottom-form joke no doubt, but I have always thought that in simple things we miss a number of tricks which could keep our humourless Communist neighbours harmlessly engaged.

At any rate the signature of the Treaty caught the imagination of the world and of Britain; but in home politics the anxiety remained, and the malaise was not cured.

I returned from a visit to the General Assembly of the United Nations in September to find that Harold Macmillan had been feeling tired and was not too well. That, on top of everything else, was an anxiety; but much worse was to come.

In a talk one evening at Chequers I told him that there was a lot of restlessness in the Conservative Party, and that many doubted whether he could recover the image of the 'super-Mac' sufficiently to win an election. I said that there was absolutely no question of revolt or plot, but that it would be much appreciated by the Party if he would put an end to speculation, and would say whether he intended to lead the Party into the next General Election, and thus prove that there was a firm hand at the wheel. We discussed the matter and he then said absolutely clearly that it was his desire and intention to lead, and that the forthcoming Conference in Blackpool would give him the opportunity to raise the Party's spirit by a forthright statement.

That was fine; but fate had a hand to play and soon. When we assembled for Cabinet on 8 October we found that the Prime

Minister had suffered a severe attack of his prostate gland trouble during the night and had to see his doctor again. It was apparent that his attendance at the coming Party Conference must be assumed to be very unlikely, and that the question of replacing him as leader could arise.

In Cabinet in his absence we had a short discussion. The Lord Chancellor (Viscount Dilhorne) said that, as he was not himself a candidate for the leadership, if anyone wished to have any private talk he would be available. I said that the same applied to me. Enoch Powell later cited this indication of my position as a kind of pledge from which, when events turned out as they did, I should have had the whole Cabinet's leave formally to withdraw. It was, however, nothing so dramatic or pompous – merely a statement revealing that at that time the question of my succession to Macmillan had simply not crossed my mind.

When the others went off to Blackpool I stayed behind to attend to Foreign Office business, as my speech to the Conference was not to be until later in the week.

On 9 October I went to see Macmillan in the nursing home and he talked about the future leadership. He asked me whether I had thought of taking it on, and if not why not. I replied that I had not done so – that I was happy in the Foreign Office, and in the House of Lords which I had never contemplated leaving, and that it was in these fields that my strong preferences lay. He seemed to accept that, and said that he had concluded after much thought that Lord Hailsham might be the best choice. I had watched Quintin under pressure during the Suez crisis where he had shown admirable calm at the Admiralty in testing circumstances; and while I had some misgivings about his famous 'judgement' I felt that he could take on the leadership and the job of Prime Minister, and make a success of it. I left it with Macmillan that he would continue his talks with him and others. He asked me to take a message to the Blackpool Conference conveying to the delegates that he felt that he could not lead the Party at the General Election, and inviting those whose business it was to do so, to take soundings about the future leadership.

I did not enjoy the journey to Blackpool with these grim tidings; and when I came to the platform to deliver his message to the audience of 4,000 the hall was hushed with anticipation that something ill was in the wind.

As President of the National Union for the year I read the message which contained Macmillan's decision. 'I will not be able to carry the physical burden of leading the Party at the next General Election. I hope that it will soon be possible for the customary consultations to be carried out within the Party about the leadership.' All of us felt a long way from the happy days when 'we never had it so good'.

I walked back from the Meeting with Quintin who knew by then that he was Macmillan's selection, and I told him that the idea had my support. Had I known that he intended to throw his claim to the leadership into the ring within a matter of hours, I would have tried to dissuade him from it then and there, for people never like being bounced, and least of all at a time of emotional stress. As it was, others advised him against precipitating the issue, and I had a late word with him shortly before his evening meeting with the Conservative Political Centre; but by then it was too late for he considered himself to be committed to his friends. In his speech he declared himself a runner. The immediate instinct of his audience was to acclaim, but there followed a swift reaction against his candidature, and the tactical advantage which he had seemingly tried to gain by such instant action fell right away. This had been predictable; and the opposition increased rapidly in the succeeding days. It was sad. He had many of the qualities of an inspiring leader; for he combined a keen intellect with an ability to speak from the heart; and over and above that the power to make up his mind and to decide.

It was after this débâcle that a number of Conservatives came and told me that I ought to consider coming forward as a leader of the Party and a potential Prime Minister. It was the last thing which I had anticipated, and the last thing which I sought. At first my reply was that which I had given to Macmillan. I was happy in my Office; it was exacting but I could carry it easily in the House of Lords; and I had no wish to re-submit myself to the rough and tumble of electioneering and the House of Commons.

But the visitors to my hotel room became more and more insistent and more numerous, and represented substantial and influential bodies of opinion in both Houses. Lord Blakenham, Mr Selwyn Lloyd, Lord Dilhorne, Sir William Anstruther-Gray (later Lord Kilmany) and others were among them. They argued that Hailsham would not be acceptable to the Party, and with that I was compelled by the recent events to agree; they said that Butler would not have the support which was essential if confidence was to be restored to the Party in time for the General Election, which was due at the latest in October 1964; and that, too, I thought to be true. More positively they insisted that I could command the support of a solid majority in the Commons and in the Lords; and that, although they recognized that I had not looked for and did not want the leadership, the well-being of the Party must be put first.

My brother was later to write a play with the title of *The Reluctant Peer*, but at that moment I was filled with deep doubts about becoming a commoner once again. It entailed renouncing a peerage which had been held for many hundreds of years; it meant taking on a new constituency, and fighting a by-election in order to be able to sit in the House of Commons; and it meant assuming the most testing and responsible of all the political offices in Britain, with all the physical strains which go with the occupancy of No. 10 Downing Street. It meant, in short, a convulsion in my life for which I was unprepared and which to say the least was unnerving.

One thing was clear in the confusion – that I could not even let myself think about the matter unless my physical health was up to it. Overstrain had brought on tuberculosis in 1939 and I had been having a lot of trouble with my eyes. I told Lord Dilhorne that I would ask my doctor whether in his opinion I could last the course if the task were laid upon me. After a thorough examination he said that I was well enough to hold it down. That escape route was closed.

I then had to consider all the political and governmental aspects of the matter. There was one rather serious minus in the count-down. I was not trained in economics, and economic matters were sure to figure largely in the run-up to the election and in the years to come. Unluckily, in 1962, in an interview with Kenneth Harris of the *Observer*, I had publicly admitted this deficiency. He had asked me whether I felt that I could ever be Prime Minister, and I had answered light-heartedly, 'No, because I do my sums with matchsticks'. It did not worry me unduly because all that was needed would be to choose a good Chancellor of the Exchequer; but Harold Wilson was not likely to miss a trick like that.

On the plus side was the fact that the Foreign Office and the years spent in Cabinet were a good apprenticeship, while in addition I had never been afraid of taking decisions. That, above all else, is what a Prime Minister is for.

Naturally I talked over every aspect of it with Elizabeth and the family; and in the end I concluded that if – and only if – convincing evidence was brought to me that a substantial majority in both Houses wished me to take on the job I would do so. The procedure for ascertaining the opinion of members of the Commons and of Peers and of prominent people in the Party Organization was then conducted by persons who were later to be christened 'the Magic Circle'. They were in the main Conservative Whips in both Houses, for if they did not know the form then nobody else would. When the result of the canvass was conveyed to me I had no doubt whatever that it had been thorough and honest and that I could command the necessary support in Parliament. There was therefore no longer any reason for or point in hesitation; and I said that if I were the choice that I would respond to the best of my ability.

I heard then that a bet had been struck at Blackpool which must be unique. It coupled at long odds Breasley to win the Flat Race Jockeys' Championship and me to be Prime Minister. It was a spectacular 'Autumn Double'. I did not have time to tell Elizabeth the final decision. She heard on the wireless that I was off to the Palace. Her comment to my son was, 'Heavens – in that suit!'

On 18 October I was sent for by Her Majesty and invited to form a Government. I expressed my gratitude, but explained to the Queen that I must ask leave to go away and see if I could form an administration. I was by no means sure, after the drama of the recent weeks, what the attitude of some of my colleagues would be. I had to enlist Butler, Maudling and Hailsham at the very least, to have the foundation on which to build a Cabinet and Government which would command support in the country and respect overseas.

Butler had for long been heir-apparent, and had given devoted and distinguished service to the Conservatives. Maudling was the best equipped on economics, and Hailsham was the possessor of a keen brain and was a colourful and popular figure. None of them could have been happy at that time. With kindness and loyalty and sacrifice they gave me their support, as did all but two of my colleagues in Macmillan's Cabinet. They were Ian Macleod and Enoch Powell, who were not natural bedfellows, but who for the moment had got into a huddle. The reason which they gave to me was that they did not believe that a man with my social background could win a General Election for the Conservative Party at that time in the twentieth century. I said that I thought they were wrong; but that if that was their reason for declining to serve I could only accept it and be sorry. I had a feeling that at the back of their minds was the calculation that, although we might lose in 1964, the next opportunity would not be long and that then we would win under another leader. But in politics one cannot do such clever mathematical sums and hope that events will conform. When a General Election comes it is necessary to fight flat out to win.

It was a pity that the two of them virtually stood aside from the team, because they carried a lot of influence in the Universities and among young Liberal-Unionist opinion. I was personally sorry at their refusal because I had a considerable respect for their intellectual qualities. I had not seen eye to eye with Iain Macleod on Africa. He once told me – and clearly he believed it – that Lumumba was the greatest man in Africa. That indicated to me an alarming lack of judgement; but then as Colonial Secretary I had always thought him to be the wrong man in the wrong place. His strength was shown in domestic politics where his brilliant oratory could be relied upon to leave his political opponents speechless.

Enoch Powell, too, had a fine mind, which I flattered myself I could have harnessed to constructive policies. Perhaps I was wrong.

Had these two pulled their weight, I have no doubt at all that our short-head defeat would have been converted into a narrow victory, and a win at that time for the Conservative Party could well have smashed the Socialists, for they could scarcely have survived four defeats in a row.

In the immediate aftermath of accepting office I had one piece of luck. In an interview on TV I was asked whether I did not resent Mr Wilson's jibe that I was the fourteenth Earl of Home? I replied that I presumed that Mr Wilson was the fourteenth Mr Wilson. I heard no more of that particular line of inverted snobbery.

I now had to find a constituency, and George Younger who had already been adopted as the Conservative candidate in the coming by-election in Kinross and West Perthshire, with great kindness made way for me.

The campaign which followed was turned into an unprecedented circus by the multitude of journalists who joined the caravan.

Major and Mrs Andrew Drummond-Moray had generously offered their small house in Comrie to be our headquarters. Every chair in the house had to be pressed into service for the twice-daily Press conferences, and in general the peaceful villages of Kinross and West Perthshire entered into the gala spirit of the affair. The weather was glorious, and the local hospitality so good, that only a minority of the Press stayed the course to the last meeting of the day in one or other of the remote glens. The result of the campaign was better than I could have hoped for, and I was returned to the

House of Commons with a comfortable majority of 9328.

My first appearance at the Box in the Chamber was nearly my last. I was quite unprepared for the sheer impact of noise after the quiet and civilized proceedings of the House of Lords; and if it had not been for the solid table between me and the Opposition I should have been seen to be shaking at the knees. Somehow I managed to get through my speech on the Loyal Address, which lays down the programme for the Session, but the signals were clear – no quarter was going to be given by Mr Wilson and his colleagues, and the going and the way ahead between then and the election was going to be hard and rough.

Sir Michael Fraser (now Lord Fraser of Kilmorack), who was in charge of the Conservative Central Office, felt that it would be useful to those who were to plan the election battle if I were to try and distil on a few sheets of paper something of my political philosophy and of my interpretation of the way which the Conservative Party should take in the years ahead. In any political office which I had held I had always tried to keep open as many policy options as possible, and that is why I like the definition of Conservatism as 'doing the right thing at the right time'.

The 'confession' to Sir Michael was scrappy, and does not bear repetition, but there were certain propositions which can stand. I still believe that politics is a public service, and that the great majority of politicians enter the profession to pursue it.

I still contend that 'Socialist recipes for equality' are merely another way of saying that the pace of the slowest will govern Britain's affairs.

I still think it to be 'touch and go' whether democracy – one man one vote – will last.

It is even clearer than it was then that we can 'well relapse into some more authoritarian form of government unless the great majority are really well educated to the basic facts of community and international life'.

My plea in 1963 was for plain speaking about true values, and I would certainly repeat that now with a fresh sense of urgency. For some reason which I cannot quite diagnose the people of Britain seem to have a picture of democracy which is less clear-cut than it used to be.

There seems, for example, to be a doubt creeping in concerning the right of the majority to rule, or as to the duty of a minority to accept the law, or even the validity of the essential freedoms of speech and choice.

Perhaps older generations were too simple, but it is surely a dangerous practice to pull up the roots of a delicate plant – and democracy is that – unless one has a substitute with which to replace it if it dies.

Loyalties are not necessarily everlasting or sacrosanct, but before discarding such concepts as Parliamentary Government, obedience to the law, the freedom from arbitrary arrest, and the freedom of speech and choice, it is as well to ask whether the alternative would serve as well.

My feeling in the early sixties was that as Conservatives we had allowed the definition of democracy to become blurred and that there was a danger that people would reject it, and be led away by the seductive cry that what was needed was a strong man with strong policies.

There is no better system than democracy, because its actions stem from the will of the people, but they must be educated in its obligations and responsibilities if it is to work.

The fourth and last year of a Parliament is not the ideal time to take over the leadership of a Party and Government. The main legislative programme is virtually finished, and the Opposition naturally makes the best use of the vacuum. The two rules of conduct for a Prime Minister at such a time are; first, not to allow any division in the Cabinet which could be represented as a split on principle or on policy, and thus dishearten the rank and file of the Party; and secondly, to show a confident face to the nation.

Unluckily there were on this occasion plans to complete a comparatively small measure known as the Resale Price Maintenance Bill. It was a minor piece of legislation, but its opponents had whipped up a determined campaign against it, on the grounds that it would do damage to the small shopkeepers who were the Conservatives' friends. Quite a number of the Cabinet were opposed to going ahead with it, as were a large number of Conservative Members of Parliament.

Heath, who was in charge of the Bill, was strongly in favour of proceeding. The Cabinet being about equally divided I, as Prime Minister, had to decide. I thought that the Bill was right, and that on balance to drop it at that late stage would be interpreted as putting the Party interest before that of the Country. To give way to pressure seldom pays, so I decided, although with many misgivings, to see the Act through Parliament.

The refusal of Macleod and Powell to serve in the Cabinet had already cost us a number of votes, and the passage of the Resale Price Maintenance Bill undoubtedly lost us some more. However, we were on every other issue a united team, and as such we prepared to face the electors.

At the time of the change of leadership in October 1963 most of the commentators had forecast that the morale of the Party had fallen so low as to be beyond recovery within the year available before an election; but in the event, by Christmas there were some signs that the spirits of Conservatives had begun to rise.

One of the decisions which cannot be taken by anyone other than the Prime Minister is the date of an election. That is for him, and him alone. The chances are that he will receive conflicting advice from the Party managers and from colleagues. In 1964 there were in reality only two alternatives – June or October, and there was the usual see-saw of argument.

The danger of running until the last possible day is that some capricious and unforeseen happening can give the Opposition a chance to divert the attention of the voters from the solid issues on which the Government has chosen to fight.

The estimate of the Chairman of the Party – Lord Blakenham – was to the effect that we were likely to lose by 60 to 70 seats in June, whereas by October there was just an outside chance that we could win. So for better or for worse 15 October was fixed as the day of decision.

XIV

The office of
Prime Minister

Harold Macmillan had been a stimulating political chief under whom
to serve, and he managed to make the conduct of government
interesting, agreeable and entertaining. He would enquire of
Ministers how things were going from time to time, but would
seldom interfere. If he wanted some course of action he would say
so, and expect it to be done without constant supervision. He was
easy to reach, and easy to talk to freely. We would therefore go to
him for advice only when we really needed it, and we were sure of
a ready and understanding hearing.

Lady Dorothy, too, kept open house, and the whole was a family
affair. Harold was also incomparably amusing even on official
occasions. I recall walking with him through the miles of statues
which the Vatican houses, and arriving face to face with the ultimate
reward which was the famous bust of Julius Caesar. He gazed upon
it reverently, and twenty or thirty Italians waited hanging upon his
words. He turned to me and said, 'It's terribly like Douglas Jay.'
And that was all.

In Cabinet he deliberately used to illustrate his points with
analogies from the shooting-field, which he knew nine-tenths of
the members would not understand. I remember one such beginning,
'Of course, if you brown into a covey of partridges –' He took an
impish delight in the general bewilderment.

One morning I came into the Cabinet room rather early and found the Cabinet Secretary, Sir Norman Brook (later Lord Normanbrook) changing all our places. I asked what had happened – Had there been a shuffle? – or had one of us died in the night? 'Oh no,' said Sir Norman, 'it's nothing like that. The Prime Minister cannot stand Enoch Powell's steely and accusing eye looking at him across the table any more, and I've had to move him down to the side.'

The secret of Macmillan's political success was his absolute mastery of every parliamentary occasion. It involved a lot of preparation, but it paid a high political dividend. As an historian, too, he had a finely developed sense of perspective.

If he had been given the health – even after the Profumo affair – I would not have put it past him to have led the Party to a fourth Conservative victory.

He was, apart from his great ability, a supremely successful showman. Years later, in a private house, when he was discussing politics among a group of friends, he said musingly, 'Of course, when a man becomes Prime Minister, he has to some extent to be an actor.' We kept our faces and behaved remarkably well.

It has often been said that a Prime Minister is a lonely person, and I suppose that is true of anyone put on a pinnacle where there is only room for one, and especially where the ultimate decision and responsibility cannot be shared.

But he is certainly not lonely for company and occupation, nor, if he is a natural devolver of work, will he sit anxiously twiddling his thumbs because his colleagues do not come and tell him what they are doing day by day. There are in fact dozens of people around ready to advise and help and generally to oil the wheels so that a Prime Minister's life may run smoothly and safely. He becomes accustomed to never being alone out-of-doors. I was extremely fortunate both as Prime Minister and as Foreign Secretary in my detective guardians, for all were efficient, adaptable, interesting and delightful companions.

I had only one perpetual skirmish with them, for I cannot live a London life without walking. They would use every argument and device – weather, pressure of time, security – to get me into the motor car. These contests I always won, and grudgingly in the summer holiday they would admit that they would not have lasted a week in the Scottish hills but for the circuits of St James's Park.

I can only recall one encounter where a member of the public inflicted physical damage on me. It was a roasting day, and I was wearing the thinnest of tropical suits, when, as we were walking through the main gate of Palace Yard, Westminster, a woman launched herself at me. I had my hands in my pockets (a bad habit) and she entwined herself round me, pinning both my arms to my sides with strong hands and pointed talons. Gradually I was disentangled, and my detective said, 'I know her – she's quite harmless.' I then revealed ten bloody nail-prints in my arms. But all the sympathy I got was, 'It wouldn't have happened if we had gone by car.'

All important to a Prime Minister and a senior Cabinet Minister is the organization of his private office. Here again I was blessed with private secretaries who were skilled, helpful, equable and good company. Great care was always taken with the selection of these young members of the Foreign and Home Service who were to fill such posts; for they require a blend of discipline and informality which is a real test of character. The individual needs physical and mental stamina, for neither in Downing Street nor in the Foreign Office are there set hours for work. Anything may happen at any time, and whatever it is it will be sure to spring upon you when least expected. Owing to the change of time, telegrams from the United States do not begin to arrive until late in the Foreign Office day, so that is always a hazard.

In No. 10 the secretaries and typists in the 'Garden Room' cheerfully doubled up their duties with watching over a grandchild parked in a pram outside their windows. This was necessary so as to prevent disturbance to my colleagues sitting in the Cabinet room a few feet away.

In Macmillan's day one of the private secretaries was drawn from the Foreign Office. I gladly continued this practice. He would keep in close touch with his colleagues across the way, and thus anticipate and prevent any friction between the two sets of advisers. Of one thing I am sure; it is a great advantage for the Prime Minister and Foreign Secretary and for their respective staffs, to be within close walking distance of each other. If the Foreign Office is rebuilt, I trust that it will be on the same site and within the same façade, for above everything else the Prime Minister and the Foreign Secretary must have rapid communication.

Life for a Cabinet Minister today would be an impossible strain without an orderly and disciplined schedule for the working day. Mr Arthur Balfour, whose home was in East Lothian, used to complain bitterly if he could not spend six months of the year at Whittingehame; but from the 1930s onwards Parliament and politics have become more and more exacting, and today a Cabinet Minister has to be always on call.

In order to work through the piles of minutes and telegrams, even after the private secretaries have sieved it ruthlessly, it is necessary to work late into the night, or to rise early in the morning. People, I found, are almost equally divided into late or early birds. It was no hardship for me to wake myself at 6.45 every morning, and to embark on serious reading by 7 o'clock. By breakfast at nine, I had broken the back of the telegrams from overseas, the dispatches from Ambassadors, and the briefs for the agenda of the day. At the Foreign Office there would be another two hours' reading during the afternoon and evening. Of course one acquires the art of finding the meat in a document, but on any count it is hard slogging.

Some days of the week are heavier than others with agendas for Cabinet Committees to be mastered, and once in three weeks, House of Commons questions for a departmental Minister, while the Prime Minister is put through his paces for a quarter of an hour each Tuesday and Thursday. That is looked upon by all sides of the

House as a sporting occasion, and a Prime Minister, who must above all else hold the ascendancy in the Chamber, is well-advised to search every question for the trip-wire which is usually well-concealed, but almost sure to be there, and to think up the riposte which will turn the tables on the Opposition.

A Prime Minister's sheet-anchor is without question the Cabinet Secretariat, and in particular the Secretary to the Cabinet. Any Prime Minister leans heavily on him for the management of Government business and for advice. Lord Hankey, Lord Bridges, Sir Norman Brook, and Sir Burke Trend (later Lord Trend) over the years, proved conclusively the supreme value of continuity in the Civil Service from Government to Government, and their individual standards of service were of the highest quality. During my years in politics I have worked with Civil Servants from many government departments, and in the huge majority of cases I have found them competent, skilful, inventive, resilient and careful of the public good. Doubtless some from time to time are properly targets for criticism, but usually when they are labelled with this or that offence it is because people will cast them for rôles which they were never intended to fill. It cannot be too often repeated that it is the politicians who make policy and are responsible for the laws which are made.

The Civil Servant is the person who advises the politician how the law can be best put into shape, so that it can pass the scrutiny of Parliament, and will work in practice when it becomes the law of the land. The good Civil Servant, too, will provide his Minister with the pros and cons in any situation, and, if he is to earn respect he will not modify a view which he feels to be right until he is over-ruled by his political master.

A valid criticism against members of the profession is the rate at which they reproduce their kind, but even that is the fault of the politician who is always inventing more work for them to do.

I have seen one or two Civil Servants who were eccentrics. One morning I was turned out of my room in the Foreign Office because a bomb was suspected in a locked car outside. It turned out to belong to a member of the Service who had invented a kind of Heath Robinson device for charging the battery. He was not pleased when he discovered later in the day that it had needed a major operation on the body of the car before the police could break in.

Another, in a Home Department, had written on his desk 'never forget Scotland, Wales and women'.

Paper is the curse of Whitehall. Between my two periods at the Foreign Office – a gap of seven years – the paper work had increased by about half as much again. It is true that the Commonwealth countries had been added to the clients, but even so the addition was much too much. The dictating, recording and duplicating machines are largely responsible, for once something has been put into the stream, there is nothing to stop it circulating round the world.

There is little to be done about verbosity for, with the decline of the classics in schools, the discipline of economy of words has largely gone.

In my first period in the Foreign Office, in an effort to save myself and my successors in the office from suffocation by paper, I circulated the Ambassadors, saying that I was always happy to hear the story of their lives, but would they please tell it in serial form. Ten years later something more drastic was needed, and I put my Principal Private Secretary on his mettle to cut outgoing and incoming telegrams by 20 per cent. After three years the reduction was 14 per cent and only loss of office prevented the target being reached. In self-defence a Foreign Secretary must wage this war ruthlessly and with a hard heart.

Into the day, in addition to the routine work, a Prime Minister has to cram a host of other activities both political and social. The penalty of failing to keep contact with Members of Parliament or with the country is high, while entertainment given and received is a constant health hazard. Very seldom during the years when I was Foreign Secretary did Elizabeth and I lunch or dine alone at home. Two rules enabled me to get by. The first to eat sparingly at night;

and the second to balance each glass of wine with one of water. These are life-saving tips.

With so many important visitors coming to London, introducing variety into the programme of hospitality presented quite a problem. We found that our visitors delighted in the beauties of Hampton Court or the Painted Hall at Greenwich; alternatively with the ready co-operation of Covent Garden, we rang the changes with the opera or the ballet. The latter, after a heavy working day for Minister and visitor, has the advantage of removing any difficulties of conversation in a strange language, and is restful. So much so that I recall an occasion at the opera – *La Somnambula* appropriately enough – when all our distinguished visitors from overseas were unashamedly asleep with their heads resting on the front of the Royal Box. The moment came when the famous leading heroine swooned into a haystack on a note which soared up to the heavens. In the hush, one of our own celebrities said in a voice which echoed round the Opera House – 'Any chance that the woman is really dead and that we can all go home?' Protocol and culture do not always go hand-in-hand.

However carefully a Prime Minister's programme is rationed it will still be too full; for there are many clients for his attention and over and above these he is claimed by events which no one can anticipate.

I had barely taken charge of the Government when President Kennedy was assassinated. I had motored on the Friday evening to Arundel in the hope of the first day of relaxation that I had been able to snatch since the election. I arrived to be met on the doorstep by the Duke of Norfolk with the news that the President had been shot. It was a personal shock and loss to me, for from the moment we had first met our thinking about world affairs had been in tune.

If I was to be able to pay the expected tribute after the 9 o'clock news there was no choice but to turn back on my tracks, preparing as best I could on the way. We arrived at Broadcasting House with a margin of three minutes to spare and I got into the lift which then proceeded to stick. Luckily it would move down, but I then had to run up three flights of stairs. My lungs were bursting, and my heart was doing treble overtime, and I cannot imagine to this day how my plight was not detected by the viewers.

The authorities in Washington had only three days in which to organize the funeral. That would have put even the late Duke of Norfolk to the test; but on the day there was remarkably little confusion. Prince Philip, it is true, only got a place in the Cathedral when Elizabeth surrendered her seat to him, which was emphatically not the right position for the Consort of the Queen. Such is the power of suggestion that the thousands of security men and troops on the route of the procession had their eyes and rifles firmly fixed upwards, because it was from a roof that the fatal shot which killed the President had come.

But order and dignity prevailed. The huge crowds were still in a state of shock that an assassin should have been able to strike at their President and their constitution. Mercifully there was no racial reason for the deed, but one could feel the clammy fear – where would it end?

In total contrast – a few months later – was the cremation of Mr Nehru, the Prime Minister of India. There were millions present in the great open space provided for the occasion, and there were the minimum of security precautions. They were unnecessary because the self-discipline of the multitude was absolute. The scene, with family upon family with their picnic food sitting on the ground, determined to see the long ceremony through, and all good-tempered and friendly, resembled nothing so much as a Bank Holiday crowd on the Sussex Downs. They were reverent but cheerful in their thanksgiving for the life of their national hero.

When we approached the appointed place for the ceremony of the lighting of the funeral pyre I had expected something spectacular, and symbolic of the soul being translated to heaven in a blaze of glory. But there was nothing like that. The coffin with the body must burn slowly and evenly for three days. By that time the millions have departed, and the final leave-taking and scattering of ashes is virtually a family affair.

President Nasser's burial, which I was to attend as Foreign Secretary some years later, also attracted the millions, but from the start the crowd got out of hand and chaos resulted. Those who represented their countries assembled in the headquarters of the building of the Revolutionary Council on the west bank of the Nile; and we were intended to march for half a mile or so behind the coffin on its gun-carriage, and the procession was to be led by the Emperor of Ethiopia. The idea was that the crowds should be excluded from this the first part of the long journey.

The Emperor set off, flanked by four attendants carrying large ceremonial sunshades; but we had not proceeded further than two hundred yards, when a wailing breast-beating crowd, frenzied with emotion, burst the barriers and swarmed across the route, hurling themselves on to the coffin. The Emperor's bodyguard was swept away. The little man made a quick appreciation of the situation, and, putting his head back and his beard in the air, sprinted unashamedly back to the haven of the building from which we had started. Never have followers more thankfully followed their leader.

So far as the visitors were concerned that was that. We heard later that armoured cars had had to be brought to enable the cortège to move at all, and that there were many casualties; for the police and armed services lining the route were powerless in the face of the mob.

Some four hours later we struggled back on foot to the British Embassy and arrived unscathed. We sank into chairs in the portico, and gratefully washed away the heat and the sand with drinks. As we sat there a huge moth fluttered round and plastered itself against the white wall. It was a Death's Head Hawk Moth. Inevitably it was labelled the 'Spirit of Nasser' which couldn't leave the British alone.

Most Prime Ministers and Foreign Secretaries have been Englishmen with houses within reach of London, and it was natural that they should have preferred to spend their spare time at home. As

Scotland was inconveniently far, Elizabeth and I used Chequers a lot, and we became very much attached to it. The rolling country-side clothed with beech woods is beautiful, and there is a very attractive garden to the south and front of the house, which had been filled with a wide variety of species roses by Lady Eden.

We generally used a small room – the White Parlour – when we were alone, or with members of the family. The Long Gallery was more interesting than comfortable, but had its own attraction. In it was a link with the Home family. A ring, given immediately after Queen Elizabeth's death, to the first Lord Home by James I, as a special mark of his esteem and as a reward for his services.

On the occasion of the Prime Ministers' Conference in 1964 we invited most of the African leaders to dine and stay the night. Everything seemed to be going with a swing, when one of them said that he had urgent business in London, and could he please return there as soon as possible? It was then about 10.30 p.m. and I made the arrangements (not without difficulty, for the chauffeurs had been well regaled with food and beer) – when four or five more Prime Ministers said that it would also suit them best to go back. Dr Banda, who stayed on, could scarcely conceal his merriment, and I asked him what had gone wrong? He said that the curtained Elizabethan four-poster beds had so scared them that they were afraid to sleep in them. When at midnight one of the Prime Ministers, who was known to be at Chequers, appeared on the doorstep of his High Commissioner's residence in London, the night-watchman fell down in a dead faint – sure that he had seen a ghost.

The only real need which we felt at Chequers was for a large room in which to entertain guests before or after luncheon and dinner. Later Edward Heath converted a conference room on the ground floor into a delightful drawing-room, so that the house is now equipped to meet any need.

During my years as Commonwealth Secretary and twice later when I was at the Foreign Office, we lived at Dorneywood, a house left to the Government for the use of one of the overseas

Ministers who needed to entertain. Lord Courtauld -Thomson who made the gift had apparently foreseen the inflationary years, because so amply was it endowed that the Trustees were always pressing upon us this or that improvement. Originally a Tudor house, it had been gutted by fire in 1912 and later restored. Here again was a pleasant garden, while Burnham Beeches with its beautiful trees was but a few hundred yards away. Close to us also was Dropmore of sentimental memory where the nightingales still sang.

There is one recurring engagement of which it is safe to say that every Prime Minister has the happiest of recollections. It is the weekly audience during the parliamentary sessions with the Sovereign. The Queen, after twenty-five years of her reign, knows almost every Head of State and Leader of Government in foreign countries; while as Head of the Commonwealth she has an intimate knowledge of the leading political personalities and of their ways.

Her experience is readily put at the disposal of the Prime Minister and is invaluable to him. Few realize the exacting nature of the work which it is necessary for the Sovereign to do, if she is to keep abreast of events all over the world which are of interest to her country. Her Private Secretaries are doubtless skilled in the selection and presentation of telegrams, but there remains a mass of fact and information which needs to be absorbed if Her Majesty is to meet Ministers of the Crown and foreign visitors on their own ground. The Queen, as I and my predecessors and successors can readily testify, is always up to date and fully versed in the niceties of every national and international problem.

It is also the duty and good fortune of the Foreign Secretary from time to time to attend the Sovereign on State visits to other countries. I know of no Royal tour which has not made a deep and favourable impact on the people and Government of the country visited. On several occasions I have watched the open admiration of the crowd, rather satisfactorily tinged with envy, that they had nothing so colourful and romantic to excite and raise their enthusiasms.

The monarchy has a few political critics. I often wish that they could be at the receiving end of one of the Queen's visits abroad They could not fail to see that such appearances do more in days to gain goodwill for Britain than all the politicians and diplomats lumped together could achieve in years. Supply for the monarchy should never be skimped. It would be a totally false economy.

I confess that I would have liked to have been given a bit longer at No. 10 so as to get more grip on the machinery of government.

The keys to this are: short and precise paper-work; a chain of government committees each charged to take decisions, resulting in a Cabinet agenda which is cleared of all but the absolute essentials; Ministers who can be relied upon to insist on these rules, and personally to see to it that they are carried out; and lastly a programme of legislation for Parliament which is not overloaded.

It is not easy to control the word-mongers. Edward Heath, as Prime Minister, requested Ministers to limit the statement of their case to one sheet of paper. That was duly done, but the circumventing device of attaching an appendix was adopted so that the amount of reading was just as much as before. The ideal would be the clarity of a Churchill, combined with the economy of words of an Attlee, and the efficiency of a John Anderson; but that is one of those glimpses of perfection which I suspect will always remain a dream.

The pattern of committees below Cabinet level has usually been about right, but there the brake on the progress of business is usually the reluctance of the Ministers who chair them to take a chance. Somehow the ground must be cleared so that the Cabinet can give its mind more frequently to the broad strategic issues of policy. So great is the pressure of business that a Prime Minister must be prepared to devolve decisions over a fairly wide field, if he is to keep the heads of his senior colleagues above water. There is a hazard for him, for it is the comparatively trivial things which often create the most parliamentary trouble, and the public media are always on the alert for any ministerial error. But he must run the risk.

In the sixties and seventies Prime Ministers have been expected to create for themselves an 'image' on television. It is something from which our predecessors were spared, and I often wonder how Churchill would have treated the 'box'. Probably with the same physical revenge which he used to apply to a telephone which 'would not respond' or to the mechanical amplifier and aid to deafness which was once tried out in a Cabinet meeting, but was short-lived because a taxi-driver in Whitehall, through faulty mechanism, had picked up most of the discussion.

I fear that I could not conceal my distaste for the conception that the political leader had also to be an actor on the screen.

In 1963 I had an unpromising start when I was being made up for some Prime Ministerial performance; for my conversation with the young lady who was applying the powder and tan went like this:

Q. Can you not make me look better than I do on television?
A. No.
Q. Why not?
A. Because you have a head like a skull.
Q. Does not everyone have a head like a skull?
A. No.

So that was that. The best that I could do for the cartoonist was my half-moon spectacles. Elizabeth always said that they lost the 1964 election. So one cannot win.

However, now that television is one of the main channels of communication with the public, a Prime Minister must discipline himself to be 'presentable'; but I confess that I still prefer my politicians in the flesh to their bloodless image.

I have a strong prejudice too, in favour of making my speeches in my own words. However, such is the pressure on a Prime Minister's time, that he is bound on many occasions to rely on other people's drafts.

But there are traps. In the old days when ministerial speeches were read in the House of Lords by members of the King's Household, one proceeded so literally that he completed the brief which ran – 'This is a rotten argument, but should be good enough for Their Lordships on a hot summer afternoon.'

Ernest Bevin, once presented with a script which he was expected to deliver with conviction said, 'Good, gentlemen, very good, but it ain't me.' I know exactly how he felt.

XV

Scotland's government

While we were in Opposition from 1964–70 there was one matter with which I was saddled which was off my foreign beat. In 1968 Heath had asked me to undertake a domestic chore of considerable importance for the future – to chair a committee on Scotland's government.

After an interval of twenty years Scottish nationalism had once again come to the fore. Any proposals, therefore, in the context of the devolution of powers which might be framed by the Westminster Parliament would clearly be the most important constitutional event since the Act of Union in 1707.

One of the paradoxes of modern life has been that, while communications have brought people closer together, and made them more dependent upon each other, nevertheless the smallest unit has insisted on asserting its personality and independence. It is understandable in that super-powers are apt to dictate conditions of life, while bureaucracy in the technological age has become impersonal, inconsiderate and undiscriminating. But narrow nationalism is selfish, divisive, and dangerous, and Conservatives saw the need to steer the patriotism of the Scot into channels which were unifying and constructive. Hence our committee.

There is, of course, historical reason for special treatment for Scotland within the United Kingdom. Scottish law and the Church of Scotland are distinctive; Scottish education, too, had a particular flavour; while the twentieth-century innovation of a Secretary of State for Scotland who is a Scotsman, and is always a member of the United Kingdom Cabinet, and who presides over an office in St Andrew's House in Edinburgh, is Scottish Government in all but name.

The first proposals for an element of devolution were put forward by Mr Gladstone in the 1890's. From then and for ever after the argument has swayed back and forth between 'a stitch in time' and 'the thin end of the wedge', and the latter has always won. It is in itself an irritating argument, and the itch for some further de-centralization of power from Westminster to Edinburgh has never been far under the skin.

I had some understanding of the plea. It seemed to me that the history of Ireland tended to justify Mr Gladstone's premonition; that the Westminster Parliament should make up its mind to shed some of the clutter of legislation which should be capable of local treatment; and that in practice the larger departments of Whitehall were apt to think of Scotland as somewhere near the North Pole, and to issue prescriptions for Scotland's ailments and needs which were quite frequently off-beam.

No Borderer, however, after the centuries of misery before the Union of 1707, would ever contemplate the separation of Scotland from England; and as the great majority of Scotsmen apparently felt the same way, the pattern of devolution which I felt was required to satisfy reasonable people was one in which more decisions on Scottish matters should be taken in Scotland by Scotsmen. That would not be an exercise in nationalism, but a charter for efficient government. The 64,000-dollar question was: 'Should there be an Assembly in Scotland with a legislative function, and what should the limits of its authority be?'

Unhappily all political parties had funked the issue for so long that a Scottish Nationalist Party had grown up which had begun to advocate separation from England; naturally this fed the fears of the 'thin-end-of-the-wedge' school.

Heath therefore assembled a Committee to examine the problem. Its membership (see Appendix D) included some very distinguished people, well-qualified in constitutional law, and the practice of politics; and these were reinforced by others with experience of the economy and the different aspects of Scottish life.

After hearing evidence from over a thousand individuals, and from many bodies representing different aspects of Scottish opinion, we made our Report.

We began by asserting – and on this the Committee was unanimous – that Scotland's economic, political and social interests required that she should remain within the United Kingdom. We found, too, that the United Kingdom was too small, and the units composing it too disparate, to justify a Federal experiment on the pattern, let us say, of Australia. Nevertheless 'Federal' is a label which can be attached to a number of devolutionary schemes without exactly reproducing one of the existing models.

In the context of Devolution we borrowed a paragraph from the Balfour Royal Commission of 1954 on the same subject, which stated: 'Scotland's needs and points of view should be known and brought into account at all stages in the formulation and execution of policy – that is to say when policy is considered, when policy is decided, and when policy is announced.'

The clear implication of that was that Devolution meant an extension of the United Kingdom Government to Scotland.

We rejected an Assembly which would be purely consultative. There was much to be said in favour of it, for 'parleying' was, after all, the origin of Parliament. But we felt that moderate Scottish opinion would not be satisfied unless the Assembly had a part in shaping that legislation which applied specifically to Scottish affairs. There was such a definition ready to hand, for the Speaker of the House of Commons already designates a number of Bills as purely Scottish. At present they are taken through their various legislative stages by the Scottish Standing Committee, and Scottish Grand

Committee, and the majority of us felt that some of these proceedings could well be transferred to an Assembly sitting in Edinburgh. Having taken the view that such a body would have a legislative function, we felt bound to advise that it should, according to our constitutional practice, be directly elected; but we left open the question as to whether or not some form of proportional representation should be used.

We advocated, in conformity with the conception of the Scottish Assembly as part of the United Kingdom Government, the retention of the office of Secretary of State for Scotland, for he had become over the years the personification of Scotland's interests as a whole, both inside Scotland and in the United Kingdom Cabinet. He and his Ministers would remain the link with the United Kingdom Parliament.

Political devolution is unreal unless it involves some delegation of control over funds, and we strongly recommended that a block grant for Scotland should be provided, from which the Assembly would decide priorities in expenditure. Scotsmen would then feel that their influence over their own affairs had substance and was real.

Inevitably there were grey areas which could only be filled in by the government of the day, which was ready to assume the responsibility for introducing the constitutional changes. For example, the duties of the Assembly must be precisely defined, and the method of working with the Secretary of State must be laid down, so that business is conducted in an orderly way with the minimum of friction.

Again the question arose – whether the promotion of economic development in Scotland should be the function of the Scottish Assembly. There are very strong arguments against the fragmentation of the United Kingdom for economic purposes, and our strong preference was, in so far as politics intruded at all, for a partnership between the Scottish Development Council and the Assembly and the Secretary of State.

Following our Report, Heath at the Scottish Conservative

Conference in 1968 made what he called 'The Declaration of Perth' which accepted our main recommendation for a Scottish Assembly. Unhappily, for public opinion was then ripe for change, nothing was done to translate the proposals into legislative form.

It was understandable, for in domestic affairs inflation occupied our attention, while the negotiations for entry into Europe took up a lot of our time; but we have paid a heavy price for delay as Scottish nationalism has stolen a lot of the stage.

Their platform is now the strident cry for independence from England. It is fair to say that the majority of the Scottish people would reject separation from England if there was a referendum on the subject, but they vote Scottish Nationalist because no one has yet given to the moderates the measure of control over Scottish affairs which they feel that it is reasonable to ask.

The leaders of the Scottish National Party, in declaring for independence have done a great disservice to Scotland, for it is virtually impossible to debate Devolution sensibly, while every step towards it is hailed as advance towards separation from England. Their action has put fresh cards into the hands of the 'thin-end-of-the-wedge' school.

What then after eight years of inaction should be done?

Certain of our conclusions are still valid. Westminster is overloaded with legislation. Whitehall is too large and top-heavy. Scotsmen should be able to decide the priorities for the spending of public funds. The Scottish Development Agency – the successor of the Scottish Development Council – could well be associated with an Assembly in planning the pattern of industrial expansion.

There are still Parliamentary Bills which in content are purely Scottish. There is no reason why they should not be taken through all or most of their legislative stages by a Scottish Assembly. It would be possible to retain a Report Stage or Third Reading in the Westminster Parliament, in order to emphasize the unity of the United Kingdom, and rely upon a background power of disallowance.

The Assembly should also debate, on a First Reading procedure, Bills which have a Scottish content, but are of United Kingdom application. Their remaining stages should be taken at Westminster. The Assembly should begin the task of producing a sensible pattern of Local Government for Scotland.

Another way would be to devolve by subjects on the Northern Ireland Stormont pattern.

One way or another this devolution should be effected.

It is, of course, possible to conjure up all sorts of difficulties. Some are real; as for example, the future rôle of the Secretary of State. If there is to be an Executive in the Assembly what will remain for him?

The broad answer is that there must be a representative from Scotland in the United Kingdom Cabinet – with a general oversight over the economy and the framing of Scotland's budget – to represent Scotland's interest on fuel policy and on defence, in European and foreign affairs. There will be quite enough for a Secretary of State to do.

Finally there is the size and composition of an Assembly. It should not be too large. It should be directly elected, and because there will be at least four parties in Scotland, and it is undesirable that the country should be governed by a party elected on a minority vote, there should be election by a form of proportional representation.

There is one argument in the nationalist case which is unworthy of the character and the intelligence of Scotsmen, and that is the link which is made between Scotland's independence and the prospect of expanding oil revenues. There would, of course, be matters of international law to be taken into account; for the continental shelf which determines the ownership of the oil is that of the United Kingdom and not of Scotland. On the precedent of Australia it would so remain even if Scotland was part of a Federation.

But there are more powerful arguments than these. Almost all the reasons which are given in favour of unity in Europe apply to the United Kingdom. Scotland's primary market is England; investment comes to Scotland because the country is part of a United Kingdom, with no trade barriers or currency restrictions between the component parts; Scotland's influence in international affairs is immeasurably enhanced by being part of a British voice, nor can the United Kingdom be defended piecemeal.

It is by these strategic considerations that the question of the limits of devolution should be decided.

To allow oil, which anyhow has a comparatively short life in the history of the country, and a precarious price-level, unduly to influence the findings would be to abandon our heritage for a mess of pottage.

In the preface to the 1968 Report I wrote: 'Our proposal does involve an act of faith in the common sense, objectivity and tolerance of the Scottish people.' That is true of any scheme of devolution, but I still believe that such a risk as there is should be run. The alternative, which is there for all to see, is continued agitation, and in time a majority in Scotland for the kind of narrow introspective nationalism which is the curse of the modern world. That would be the end of the United Kingdom.

If the Scottish National Party really intend to campaign for the separation of Scotland from England, then they will surely be rejected by their fellow Scots in favour of those who seek genuine devolution, and those who know the value of their British citizenship, and who have been and always will be men of the world.

XVI

General Election 1964; resignation of party leadership; shadowing foreign affairs

In retrospect General Election campaigns make dull reading. On 9 April 1964 I had thought it right to announce that I intended to carry on the Government until the last months of its legal life. One reason for that decision was that Lord Blakenham – the Chairman of the Party, who was wise in matters of organization, and had a keen political 'nose' – felt that with time we had a chance to win. An announcement, too, would steady confidence, for the public media had been carrying on a running speculation which was unsettling to everyone.

I have always believed it to be a mistake to clutter an election campaign with too much detail; so, while in our prospectus we covered the whole range of political medicine for the nation's ills, and recipes for progress, I decided the fight should be conducted on three main fronts: the first, ways and means of reconciling the two objectives of full employment and a tolerable price level; the second, the retention of the nuclear deterrent which we had secured at the Nassau Conference with President Kennedy, and the possession of which I considered to be literally vital to our national security; the third that, on the hard evidence, Socialism always made things worse.

During the years when 'we never had it so good' inflation was mild and controllable, but that happy state did not last beyond

1964, and the argument whether – and if so how – inflation is to be beaten has been carried on ever since.

In 1964 we had certainly made a creditable shot at it. Mr Maudling, who was Chancellor of the Exchequer, had deliberately budgeted for a modest deficit, in the anticipation that the winter and spring would see it redressed. His forecast was later to be vindicated.

But August and September are months when the bills come in; and for temporary cover we had to go to the International Bank for a loan to tide us over until December. The deficit, which Harold Wilson later quantified at £800 million, was small and half of it was covered by an increase in our invisible earnings, but it was a gift to our opponents.

I knew, of course, that application for a loan was the kind of cue for which the Leader of the Opposition had been waiting, but I decided that the operation must be open and above board, and that he might hesitate to knock the prospects for sterling too hard if he felt that he had a chance to inherit. In the event he said enough, and hinted at more than enough, to stir the people into a nervous state. He could not resist the rôle of a prophet of doom.

On the retention of the 'Polaris' he was, to put it bluntly, ignorant or irresponsible. A lot of people, in spite of the Test Ban Treaty, were anxious about nuclear contamination of the environment, and fears arising from a nuclear balance of terror were real. Mr Wilson did not hesitate to play on these emotions, to condemn the morality of nuclear armament, and to ridicule the possession by Britain of a nuclear weapon as being about as effective as 'a pea on the top of a mountain'.

I have no doubt at all that he frightened many electors who voted for his promise to re-negotiate the Nassau agreement, with the strong implication which went with it that he would abolish British owner-ship of the weapon, and Britain's ability to use it independently in the event of a dire national emergency.

He was either unaware of the potential of 'Polaris' as a deterrent, or careless of the first duty of a government which is to provide security for its country. At any rate when he had assured himself of office he kept the weapon, he made no attempt to re-negotiate Nassau, and the submarines and their equipment, with all the original conditions for their use, are still ours.

Life is too short to harbour grievances against political opponents; and the pace of politics too rapid to catch up with one who falls down on acceptable standards in electioneering, but Members of Parliament who have carried responsibility in Government should in no case mislead the public on matters of national security.

The Conservative campaign had been intelligently planned, and it was decided that I should tour the country, speaking in towns and villages, so as to make myself known to as many people as possible in the short time available.

We had, however, reckoned without one tactical move by the Socialists which helped towards our undoing. At open-air meetings they used to pack the area immediately below the platform. Two or three hundred young hooligans would collect under the microphone, and proceed for the necessary time to bawl their heads off. The noise was so literally deafening that I could not hear what I was saying. I had not realized until then that it is necessary to hear one's own words in order to be reasonably sure that one is using a coherent argument. Speaking, and simultaneously trying to hear, produced an appearance of strain which inevitably conveyed itself to the television onlookers, who began to feel that the Conservative leader was on the defensive.

The climax came at the Birmingham Rag Market where an audience of 10,000 was collected with no semblance of order. Groups of Socialists in hundreds had been planted all over the place, and when one bunch ran out of breath another took up the chant. The result was pandemonium and no one in the audience could hear a word. There was only one bit of light relief. On the way out, one heavy-weight lout aimed a kick at my leg with hob-nailed boots. I took evasive action, and the victim was his equally ugly neighbour's knee-cap. When last seen they were at each other's throats.

Lord Blakenham was convinced that it was after the Rag Market spectacle, which was seen on television all over Britain, that support began to slide away from us. I think that he was right. It was then too late to vary the programme and to stage a recovery by a change of tactics; but anyhow the truth of the matter was that the Conservatives would have needed a large slice of luck to win. After thirteen years far too many felt that it was 'time for a change'. We nearly got the lucky break, for on the day of the Poll the Chinese exploded their first nuclear bomb. The knowledge of it a few days earlier would possibly just have weighted the scales in our favour.

If Macleod and Powell had rallied with us in October 1963; if we had postponed the Resale Price Maintenance Bill; if I had not insisted that a normal borrowing operation should be publicized; if the Chinese had happened to give out the news of the explosion of the bomb a day or two earlier . . . Happily we shall never know the answer to these and the other 'ifs' of history, or the politicians would one after another have long ago worried themselves into their graves.

An exit of a Prime Minister from No. 10 is almost as dramatic as the entrance, in that it has to be accomplished in a matter of hours to prevent the embarrassment of old and new actors occupying the same stage. In another sense it is furtive. The crowds assemble in Downing Street to hail their successful hero; and that is his due, and must not be diluted with tears for the departing incumbent. So Elizabeth and I slunk out of the 'Garden Door' to recover our breath and to take stock of the future.

The Prime Minister kindly put Chequers at our disposal for a day or two, and then Sir Hugh Wontner, with great consideration, allowed us to stay in the Penthouse at Claridges for a fortnight, so that a sense of perspective and poise was gradually regained.

How did I feel looking back on that year?

Only a fool would deny a feeling of gratification at occupying the honourable place of First Minister of the Crown, and there are many facets of the office which are exhilarating and exciting and interesting. Direct dealings with the Prime Ministers and Heads of Governments of other countries was one such activity. Some of these things I had enjoyed as Commonwealth and Foreign Secretary, but the Prime Minister is responsible for policy and for taking the final decisions about everything of substance. That duty keeps him on his toes.

If I have a regret, it is that by reason of the fact that I never dreamed of holding the position, I had taken no particular steps to prepare myself for it. Had I done so I would have soaked myself more thoroughly in domestic issues, rather than specializing so completely in the foreign field.

Then, much as I would have detested the exercise, I would have taken trouble to master the techniques of television. On question and answer I was adequate because that is a reproduction of a natural occasion, but on the set-piece unhappiness and distaste was written all over my face. That could with pain and grief have been got over.

'Imagine that you are speaking to two other people in a room,' the producer would say. In vain I would retort that I usually let them get a word in.

Happily, with more experience, the solid twenty-minute or half-hour talk to the electors is being replaced, but then I was a victim of the vogue of the day.

There was one other fashion which was tiresome and, even when one hardened oneself against it, was diverting. In 1963–64 satire, so-called, was at its height with a programme of Mr David Frost's called *That Was the Week that Was*. It was aimed at the establishment, and the Prime Minister was an irresistible target. I do not think that I was unduly sensitive, but such personalized attacks place the exposed politician in a dilemma. If he reveals that he is affected he is an even more tempting target, so the only alternative is to present the hide of a rhinoceros, which is singularly unattractive.

Loyalty of colleagues, and the pleasure of working with them, is a Prime Minister's reward. All in all with the Cabinet working as a harmonious and friendly team; with Elizabeth as hostess taking every situation in her stride; with a young and lively family to give No. 10 a new look, it was a happy and rewarding year.

Defeat at the October General Election was a disappointment, and a Prime Minister is always bound to feel if only he could have pulled out some more stops the victory might have been won. That was so in particular when in 1964 we lost by a short head. But post-mortems are unsatisfactory affairs. We had kept the Conservative flag flying, and the Party lived to fight another day.

Some politicians thrive in Opposition. Those who are masters of procedure can harry Government Ministers, and those who need little preparation and can whistle up arguments for a debating speech in quick time get considerable satisfaction from it. Parliament always contains enough of these, and that is as well; for the friction of spontaneously debating one idea against another provides the generating power of a democracy. When defeat came in 1964 I did not greatly relish the prospect of leading the Conservative Opposition. A habit of Tweedledee-Tweedledum politics had grown up in which whenever the Prime Minister spoke, whether sense or non-sense, the Leader of the Opposition was expected to knock him on the head, and vice versa. For me these crude tactics made little appeal. At the wicket, at least until one's eye is in, it is wise to wait for the half-volley or the long hop. That is the way to build up a score. Blind slogging at every ball soon receives its deserts. I did not like the game any better because the slick knockabout was something at which Mr Wilson excelled.

The leadership of the Opposition, too, is a frustrating business, in that the holder can do nothing but talk; and there is a limit to the satisfaction which can be drawn from that.

In recent Parliaments much more is expected of the Opposition Front Bench than used to be the case. In Churchill's day the prep-arations for the Parliamentary fray used to be made at a fortnightly luncheon at the Savoy Hotel, where discussion of politics was almost perfunctory. It was reputedly at one of these that Churchill said to the waiter: 'Take away that pudding – it has no theme.'

There was then no system of 'shadows' where one chosen member of the Opposition marks a particular Government Minister. The Leader and the Chief Whip would allocate the person who seemed best suited to the particular occasion, and thus there was greater flexibility and variety in the Opposition's conduct of affairs. A larger number of backbenchers and potential junior Ministers had a chance to shine.

Economics, which now take up so much of Parliament's time, have killed oratory in Parliament, and the specialist is deemed to be necessary to meet the opposing expert – a rather curious development, as economics is surely the most inexact science of all.

On balance, however, I felt that I should continue to lead, at any rate until the Party had been given time to shake down after defeat, while there were also some necessary chores to be done.

After the widespread criticism of the methods which had been used in my own selection as Leader, I decided that for the sake of any future holder of the post, the processes of choice must be reviewed.

The 'Magic Circle' of selectors had almost everything to be said for it. The Whips and the experienced Conservative Parliamentarians knew the form of every runner in the field; they knew the Members of Parliament who had to work and live with the chosen Leader; and they could operate quickly and quietly in collecting views. It was the latter 'advantage' which caused the trouble. Some felt that candidates favourable to the establishment had the edge over anyone who might at any time have been rebellious, and there were always those who, stirred up by the media, were ready to charge the 'Magic Circle' with rigging the result.

I was not particularly worried about such happenings until the accusation that the last result had been jobbed began to reverberate through the Constituencies and to affect Party morale outside Parliament. I then came to the conclusion that, with all its disadvantages, it was necessary to adopt a system of election of a leader, where from start to finish everything was seen to be open and above board. I was in the best position to see that business through. There was a lot of talk about the procedure to be adopted if the result was not clear-cut on the first round, and it is possible to argue the variations and details of any scheme until the cows come home; but the new rules were debated, adopted and ready when some months later I decided to hand over to a successor.

Gradually in the early months of 1965 Conservatives regained confidence; and as there was always a chance that with their narrow majority the Socialist Government would be thrown out, the Parliamentary Party remained reasonably well united. Nevertheless there was a persistent demand for more instant politics in the sense of attacking the Government whether they did right or wrong.

I had declared the approach to our function as an Opposition to be support for the Government when they acted in the national interest, and implacable opposition when they did not. That was thought by an increasing number to be weak if not wet. I thought then, and I think now, that the essence of successful opposition in Parliament is timing, and that indiscriminate bludgeoning is boring to the great majority of thoughtful electors. Nor can a clarion call to the nation be made once a week. But that was not then the popular view, and criticism grew.

There cannot in fact have been very much wrong with the conduct of Conservative affairs or with Party morale, as very considerable gains were made in the Local Elections in May, and the Party's reputation was on the rise.

But some of the younger Conservatives – front bench and back bench – were restive, and desired more dynamic leadership. Groups began to meet and rumour to stir, and the Press began to circulate stories of 'plots'. These inevitably began to affect the confidence of some of the Conservative Associations in the country.

The Finance Bill is always the main Parliamentary feature of the summer; and the Socialist proposals in it were contested clause by clause by a team of young Conservative members under the skilful leadership of Heath. He came through the debates with a greatly enhanced reputation as a Parliamentarian – able and always ready to hit the Government hard, and to make the Conservative case with clarity. Here was the quality of leadership which seemed to these young crusaders to be lacking at the top; and there was a movement to displace me from the Leadership. Ted Heath took no part in it, and it didn't amount to anything very much; but it was there and it was unsettling.

All this was duly reported to me and much advice was tendered. My reaction was boredom with the whole business. I had been chosen as Leader to fight the Socialists, and I did not see why I should now be asked to battle with my own side. I knew, of course, that all political leaders had been faced with revolts – Baldwin, Chamberlain and Gaitskell within my own parliamentary recollection. I dare say that, had I been ten years younger, I would have summoned up the necessary spirit to assert myself, as could undoubtedly have been done. But I had spent a decade consecutively in responsible office; I had been Commonwealth Secretary; Lord President and Leader of the House of Lords; Foreign Secretary and finally Prime Minister; and I simply did not feel inclined to go into the arena for the doubtful satisfaction of confounding a number of those with whom I had campaigned on the same side. Nor had I ever believed in the doctrine of political indispensability. There are always good fish in the sea.

Dutifully I listened to all the counsel, and was grateful and touched by the many friends who urged me to fight, but I had no stomach for it, and on 22 July I went to the weekly meeting of the 1922 Committee and spoke as follows:

When I took over the Leadership of the Party in 1963 there was nothing that I could do but ask the Party to fight on the ground on which we stood. Unity was too fragile, and time too short for anything else.

After our narrow defeat in 1964 I knew exactly what I had to do. First, to strengthen the organization of the Party and to eliminate its weaknesses. This I am satisfied is being done by Edward du Cann. Secondly, I was determined that the Party should re-think its policies to make certain that they would be up to date and meet the needs of our countrymen who are not Socialists, but who are progressive and radical. This work has largely been done, and we are ready with policies either for a Manifesto if there is an election, or for the Party Conference.

The Labour Party Conference will be a bitter wrangle; ours will be full steam ahead. Thirdly, I tried to organize our Party in Parliament so that we would present an effective Opposition. In this we have been successful.

The object of all these moves has been to turn public opinion back to the Conservatives, so that we would be in a position to win a General Election. You have only got to look at the results of the local elections in May and since, to see that this is happening.

I believe then that we are in a position now when a Conservative leader can lead the Party to victory at a General Election. All that being so, I come to two promises which I have always made to you. The first is that I would never allow disunity in the Party, least of all over myself; the second, that I would tell you when I considered that the time was right to hand over the Leadership to another. The decision had to be mine and mine alone.

I have to tell you that, having weighed to the best of my ability all the considerations, I have asked our Chairman - Sir William Anstruther-Gray - to set in motion the new procedure. I myself set up the machinery for this change, and I myself have chosen the time to use it. It is up to you to see that it is completed swiftly and efficiently and with dignity and calm. I do not intend to stand for election.

It only remains to me to thank all of you for the kindness and understanding and support which you have given to me and my wife during these two eventful years, and to ask you to preserve absolute unity behind the new leader of our choice. It goes without saying that I will give him, whoever he may be, my full support at all times.

Let us now look forward to a resounding victory.

I had deliberately kept my own counsel, because once I had made up my mind, it was best that the break should be quick and clean. Few at the meeting had any idea of my intention, and there was clearly a sense of shock. However, I was mentally content because there were anyhow strong arguments in favour of a younger and fresher man at the helm, and if there was to be an autumn election the new Leader would have time to collect his team around him and to prepare for the campaign.

There were two men at least – Heath and Maudling – who were well qualified to lead.

When Ted Heath was elected, he invited me to cover Foreign Affairs for the Shadow Cabinet; I was glad to do so for it was there that my prime interest lay. Kinross and West Perthshire were extremely considerate, both when I was in Government and in Opposition. It can certainly lay claim to be the most beautiful constituency in Scotland. The electorate was steeped in farming and all that goes with it, so that we talked the same language. My Chairmen and the Conservative executive always understood that elections are won by organization and a paid-up membership which will hold in good times and bad. In Mr John Robertson too I had an Agent who never wearied in keeping the Branch committees up to the mark. Altogether the partnership proved itself for eleven happy years.

My constituents understood that frequent journeys abroad were an advantage if the Party was to keep abreast of international developments. So what with Parliamentary debates at intervals, Party Conferences and Meetings in and out of the Constituency, and excursions overseas there was enough to do. That was as well, for it was to be six years before we sat on the Government benches again.

There were a number of countries to which visits were due. South Africa clearly held the key to a solution of the Rhodesian deadlock; a problem which was bound to recur again and again in our Parliamentary debates; while the attitude of Israel was crucial to a Middle-East settlement.

With the victory of the Socialists in the British election, the patience of Mr Smith, the Prime Minister of Rhodesia, was beginning to wear thin, and noises about a Unilateral Declaration of Independence began to be heard. They grew louder, until on 11 November 1965 Mr Smith declared Rhodesia to be independent from the British Crown. He might protest that Rhodesians wished the Sovereign to remain as their Queen; but there was no denying the fact that his action was illegal, and not even the best friends of Rhodesia could deny it. It was a foolish act, because no British Government had intervened in the internal affairs of Rhodesia since 1923, and they were for all practical purposes self-governing.

What in the circumstances should Britain do about the rebellious territory?

Mr Wilson, on all the advice which was given to him, decided to try and break the revolt by economic sanctions. There was a case for temporarily suspending from Rhodesia such credits and preferences as she derived from the Commonwealth association. If she deliberately broke the rules it was reasonable that she should forfeit advantages such as economic preferences and access to the Bank of England, enjoyed by Commonwealth countries which remained loyal to the Crown. As Conservatives we agreed to Mr Wilson's request that these limited restrictions should be applied. It is difficult to see how we could have done otherwise.

But Mr Wilson did not stand on that ground for long. His subsequent action in turning the matter over to the Security Council of the United Nations, and in applying mandatory sanctions, was entirely different, and in our view wrong. Conservatives, therefore, voted as a Party against giving any authority to the United Nations and against the concept of mandatory sanctions; but the distinction between penalties brought by the Rhodesians on themselves in a Commonwealth context, and those applied by the United Nations, was too subtle for the public mind, and some of the odium rubbed off on us. Unfair it might be, but that is always a political hazard.

I visited South Africa partly to discover from Mr Vorster how far he would feel able to apply pressure on Mr Smith to withdraw his illegal declaration. His answer in short was that a quarrel between Britain and Rhodesia did not suit South Africa's book at all; but that if he was asked to apply an economic squeeze his answer would have to be 'no' because his supporters would not stand for it.

So if Mr Wilson wished to see Rhodesia restored to legal relations with Britain, he was thrown back on his own resources. He had made his task of finding a settlement far more difficult by agreeing to the proposition made at the Lagos Conference of Commonwealth Prime Ministers in 1966 that there should be no independence before majority rule. 'NIBMAR' was an added weight in the scales against settlement when in all conscience things were hard enough already.

A negotiation was only possible if Mr Wilson would agree to meet Mr Smith, and if he would suspend NIBMAR for the duration of the talks. In spite of the Lagos declaration he decided to do just that, and to convene a meeting on board HMS *Tiger*.

The story of that discussion has been told. It was a cheerless party, but nevertheless the Prime Minister obtained a result in terms of an alteration to Mr Smith's Rhodesian constitution which satisfied him, and which he was prepared to recommend to the British Cabinet and to Parliament. There had been no consultation with Rhodesian Africans, but he was evidently confident that the agreement was in all the circumstances just and saleable, for the table was actually laid and the champagne ready for the celebration dinner. Unhappily Mr Smith, who had referred to Salisbury for approval, was invited to go home and explain the terms before his Cabinet would assent. He arrived exhausted and failed to carry conviction.

It is easy to be wise after the event, but I have always thought that, having agreed the terms, Mr Wilson and Mr Smith ought to have summoned the Press of the world, and been photographed toasting in champagne a remarkable achievement, along with Sir Humphrey Gibbs, the Governor. In those circumstances I do not believe that the small men of Salisbury would have dared to challenge Mr Smith, whose popularity with the white electorate was absolute. Alternatively, if Mr Wilson had gone to Salisbury with him, their combined authority would certainly have carried the day.

Mr Wilson was to have one more try, and this time on HMS *Fearless*. I had been to South Africa, and had also visited Mr Smith; and on my return I had given the Prime Minister my opinion that a formula could be negotiated which would fulfil the aim of uninterrupted progress towards majority rule, although NIBMAR would have to be dropped.

On *Fearless* I am inclined to think that failure derived from the rigidity of the counsel which was given by Mr Wilson's principal legal advisers.

Once again the Prime Minister had apparently concluded a satisfactory settlement on the main points at issue; once again he had found it unnecessary to talk matters over with representative Africans; but he did feel that it would be well to try and get agreement on some machinery for guaranteeing the terms of the settlement which would operate if Mr Smith broke his word.

It was proposed that the Privy Council should fill this rôle, but Mr Smith would not agree to this suggestion or any other form of second guarantee. It should not in my view have been a breaking-point; for the use of the Privy Council in supervising constitutions was, however regretfully, being discarded by the great majority of Commonwealth countries.

It seemed to me then, and I continued to hold the same view when I was negotiating in 1971, that once Mr Smith was committed to putting his personal prestige behind piloting a reformed Constitution through the Rhodesian Parliament, he was bound thereafter to abide by it. Should he have failed to do so he would have lost all credibility. External guarantees therefore were not necessary.

At any rate *Tiger* and *Fearless* were near-run things; and in spite of the fact that Africans were not invited to give their opinions, had the two Governments agreed the terms they would, I believe, have stuck. If that had been so the whole history of Southern Africa might have been changed.

I had always felt that in Rhodesia we had an opportunity to establish a State which, by its orderly constitutional advance, and by its practice of racial tolerance, would set an example to the one-party black countries to the north, and to South Africa which practised 'apartheid' to the south.

Rhodesia had many of the ingredients of a non-racial society; for the original pioneering settlers who lived on the land had the interests of their workers at heart. They may have been paternal; but they were good employers, and although there were some exceptions, race relations all over were good. The situation was quite different from South Africa where there was discrimination against the African in every aspect of life.

In South Africa change is taking place, but it still presents a very difficult problem. The proportion of Africans to Europeans is roughly four to one, compared with fourteen to one in Rhodesia. The Cape Coloureds would like to be able to join forces with the white South Africans.

The urban African, too, is earning big money; and many of the workmen come in from Malawi, Basutoland and other countries, and return home with wealth beyond anything which they could earn elsewhere.

As long as prosperity continues there may be sporadic outbursts of discontent against the petty irritations of 'apartheid' which are numerous, but the chances are that serious violence will be contained. The intellectual opposition in the Universities is probably a greater menace to the establishment than an organized revolt of African workers.

In 1968 I was given varying estimates as to how long South Africa could continue to go along without a social explosion. The pessimists gave it five years (now well past), the optimists far longer.

One African to whom I spoke gave me a clue which seemed to me nearer to reality. He told me that, although he was worth a lot of money, he was content to live in his African township with the

friends with whom he had grown up. But he added, 'I am a cultivated man, with a knowledge of history, and philosophy; and when
my children grow bigger and I want to build a house on that lovely
hill, and I am told that I cannot do so because I am black – then I
shall become angry.' So far there are few such men; but the South
African Government should take heed of their plea, and in time.

There are two particular aspects of South African life which in
their different ways cause concern. The first is the official Government
policy of creating 'Homelands' which will in time become areas of
African Home Rule, and will then acquire the status of full national
independence. It is a defensible policy, but there is a flaw. I caused
three separate enquiries to be made by qualified persons as to the
total capacity of the Transkei and other designated areas, taking a
time-scale of thirty years from that date. All of them arrived at
much the same conclusion. It was that the 'Homelands' could absorb
roughly fourteen million people, but that over and above that
number there would be some ten to twelve millions remaining, and
required in the large urban areas of the Republic, in order to keep
the economy afloat and prospering.

The official policy of the South African Government of separate
development therefore is no final solution of the country's racial
problem. If South Africa is to cultivate a harmonious society the
political leaders must take steps, however gradually, to confer upon
the Africans and the coloured population the dignity of full citizenship, including political representation. Dr Vorster is clearly aware
of the need for steady progress in this direction. His political difficulty is to carry Afrikaaners along at a sufficient speed. He has made
a beginning in sport.

During my journeyings I always raised the subject of 'apartheid'
in order to test the reactions of my hosts, or my audience. I quickly
discovered that if one opened with a tirade against the system, the
listeners would shut up like clams; but if the subject was approached
as a difficult legacy which the history of South Africa had left with
them, and enquired how they thought they could solve it, they

would talk into the small hours of the morning, seeking ways and means of extracting themselves from a situation which they knew in their hearts was untenable, dangerous and harmful.

That experience confirmed my belief that precept and example must be better than ostracism, and that perception and understanding would bring apartheid to an end far more quickly than boycott. The more tourists and sportsmen, businessmen and politicians whom we can send to South Africa the quicker will be the process of the dilution of 'apartheid' – the more we send them to Coventry the more obstinate they will become, and the more they will retire into their hard protective shell of intolerance. South Africans, too, should be encouraged to come to Britain and Europe in the largest possible numbers.

The Western world and the free countries of Africa simply cannot afford to alienate a country of such strategic importance in the context of the freedom of the seas. Anger against injustice is right; but self-righteousness is ugly, particularly in those with a beam in their own eye. There are a number of them in the continent of the 'wind of change' and at home. It is indeed a double standard to censure South Africa and to court the Soviet Union. In the sixties Rhodesians could not see the dangers ahead. In 1971 I was able to offer them another chance; but by then it was the black African who was blind.

My second journey was to the Middle East. Israel in 1967 was buzzing with rumours of war. The Arab countries, led by Egypt, were running a continuous and blaring propaganda campaign against her existence, and the slogan 'Push Israel into the Sea' still fanned the flames of hatred.

Although this constant noise was partly to boost Arab morale, Israel certainly had cause to fear an attack from Egypt or Syria or both.

When I was in Galilee in the early spring of 1967, shells from the Russian-built emplacements on the Golan Heights were lobbing into the villages; and although the spirit of the inhabitants seemed to be high, it was an unnerving and unsettling state of affairs which clearly could not be allowed to continue indefinitely.

I had never visited Israel before, and it was impossible not to admire the dedication of young and old to the building of their new home, and the self-discipline with which they all set about their appointed tasks, whether in the life of the agricultural Kibbutz, or in the infant industries which were springing up in the cities. They were to be manned by the flow of new Jewish immigrants, largely from Russia, which it was confidently anticipated would swell the population and render the State more self-supporting and less vulnerable.

The Israelis had been fortunate in leaders like Dr Weizmann and Mr Ben Gurion, who had brought inspiration to their task of national construction; while Mrs Golda Meir was the embodiment of patriotism; and a woman who combined an almost masculine strength and determination with a maternal care for every individual in the land. In Mr Eban, the Foreign Minister, Israel had one of the most persuasively articulate politicians in the world.

I was able to see something of their military planning for defence; and could only conclude that should Egypt launch an attack Israel would win, and quickly. The military machinery was in a high state of efficiency and preparation, and always on the alert.

But there were other signs that did not augur so well for the longer term. The source of new population of Jews from the Soviet Union was being severely curtailed; labour was at full stretch, building up the economy, and conscription was a constant strain; the experience of the guns sited on the Golan Heights was a daily reminder in the age of missile artillery, of the vulnerability of a small country surrounded by hostile neighbours; while the Russians, although they had been the first to recognize the State of Israel, were now busily arming Egypt and filling that country with 'technicians' and giving them instruction in the use of modern weapons.

One matter I was unable to decide in my own mind. Did Israel plan to expand further in order to give herself more territorial elbow-room and more physical security?

The Egyptians clearly anticipated such a move, and were therefore tempted to launch a pre-emptive attack, while with the morale of Nasser's army at rock-bottom, it was always necessary to whip up an atmosphere of frenzied excitement. War seemed to be unavoidable. So it proved, and the result was the rout of the Egyptian forces.

On the face of it the Israeli victory was complete. By establishing their troops on the Suez Canal they had gained that additional airspace to give them the warning of attack which in their reckoning could mean the difference between life and death. The Russians had put a lot of eggs into the Egyptian basket, and had seen them broken; the State of Israel was proved beyond doubt to be a reality, while Arab spirit, already low, had fallen seemingly beyond recovery.

But there were two basic considerations which could not be ignored. First, an Arab is proud, and though he may have to wait, humiliation demands revenge; secondly, to an Arab his land is sacred, and he will never rest while it is in alien hands.

In the wider international scene the Middle-Eastern situation was important in the extreme, as it was an area in which the United States and the Soviet Union were ranged on opposite sides, and whenever the United States was seen to be actively involved in support of Israel, Arab passion would rise to the boil.

The full implication of this knife-edge situation at long last started to sink in; the international community began to sit up and take notice with the result Resolution 242 was passed by the United Nations. It read:

The Security Council,
Expressing its continuing concern with the grave situation in the Middle East.
Emphasizing the inadmissibility of the acquisition of territory by war and the need to work for a just and lasting peace in which every State in the area can live in security.
Emphasizing further that all Member States in their acceptance

of the Charter to the United Nations have undertaken a commitment to act in accordance with Article 2 of the Charter.

1. Affirms that the fulfilment of the Charter principles requires the establishment of a just and lasting peace in the Middle East which should include the application of both the following principles:

    (i) Withdrawal of Israeli armed forces from territories occupied in the recent conflict.

    (ii) Termination of all claims or states of belligerency and respect for and acknowledgement of the sovereignty, territorial integrity and political independence of every State in the area and their right to live in peace within secure and recognized boundaries free from threats or acts of force.

2. Affirms further the necessity:

    (a) For guaranteeing freedom of navigation through international waterways in the area.

    (b) For achieving a just settlement of the refugee problem.

    (c) For guaranteeing the territorial inviolability and political independence of every State in the area, through measures including the establishment of demilitarized zones.

3. Requests the Secretary General to designate a Special Representative to proceed to the Middle East to establish and maintain contacts with the States concerned in order to promote agreement and assist efforts to achieve a peaceful and accepted settlement in accordance with the provisions and principles in this resolution.

4. Requests the Secretary General to report to the Security Council on the progress of the efforts of the Special Representative as soon as possible.

It was ambiguous, for it was not clear whether the Israelis' withdrawal was to be 'from all Arab territories which had been conquered'; but it did at least provide a framework within which a peace settlement could be negotiated; and no one could devise anything more positive and definitive which would command unanimous support in the organization.

With Egypt licking her wounds and in a state of moral and economic bankruptcy, President Nasser was faced with a most testing decision. He had to try and rebuild the strength of his forces. He could reasonably expect Russian assistance for that for the Russians had also to restore 'face'. But equally Egypt's economic base was weak, and he was confronted with a new and confident State of Israel which had clearly come to stay.

By 1970 I began to see signs that Nasser was gradually bringing himself to realize that there was no gain for Egypt in war, and every advantage in peace. In spite of defeat his stature with his people was such that if he advocated a course of peaceful action they would certainly follow his lead. But he was soon to die.

For six years then I and my political team in the field of Foreign and Commonwealth Affairs had shadowed the Government spokesmen – first Mr George Brown (later Lord George-Brown) and Mr Stewart; supporting them when we judged that their actions were in the nation's interest, as in the case of the Nigerian Civil War, and criticizing them when they made a mess of things.

Conservatives have always sought the greatest possible degree of consensus between the parties on foreign policy and defence. It is an area of politics in which continuity presents great advantage to the nation.

NATO, since it was created with Ernest Bevin as a founder, has always provided a common platform for the parties; while during the sixties, when America increasingly had her back to the wall in Vietnam, Mr Wilson and his colleagues, although the target of sniping from the Left, broadly supported the right of the United States to conduct their Far Eastern policy in their own way. Neither of us felt inclined to criticize when Britain could do nothing to help an ally in trouble; for both sides of the House were agreed that we could not commit forces to battle in that part of the mainland of Asia. The French had employed many crack divisions of soldiers in Vietnam and I remember M. Couve de Murville telling me of the disadvantages which their troops suffered when the enemy could always outflank and arrive behind their lines. The Americans had become involved from the highest motives, but clearly Vietnam was a graveyard, and it was no place for us.

In the Commonwealth too there was little about which to disagree. The Left of the Labour Party, during the Biafran revolt in Nigeria, constantly attacked Mr Michael Stewart, the Foreign and Commonwealth Secretary, for allowing supplies of arms to continue to go to the Nigerian Government. The most retiring and reticent of Ministers, he stood up to his critics with real courage. We as constantly supported his decisions; for a contract had been made with a friendly Commonwealth Government which had relied for years on British equipment. We took the view that to fall down on our obligation would be a breach of faith for which we should not be forgiven, and that we should lose the confidence of the one country in West Africa which had a real chance to influence events in that part of the continent, in the direction of order, moderation and unity. Once tribalism was allowed to triumph the continent of Africa could be written off as a dead loss for at least fifty years.

Rhodesia was a running sore; but as each side of the House sought a solution within the framework of the Five Principles of settlement, the engagements were somewhat desultory and routine.

There was one singularly inept piece of diplomacy on the part of Mr Wilson, which was so obviously an example of how foreign affairs should not be conducted, that I decided that it deserved a rebuke from the Opposition Front Bench. It became known as 'The Soames Affair'.

Mr Wilson, after a private conversation between our Ambassador, Sir Christopher Soames, and General de Gaulle, at which the French President had hinted that Europe might be run by a triumvirate, had spoken of it without the General's leave to Chancellor Brandt, and the news had got back to Paris before Mr Wilson could explain.

I spoke as follows:

My Hon. Friend the Member for Mid-Bedfordshire (Mr Hastings) and the Right Hon. Member for Leyton (Mr Gordon-Walker) have made it clear what the debate is about. It is not about the general relationship of the various countries in Europe, or at least only indirectly. It really concerns, and is a short debate about, a specific episode of diplomacy and foreign policy conducted personally and primarily by the Prime Minister and the Foreign Secretary with the President of France.

In his general approach to the problems of Europe's future, the Right Hon. Gentleman can rightly claim much support on both sides of the House and elsewhere, but, in this particular case, there are certain points which must be made, if only for the sake of the conduct of British foreign policy in future.

The relevant facts which could be ascertained from the tangle of speculation after the Foreign Secretary's statement yesterday were these – that the President of France and the British Ambassador in Paris regarded the exchanges which they had as confidential to the two Governments, at any rate for the present. The second fact is that the Prime Minister disclosed the content of those talks to the German Chancellor without obtaining General de Gaulle's consent, or that of the French Government. There is no dispute, therefore, about these facts of the case.

I do not want to labour this point, but it is essential to establish, and at once, that this is not the practice of British diplomacy, and for a very obvious reason – that, if foreign statesmen were to believe for a moment that confidences could and would be related to others, no one would say anything worth while to us again. So this must be said at once, and unequivocally, and I hope that it will go out from this House that this is not our practice; otherwise, our usefulness in the international councils of the world would be at an end.

The more one hears of this affair the more it is clear that the Foreign Secretary is pleading that this was a special situation in which special treatment was necessary. He says, first, that the substance of the matters discussed by General de Gaulle and the British Ambassador was so important to our friends that they had to be told of it; secondly, and I think that the House recognizes that this is the feeling behind the Right Hon. Gentleman's mind, that the General is considered capable of setting a trap which would, unless one were careful, discredit Britain in the minds of the other five members of the Community, and that for those two reasons – maybe for others too, but for those in particular – the Prime Minister's action in telling the German Chancellor without General de Gaulle's consent was justified.

In this, if I may say so with respect, I think that the Foreign Secretary has underestimated the resources of diplomacy, and because he underestimated them he did not use them. Our friends and allies in the European alliance and in the European Economic Community are adult members of international society. They are as anxious as anyone, because they suffer acutely from the hostility between Britain and France, to see the deadlock between Britain and France ended.

At least two options were open to the Rt. Hon. Gentleman conducting this affair. He could have told General de Gaulle that the British Government thought that they must inform the German Government, and invited the co-operation of the General either to explain his own ideas to his partners or agree that we should do so. If the General had said, 'Yes' – which I admit is extremely unlikely – it would have been fairly certain that this was one of the General's long-term incursions into the future of Europe and of NATO – something which has been heard often before – and that the initiative was of no real value and had no real future. That was one course which at any rate would have left everyone in the clear, and particularly the British Government.

But there was another course which I should have thought would have commended itself to the Rt. Hon. Gentleman. That course was to tell the five other members of the Community that the British Ambassador had had a first conversation with the French President; that the result seemed to be the old mixture as before, but that there were certain things that we would like to pursue further in the interests of the unity of Europe in case there should be any substance in them; that we therefore intended to have further conversations to clarify these points that might be of substance, and that if at any time in these conversations matters of real substance arose which showed possibilities for negotiation, we would seek the General's agreement – insist, indeed, that there must be agreement – to create the necessary allied machinery so that all the members of the Community and Britain could meet together to consider them. I cannot understand why the Rt. Hon. Gentleman and the Prime Minister did not adopt one of those two courses. It would completely have safeguarded the position of the British Government.

The impression is that the Government felt that they were about to fall into a trap. I think that they were afraid of this. But surely one of the functions of diplomacy is to spring traps in order to render them harmless, so that the innocent are not caught. One must conclude on the evidence so far that the reaction of the British Government to this initiative of the President of France was too hasty, and precipitate, and being precipitate, led them into real trouble.

I cannot quite agree with the Rt. Hon. Gentleman the Member for Leyton in his interpretation, because I do not think that the General – and some of us have had experience of this sort of conversation with him – was asking the British Government to break with NATO. What I think he was asking the British Government to do was to talk with him about the differences between France and Britain on the political, economic and military future of Europe. If that was so, there was a very strong case for accepting the invitation, and I would say that our allies and friends in Europe and the other five members of the Community would also have felt that we would have been safe to undertake those talks.

I have one final reflection. Our joint purpose must now be to undo this damage, if that can be done. In a very special sense the Western European Union is a trustee for the peace and unity of Europe – and in these two senses in particular; it is through the WEU that German rearmament is controlled – and, in particular, German nuclear rearmament. It is through the Brussels Treaty, for example, and not through NATO that France is brought automatically to the aid of Germany if Germany is attacked. So it is within the context of the WEU that the peace and security of Europe in a peculiar way lies, and if WEU were to break up we could not replace those ingredients which are vital to the peace, security and unity of Europe.

There is no doubt, and many Hon. and Rt. Hon. Gentlemen feel this, that French policy during the last few years has been divisive of Western Europe. One must in honesty say this. It has been exasperating to those who have pursued in a devoted way the unity of Europe. But equally we have to remember that there can be no unity in Europe without the *rapprochement* of France and Germany. If there is to be real unity in Europe Britain must come into the partnership not with one or the other, but with both. Unless that is recognized, we may do very serious damage to the whole conception of European unity, and contribute to the division of Europe rather than to healing the differences.

I hope that the bitter experience of the last week or so will mean that the French – and in particular the French – will take a very hard and clear look at their policy in Europe and will realize now how dangerous are the symptoms of disunity which we have seen. I hope, too, that the British Government will take the lead in reconciliation.

I have not concealed from the Rt. Hon. Gentleman that the resources of diplomacy have not been used and that they could have been used with far greater skill, but I hope that we will take every possible step we can to reconcile these two points of view, keeping central to our mind all the time the thought that there is no unity in Europe; there may be something less, if we deal with France on the one hand or with Germany on the other; that there may be something less, but it will not be the unity of Europe, and it is to the unity of Europe that we all want to subscribe.

A number of members of the Diplomatic Corps perhaps improperly, but nevertheless specifically, agreed that this was an accurate statement of the way in which international affairs should be conducted and confidence between statesmen preserved.

Then there was the matter of Anguilla, which was certainly an occasion for ridicule for the heavy weather which the Government made over it.

I was able to have some mild fun at Mr Stewart's expense. He had over-dramatized the case and the dangers to Britain from this tiny island and had exaggerated the importation of arms.

I asked:

What about the arms? There were a few. Some arms were imported by Mr Webster – not, let me say, to oppose the British, but in case the Anguillans were abandoned by the British and the people of St Kitts succeeded in taking over. What about the crates of arms of which the Under-Secretary told us? Have those crates ever been found? The arms said to have been imported by these undesirable gentlemen have not been found. They have not been seen to be taken away. So what, so far, do we know? The men are faceless and nameless, the crates are unopened and invisible. All, apparently, have evaporated into thin air.

I do not know whether the Foreign Secretary saw the presentation on television. Our troops did their duty, as they always do but their advancing with fixed bayonets on to the beaches of Anguilla as though they were invading a foreign power stretched credibility too far. These Anguillans have always been simple British subjects, loyal to the Queen, and to suggest anything else was to give a totally false impression to the country.

And what about the comings and goings of Ministers of the Ministerial team, to and from this tiny State? We had Lord Shepherd, we had the Under-Secretary, we had Lord Caradon first, and then we had Lord Caradon again. I can almost hear the Rt. Hon. Gentleman, the Foreign Secretary, rehearsing:

> Tripping hither, tripping thither
> Nobody knows why or whither.
> If you ask the special function
> Of our never-ceasing motion,
> We reply without compunction
> That we have not any notion.

What a field-day that would have been for Mr Gilbert! Will the Foreign Secretary please tell us if this other noble and roving Lord is to be let loose on to this stage? If he were to join the dance there would have been nothing like it since the Lobster Quadrille.

Every now and then the staid business of Parliament is lightened by some such ludicrous affair.

Overall as a Party, I believe that we conducted Opposition under Edward Heath's leadership with reasonable competence. We did not, in spite of his liking for instant politics, harry the Government when they were right, but we did pin them down when they were wrong, so that the electorate could contrast their policies with ours, and their performance with our own.

June 1970 saw the Opinion Polls predicting a Socialist victory at the General Election, and we proceeded through the necessary campaigning days with the potential voters enjoying the glorious summer weather, but apparently detached from the great political issues of the day.

But the Polls and the apparent apathy were misleading; for there was a comparatively high vote, and the Conservatives were returned with a working majority, and with Edward Heath as Prime Minister.

XVII

The Foreign Service

I was glad, at Ted Heath's request, to return to the Foreign Office
for a number of reasons, not the least of which was the pleasure and
stimulus of working with those who have been trained in the
Foreign Service. I suppose that their choice of this particular profession was an indication at an early age of a readiness to be broad-
minded. I definitely found them so. Their business was, of course,
to identify and present the particular British interest in any given
situation, but there was never anything parochial in their approach,
and the need to seek reconciliation between our national requirement
and the international need was always in evidence.

Successive Permanent Secretaries had wisely encouraged the
younger members of the service to give their opinions in the different meetings which the Secretary of State would hold to discuss
this or that issue of policy or action. After the seniors in the particular
department of the Office had deployed the pros and cons, those in
junior positions would not hesitate to express their points of view
which might or might not agree with their elders. It was valuable
training for them, and it was interesting to watch those who would
in later years have to carry responsibility, gain in confidence and
stature.

I happened to be a rapid reader of telegrams and briefs, but given
a few hours to master the facts and chew over the arguments, a

meeting with a maximum of a dozen officials would save hours of paper work and valuable time.

It has often been said in recent years that with the advent of rapid communications, the rôle of Ambassador has ceased to be important. I cannot agree.

It is, of course, true that in the absence of modern facilities, Ambassadors of the last century and the pre-1914 years were often called upon to act without reference to their masters, and to trust to luck that when the news of what they had done reached Whitehall that it would be received with a reasonably good grace.

Now, with the arrival of telecommunications, an Ambassador, faced with a really urgent crisis, will usually try and check with the Foreign Secretary before he goes into action with the Government to which he is accredited. But that is not a bad thing, for two minds are probably better than one; while a Minister will clearly be in a better position to take an intelligent decision if he is armed with the latest on-the-spot news, and the Ambassador's personal reaction to it.

To the extent, therefore, that there is more consultation, there is change, but on the whole it ought to result in a reduction of human errors.

In one way the value of an Ambassador is increased. Governments change with startling rapidity, and it is necessary that a Foreign Secretary should have a pretty clear picture of the personalities with whom he will have to deal and the direction which the policies of such persons will be likely to take. An Ambassador's training equips him to make such judgements.

For example, I was early convinced of the view that if Rhodesia was to be saved from a horrible confrontation between black and white, that Mr Smith would have to be persuaded to take his head out of the sand; that Archbishop Makarios, unless he could bring himself to treat the Turkish minority as human beings, was inviting the invasion and partition of the island; that Khrushchev was a freak who did not conform to the pattern of dour and dedicated Communist leaders; that General Sadat was able to see in a way that

President Nasser was not, that Egypt's fundamental interest lay in peaceful relations with Israel; that General Franco's weakness was inability to hand over power. These impressions and many others were built up or confirmed from dispatches and talks with our Ambassadors who were in the best position to advise.

I imagine that the most difficult part of an Ambassador's assignment is to prevent himself from becoming emotionally involved with the policies of the Government of the country to which he is accredited. He has to gain the confidence of the Ministers with whom he has to deal, but he must resist the temptation to make himself popular by becoming an indiscriminating advocate of their views.

I had been alerted to these dangers by my experience on the approach to the 1939 war. Persons like the late Sir John Wheeler-Bennett had clearly given a much more objective picture of Nazi intentions than Sir Nevile Henderson; while the intelligence gathered about the French Armed Services by Mr Kenneth de Courcy was a great deal nearer to the true state of morale in the French army than that distributed by our service attachés in Paris.

In only one case did an Ambassador and I find it necessary to part company on policy. Sir Hugh Foot found it impossible to convince himself that a Conservative Government would not sell the Africans down the river in Rhodesia. I could not persuade him otherwise. In those circumstances we agreed that it was better that he should give up his post as our representative at the United Nations. Events proved, of course, that he was mistaken, but he was brave and honourable, both when he was down to earth and right in Cyprus, and when he was starry-eyed and wrong in New York.

As a rule a Foreign Secretary does well to give preference to the career man for a diplomatic post, if only for the reason that if the plums in the service go to outsiders, the regular members begin to become discouraged and recruitment falls away.

I found, however, a ready recognition that there should be occasional exceptions to the rule.

I never heard a whisper of criticism when Sir David Ormsby-Gore (later Lord Harlech) was sent to Washington. It was clear to everyone that he could command the ear of President Kennedy in a way that none other could, and that the arrangement was strongly in the British interest.

Nor was there any objection to the appointment of Lord Carrington as High Commissioner in Australia, for although there were many senior in age and experience, he clearly commanded in unusual degree the drive, intelligence, forthright speech and humour which the Australians particularly prize.

Nor was there opposition to the use of Mr Malcolm MacDonald in various posts in Asia, for he was so surely in tune with the Asians' processes of thought, and could even outstay them in patience.

These are the kind of exceptions which prove the rule, but a Foreign Secretary can usually find from within the service the right man for the right place at the right time.

It would be invidious to take illustrations of successes in diplomacy from our own service, so I turn to other countries for examples as to how diplomacy can be conducted to the best possible advantage.

It would be difficult to imagine diplomatic ground more unpropitious than that which Mr Dobrynin found on his arrival in Washington to represent the Soviet Union. There has seldom been much elbow-room for constructive diplomacy, but I would hazard that most Americans would agree that the *modus vivendi* which there has been for the last few years between the two super-powers can largely be attributed to Mr Dobrynin's skill, tact and special pleading.

America in turn paid Britain the high compliment of sending to us Mr David Bruce. I had heard him on a number of occasions, during the term of office of President Kennedy, sum up complicated international issues at times of crisis, with a mind sharpened to a fine point, and with a masterly economy of words with which he carried the maximum of conviction. He had to explain many things to the United States. The impact of the loss of the power that went with Empire, and its effect on the British people; the gradual conversion of successive British Governments to active partnership in the European Community. In reverse he had to interpret to Britain America's action in Vietnam, and to convince us that cutting their losses did not imply United States' withdrawal into herself and away from NATO. At the time of the Cuban crisis his presence with us was invaluable.

It is difficult to exaggerate the rôle which David Bruce played in maintaining trust and confidence at a juncture which was critical for both countries. His capacity to be totally professional whilst looking like an amateur was almost unfair.

Ambassadors from the Soviet Union, apart from Mr Dobrynin, were seldom allowed any discretion, and had usually to be content with reading out verbatim messages drafted by Mr Gromyko or by his superiors. All too often they were in the nature of complaints that we had offended against some Communist code. It was then necessary to decide whether to treat the matter with suitable gravity, or to turn wrath aside with a joke.

The individual Russian is, I think, a naturally friendly and gay person, but the Communist system is like a wet blanket and stifles fun.

Lenin was intellectually convinced that the formula 'From each according to his abilities – to each according to his needs' was so literally right that the Party which was set up to promote it could never be wrong.

Stalin, using the supreme authority conferred on a war leader, used Lenin's political apparatus to establish a dictatorial police state which was ruled by fear. No one could criticise it, and to make the State a target for humour could risk exile or life. No wonder that conversation at a Russian party is careful, and no wonder that they even look apprehensive when their British guests poke fun at democratic institutions.

In the Russia of today some discreet jokes are beginning to be made against the system, but they are few and far between.

Once in Belgrade a meeting at which I was to speak was held

up because the microphone had been mislaid. I was explaining this to a Minister who said: 'But that is ridiculous. Belgrade is full of microphones.' The interpreter looking anxious said, 'The Minister – he makes a joke.'

Life would, of course, be unbearable if official business was allowed to impinge on personal relations, and all in all the social amenities were preserved. Elizabeth and the Ambassadors' wives, uninhibited by considerations of policy, had as usual most of the fun.

There was one aspect of the rules governing service overseas which, from my earliest days in the Commonwealth Relations Office I considered to be positively inhuman. Parents were allowed the expense of travel to bring their children out to their post for only one of the school holidays of the year, or alternatively return to Britain to see them. Unless they had substantial private means mothers were therefore separated from their children for roughly three-quarters of the year, at the most impressionable and formative time of their lives. The strain on wife and husband was clear; and in a number of cases resulted in nervous breakdowns, and even the break-up of marriage, and I was determined that the system must be reviewed and resolved.

We made some progress during the early sixties, but it was only when Lord Plowden revealed the facts and proposed the remedies in his excellent Report on the Service in 1964 that I was finally convinced that a young man entering the service could feel confident that he would be able to enjoy the pleasures and satisfaction of family life, even in the remoter parts of the globe. It is strongly in the interest of the nation that in the Foreign Service morale should at all times be high.

On my return to the Foreign Office in 1970 the international scenario seemed to be 'the mixture as before', but there were in fact some subtle changes.

Communist Russia was close to nuclear parity with the United States. Apparently content with the *status quo* in Europe, she was nevertheless reinforcing the whole Warsaw Pact military area with men and weapons, and was probing any weak spot in the world where Western influence could be undermined.

China, too, had broken her alliance with Russia, and was beginning to stir as a power in her own right.

The Conservative Party had, during the General Election, advocated the merits of Britain joining the European Economic Community; and the great majority of candidates had made it quite clear that a Conservative Government would recommend membership to Parliament if, after negotiations, we judged the terms of entry to be fair. In all these international considerations, apart from Britain's physical security, membership of the European Economic Community took first place.

XVIII

Once again at the Foreign and Commonwealth Office

With so much activity on the international stage the Prime Minister, whilst giving me overall supervision of the whole foreign field, placed the detailed negotiation of entry into the European Community in the hands of Mr Geoffrey Rippon. The going was sticky, but after Mr Heath had met President Pompidou privately, it was clear that this time there would be no French veto.

Geoffrey Rippon's technique was skilful. In Brussels he would ring the changes on the different objectives to be settled, until he was reasonably sure that the package would be acceptable to Parliament. He was accused of leaving some issues vague; but his reply was always the same, whether it was the matter of New Zealand's dairy produce, or the West Indies' sugar, or preference for the developing countries, or regional policy. It was to the effect that the members of the Community had gone far enough in negotiations towards accepting an obligation to solve the problems in a way favourable to the parties concerned to satisfy him that they would in fact be so resolved. After entry his judgement has proved to be correct.

At the time the Left wing of the Socialist Party in the House were vocal in their disapproval; but when Mr George Brown (later Lord George-Brown) and Mr Roy Jenkins testified that in their opinion the terms ultimately obtained were as good if not better than their own Government would have got, the ground was cut away from under the feet of the Opposition, and a motion in the House in favour of entry was carried by a majority of 112.

If Mr Wilson, in order to placate the Left, had not already promised a future Referendum on the subject, that decisive Parliamentary approval would have settled the matter for good. At any rate the result was much to the credit of Geoffrey Rippon and Edward Heath and the Conservative Party.

I had not been back in the Office for long before I was made aware that the Russians, over the recent years, had been systematically filling their Trade Mission with spies, and that these people were conducting their espionage actively under the cover of diplomatic immunity. The scale of their operations was putting a heavy strain on our own security service. The Russians knew that we knew exactly what was happening, and yet they kept on piling in new agents. They reckoned that we would not dare to face the public outcry of rooting them out.

That was a situation which I decided could not be allowed to continue; but before acting I had to be sure, first that Mr Gromyko was aware of the scale of the spies' activities, and secondly that he had full opportunity to handle the matter personally and privately, and to withdraw the offending agents without publicity. I saw him and told him plainly of the situation, and asked him gradually to take away the offenders and to send no more. There was no response. After some months I wrote to remind him. There was again no reply. I repeated these approaches, and in all gave him a year or more in which to act. He still failed to answer or do anything about it.

Our knowledge of the gentlemen concerned was confirmed by defectors, and I decided that Mr Gromyko's time was up. We made no provocative announcement. Sir Denis Greenhill, the Permanent Under-Secretary at the Foreign and Commonwealth Office, conveyed the news to the Soviet Ambassador that 105 named individuals must leave by a given date; and that thereafter a ceiling would be placed on the numbers in the Trade Mission and in the Embassy. The operation caught the Russians on the hop. Our selection of individuals struck a blow at the KGB and its works, which disorganized their plans seriously; the more so as a number of European Governments were able unobtrusively to take advantage of our cover to rid themselves of a lot of undesirables. The Russian bluster impressed no one, and their retaliation was weak to the point of being routine.

There followed a cancellation of an invitation to me to visit Moscow; and two years of icy coolness before the Russian leaders recovered their sense of proportion sufficiently to renew warmer relations. But the operation had achieved its purpose. The Russian leaders learned that there was a limit to our tolerance; and thereafter there was a new respect in their dealings with us.

During one interview in New York Mr Gromyko gave me an opening to enquire whether there were any diplomats left in Russia who had not been trained in the KGB. It was too near the knuckle for his comfort.

Eventually they cooled down, and Mr and Mrs Gromyko came to London. One evening we took them to the play *Vivat Regina*, in which Mary Queen of Scots and Rizzio are leading characters. As we came out of the second act Mr Gromyko said to me: 'Do I not find myself in very dangerous company?' I asked why, and he replied: 'Did I not hear Mary Stuart say, as the dagger went into Rizzio, "And you, Douglas, too?"' Such are the amenities of international public life, and they are necessary to sanity.

But one must always force oneself to remember – odious and boring though it is – that all Communists are dedicated to a single end – victory over every other creed and every other way of life.

It would seem to be reasonable that, after more than half a century since Russia's revolution, the fervour might have been diluted a little. But seemingly it is not so. Czechoslovakia is still occupied; the Berlin Wall still remains; East Germany and Poland are still held in the iron grip of Soviet discipline; while the 1975 Summit of NATO leaders, although seeking a *détente*, felt bound to record that the Warsaw Pact deploys a force 'far in excess of any need for self-defence'.

The tolerant people of the Western democracies find it difficult to comprehend an approach to life which differs so fundamentally from their own. The philosophy and practice of Communism is dedicated to the purpose of complete victory. The democratic peoples must realize the fact; and however regretfully and painfully, supply the sinews for defence; for unless they are ready to do so the Communist persistence will win.

Our return to office in June 1970 gave us the chance to turn our attention to two matters of unfinished business. The first was Rhodesia; and the second, the Middle East and the Gulf.

The task of finding a settlement in Rhodesia was made much more difficult by the two previous public failures; but it seemed to me that there was an outside chance of success, provided that preparation could be careful and quiet.

The objective was certainly worth while; for to return Rhodesia to a legal relationship with Britain would redeem one of our few failures in the conversion of Empire to Commonwealth, while the alternative to a constitutional settlement and mixed European and African government was almost certainly an armed frontier on the Zambesi, and bloody war.

Sir Max Aitken and Lord Goodman, on a private visit to Salisbury, had seen Mr Smith and had confirmed the impression that I had gained – that an honourable deal might be made within the Five Principles which Parliament had endorsed as the framework to which any settlement must conform.

They were:

1. The principle and intention of unimpeded progress to majority rule, already enshrined in the 1961 Constitution, would have to be maintained and guaranteed.

2. There would need to be guarantees against retrogressive amendment of the Constitution.
3. There would have to be immediate improvement in the political status of the African population.
4. There would have to be progress towards ending racial discrimination.
5. The British Government would need to be satisfied that any basis proposed for independence was acceptable to the people of Rhodesia as a whole.

These had originally been 'guide-lines' settled between Mr Smith and me just before the General Election of 1964. They did not seem to me to present any serious obstacle to constitutional reform, although, since African opinion had become much more restive and vocal, and subversion organized from outside was rearing its ugly head, it might be difficult to obtain the approval for a settlement of the 'Rhodesian people as a whole'.

I asked Lord Goodman, who had been intrigued by the problem and was a supremely skilled negotiator, if he would undertake the preliminary investigations to establish whether or not there was a basis for official talks.

He was scarcely inconspicuous, but with luck which was uncanny, he completed his exploration without attracting attention, and by the time he was detected on the job, it was clear that yet another attempt to settle ought to be made.

He and his team from the Foreign and Commonwealth Office then set about in earnest the task of drafting, with the help of Rhodesian officials, the amendments which were necessary to Mr Smith's Constitution of 1969. They had to be drastic if they were to have a chance of being acceptable to the British Parliament, and to form the basis of legislation which would provide for Rhodesia's independence.

They had at least to include: a code of human rights applicable to all the races, and justiciable in the courts; the substitution over time of a common voting roll for the separate racial rolls which existed; visible advance for the Africans in the Parliament and the Civil Service; alteration of the voting qualification which was patently unfair; progress towards majority rule; and machinery which would diminish and then abolish racial discrimination. The problem of providing more land for the African was another question about which native opinion ran high.

When Lord Goodman reported that the time was ripe, and that in his view the ingredients were there for a settlement, I went to Rhodesia supported by Sir Peter Rawlinson, the Attorney-General, and Sir Denis Greenhill, the Permanent Under-Secretary at the Foreign and Commonwealth Office; and we joined up with Lord Goodman and his team.

I spent some days in collecting opinions of the shape of a settlement from representative Rhodesians – European and African; and the latter were apparently pleased to be consulted for the first time by the British Government. Mr Joshua Nkomo was released from prison to see me, and we had some hours of conversation. It was he who had wrecked the 1961 Constitution by resiling on the agreement to which he had subscribed in London, and I was anxious to see whether he would contemplate a compromise settlement with Mr Smith, which I presented to him, I think fairly, as the only alternative to war.

He was uncompromising, and left me with the strong impression that he would not be a party to any solution short of NIBMAR. He was clearly a clever man, and that he was so fatalistic was depressing.

The rest of the Africans and Europeans, Churchmen, industrialists, members of the professions, Chiefs and commoners seemed to be much more receptive to the kind of ideas which I was floating. Mr Garfield Todd at the time expressed his approval.

The negotiations were sticky; but we made progress under every heading, and after Sir Peter Rawlinson had gone to London to consult with my Cabinet colleagues, I signed on behalf of the

Government a provisional agreement with Mr Smith. It was certainly the best which could have been extracted from him, and in my opinion gave to the Africans many advantages over the existing situation and good prospects for the future.

The proviso was the need to discover whether our proposals were acceptable to the people of Rhodesia as a whole.

This is the account of the terms, and the justification of them, which I presented to Parliament.

The proposals have the following main features. First, amendments will be introduced into the present constitution of Rhodesia to remove the provision which precluded any possibility of progress beyond parity of representation in the House of Assembly between Europeans and Africans. This will be replaced by arrangements providing for unimpeded progress to majority rule. The present number of lower African roll voters will be increased by a reduction of the franchise qualifications.

Secondly, in order to proceed to this end, changes in the present franchise conditions will be made and the present income tax regulator abolished. The present number of directly and indirectly elected Africans in Parliament will continue, but there will be created a new higher African roll with the same qualifications as the European roll. New African seats will be added as the proportion of voters on the higher African roll increases in relation to the numbers of voters on the European roll. On the present estimates, it seems likely that four new African seats will be due to be created when the procedures for registration are completed and in that case they will be filled by by-elections in advance of a General Election. These new seats will be filled, the first two by direct election by the higher African roll, and the next two by indirect election on the same lines as the present indirectly elected members, until parity is achieved.

At parity, ten new seats will be created and filled through election on a common roll consisting of the European and higher

African rolls. At that stage, the numbers on each roll would be approximately equal. Throughout this period up to parity, the blocking mechanism for the specially entrenched clauses of the Constitution will be two-thirds of the Assembly and the Senate voting separately, plus majorities of the European and African members of the Lower House, again voting separately.

At the parity stage when there are 50 African members of the House of Assembly, a referendum will be held amongst voters on both African rolls to determine whether all the African members should in future be directly elected.

Following that referendum and any consequent elections, the ten common roll seats will be filled, unless the Assembly determines, on the recommendation of a commission to be set up at that stage, that some more acceptable alternative arrangements should be made. Any such decision, however, would be subject to the blocking mechanism which I have described. Thereafter the blocking mechanism will revert to a simple two-thirds majority. This would mean that at least seventeen African members of the Lower House would have to approve any change to the specially entrenched clauses, and at that stage the Africans would be represented by directly elected members if that had been their choice. So much for the constitutional arrangements. The proposals also involve other important changes to reduce discrimination and to promote racial harmony. There will be a Declaration of Rights that will be justiciable in the courts. This is a major advance on the present constitution. In particular, on discrimination, the Declaration will re-enact the safeguard relating to discrimination contained in Section 67 (4) of the 1961 Constitution.

Secondly, there will be a three-man Commission, whose membership, to be agreed with us, will include an African, the task of which will be to review the question of racial discrimination throughout the whole field, but with particular regard to the Land Tenure Act and to certain of its effects. Mr Smith has put it clearly on record in the proposals that it is his intention to reduce racial discrimination and that he will commend to his Parliament legislation to give effect to the Commission's recommendations which any Government would regard as overriding.

Thirdly, there will be no further evictions of established communities from Epworth or other areas, until the recommendations of the Commission have been considered.

Fourthly, further land is now available for African settlement, and as the need arises, more will be allocated.

Fifthly, when sanctions have been lifted, the State of Emergency will be revoked, unless unforeseen circumstances intervene.

Fifty-four detainees out of 116 have been released or will be shortly. For the remainder, there will be a special review, at which a British observer will be present. Rhodesians living abroad will be free to return save only where criminal charges lie against them. The Rhodesian Government have undertaken to encourage African recruitment to the public service. As a further important part of the settlement, the British Government will provide £50 million in aid over ten years for economic and educational development in African areas, such aid to be matched appropriately by the Rhodesians with money additional to their present planned expenditure.

Finally, the whole complex of these proposals is to be submitted to the Rhodesian people for approval. This test will be conducted by a Commission appointed by Her Majesty's Government, of which Lord Pearce, a former Lord of Appeal in Ordinary, has agreed to be Chairman, and will report to Her Majesty's Government. The Rhodesian authorities have agreed to allow a full and fair test, and to permit normal political activity to the Commission's satisfaction. Thereafter, if the proposals are acceptable to the Rhodesian Parliament it will be asked to enact the necessary legislation to give effect to them; and the Government will ask this House, once they are satisfied on that score, to enact the amended constitution and to give independence to Rhodesia. This will clear the way to the lifting of sanctions.

These terms were, in my view, so favourable, that, had we not agreed to a Commission to test opinion, I should have had no hesitation in asking then and there for the support of the British Parliament, once Mr Smith had acted on them at the Rhodesian end. Europeans were asked to surrender many of their entrenched positions, and Africans were offered fresh opportunities. I believe that the proposals were fair, and it would have been in the interest of all Rhodesians that they should have been applied.

The findings of the Pearce Commission are public property; and I do not believe that, as events turned out, Lord Pearce could have recorded any verdict other than that the Africans as a whole rejected the settlement.

But the reason why I shall always regret the result is that I am clear that the African opinion did not reflect their disapproval of the terms so much as their dislike for and distrust of Mr Smith.

I had tried to explain that the British Parliament would make no move until Mr Smith had passed all the necessary legislation through the Rhodesian Parliament, and had therefore committed himself to the reforms up to the hilt. But it was to no avail; for the Africans were sure that even so Mr Smith would cheat them out of the benefits of the reforms.

I think that they were wrong. Ian Smith was a man who had a lot of courage, and I believe that once he had put his name to a document, he would have kept his word. His weakness was that he could not read the writing on the wall which was large and clear. He shared that disability with many other Rhodesians. 'Where there is no vision the people perish.'

It was additionally sad because the proposals themselves combined the unimpeded progress to Government which Africans had always sought, with the responsibility which evolutionary change alone could bring. This time it was the Africans who turned down a settlement which could have averted war.

As I write, the last act of the drama has yet to be played. Rhodesians black and white will have to take the main parts, as Britain has now little power to influence events. But both races will do well to find an accommodation, because technically, and in the eyes of the United Nations, it is only the British Parliament which can confer that independence and that status for Rhodesia which will provide her with a passport into international society.

For the Middle East I felt that the Conservatives must proclaim a policy more definite than that which the Socialists had felt able to pursue.

I had become convinced that Israel's resources could not survive a long war; that Russian weaponry was placing her at an increasing disadvantage, and that the Arabs, who had never before been united, were finding unity in the cause of recovery of their conquered lands. I was also sure that the shock to Egypt's system after the 1967 war had been such that they were reconciled to the fact that they must recognize and live with the State of Israel once their territory was returned.

It was not possible to persuade Mrs Golda Meir, or Mr Eban, the Foreign Minister, that Israel's security and long-term interests would be served by any statement about withdrawal. They were confident of American military support; and the best which they would do was to offer bilateral negotiations with Egypt without preconditions, and then sit back and wait.

To that the Egyptians would not respond, feeling that facing the victorious Israelis alone they would suffer diplomatic as well as military defeat. Therefore I took an initiative, and in October 1970 I deployed the British Government policy in a speech at Harrogate. (See Appendix B)

I began by drawing attention to the fact that, parallel to the creation of the State of Israel, new Arab states had been formed and that through all the Arab world there had spread a political revolution involving violent change.

The great powers had become involved in this turbulent picture – first the French and British and then the Russians and Americans.

That part of the reason for this was oil, but that part was due to the fact that the Middle East crossed the road of Europe to the east and Russia to the south.

I pinpointed the kernel of the matter as the Arab conviction that their hereditary territory had been usurped by Israel, and their claim that the million and a half Palestine refugees was proof that their land had been unjustly taken.

That it was this deep emotional feeling which drove some Arabs to pledge themselves to Israel's destruction, and others to swear that they would never rest until all the conquered territory had been restored.

That attitude evoked the Israeli response which was that their only hope of survival was a military deterrent so strong that no Arab country would dare to challenge it. Their single-minded purpose was to deter.

I argued therefore that there could be no settlement unless there was a definitive agreement on the question of territory, and went on to say that although no outsider could lay down where the ultimate boundaries should be, the settlement was bound to involve substantial withdrawal of Israeli forces.

I was well aware that the only compensation which could be offered to Israel was paper security, so I said, 'The second main pillar on which a settlement must rest would be binding commitments which the Arab countries and Israel would make to live at peace with each other. These should include the establishment of a formal state of peace. They should cover an obligation on all states to refrain from any act or threat of hostility, and to do all in their power to prevent the planning or conduct of any such act on their territory.'

I went on to say: 'We cannot support any political programme which would involve the disappearance of the State of Israel . . .

We must work for a settlement which will attract the agreement of all the people of the area including the Palestinians, and which takes account of their legitimate aspirations and resettlement in dignity and honour.'

I was well aware that it was impossible to please both sides. Predictably the Arabs were welcoming and the Israelis angry; the more so as they had thought that I was sympathetic to them in the fight for their existence. In the latter feeling they were right; and the speech stemmed from the conviction that their only hope of survival in an age of missiles lay in abandoning their conquered Arab territories, and in retiring behind their 1967 frontiers (with minor adjustments) which would then be policed by the United Nations, and would probably require an international guarantee.

Very gradually the United States swung to this point of view, as did the policies enunciated by the European Community of the Nine. In fact the principle of withdrawal and buffer zones has been conceded and twice put into practice on the ground following the wars.

Now that Egypt and the Arab countries have been purged of their humiliation by achieving a stalemate in battle; and now that there is a possible solution for the resettlement of the Palestinians in an independent State on the west bank of the Jordan, the prospects of a permanent peace look to be more hopeful than for some time past.

In the final reckoning much will depend on how far the Russians accept that they would be wise in this area to resist the temptation to stir the pot, and to exercise discretion in the use of their power. They will only do so because they fear that otherwise a direct clash with the United States could result.

Much, too, will hang upon America's ability to persuade the Israelis that there will only be peace for them when they finally return the conquered territories to the Arabs.

At any rate, if there is to be a negotiated settlement, I believe that in the end the pattern will closely resemble the Harrogate forecast.

Just as important to Britain was the future of the Gulf States. The Socialist Government of Mr Wilson had been precipitate in their evacuation of the base of Aden, and had announced Britain's withdrawal from the Gulf States without any clear idea as to how the security of that area could be organized to fill the vacuum left by the absence of British power.

Everyone was unsettled. The Rulers because they feared that fragmentation would expose them to Communist influence; the Shah of Iran because he had always foreseen himself as the protector of the Gulf once the British had gone, but had never anticipated that we would quit and run.

There was a school of thought in the Conservative Party in Parliament which felt strongly that we should reverse the Socialist Party's policy and refuse to withdraw our troops; and they reinforced their view with the assertion that the Sheikhs would welcome it. I did not agree, having the strong conviction that, once control over their own affairs had been publicly aired, and offered to such proud and independent-minded people, to snatch back the prospect would be an unacceptable blow to their pride.

If an alternative system was to be erected, there were two essentials. The Sheikhs had to feel that they were the architects of it and to have a vested interest in it; while the King of Saudi Arabia and the Shah of Iran had to be reconciled to the plan.

We put into the minds of the Rulers that they should organize a Union of the Sheikhdoms, with its own security force, and said that we would be willing to supply the personnel and equipment which would ensure that it had a favourable start.

So it happened, and although the Union of the Sheikhdoms is young, and there have been a few stresses and strains, the experiment has on the whole been successful. Certainly our sympathy and interest in the Arabs of the Gulf helped us greatly when the first oil crisis hit the world in 1972, and it still does so.

This event is an illustration of the thesis which I advanced earlier, that it is an error to believe that because we have less power we have no influence at all.

In my second stint at the Foreign Office there was therefore more than enough to do, particularly as I had to play myself in at the Council of Foreign Ministers of the European Community.

XIX

China

During my years in the Foreign and Commonwealth Office I had visited many countries, but it seemed that the door into China was firmly locked.

Since the Long March, the Revolutionary leaders had deliberately isolated themselves from contact with the outside world. Doubtless they were wise, for the history of China had shown that unity was difficult to establish over such a huge area and such diverse people, while the disciplines involved in establishing Communist central control were better conducted away from the public eye.

The few people in the world of business and commerce who had been to China had returned astonished at the way in which the Chinese, with their strong tradition of family cohesion and loyalty, and their independent outlook, had allowed themselves to be communized.

I was anxious, therefore, to judge for myself the effect of the People's Revolution on the future role which China would play in the world.

By 1970 there were signs that Mao Tse-tung and Chou En-lai were gaining confidence in themselves, and that they considered China to be ready for international relations.

We had welcomed this prospect, being the first Western European country to establish diplomatic relations with the Republic, while we had also shown ourselves favourable to China's membership of the United Nations.

These two actions were consistent with our general philosophy and diplomatic practice, for recognition by a British Government has never implied political approval; while we have always insisted that membership of the United Nations must be universal. Both these attitudes had pleased the Chinese.

Two events opened up the possibility of a visit by the British Foreign Secretary. The first was the fact that President Nixon and Dr Kissinger were not at all averse to teaching the Russians that they would be mistaken if they believed that the United States could never establish a working relationship with Communist China, even although America continued to recognize Chiang Kai-shek. Dr Kissinger, in particular, was ready to hint at a possible squeeze on the Soviet Union; while for President Nixon, who was hard pressed on many fronts at home, a visit to China was a considerable political diversion and prize.

Mao Tse-tung had little love for the Americans, but he disliked and feared the Russians even more. In 1950, in a fit of pique, the Russians had picked a quarrel, and withdrawn their personnel and technical aid upon which the Chinese relied to construct their industrial base, and in particular their steel plant. From that time on the Chinese leaders had lost no opportunity of accusing the Soviet Union of deserting an ally, and distorting true Communism. They too, therefore, were happy to keep Russia guessing.

The second event was in the same pattern. In 1970 the new Conservative Government in Britain was clearly intent on becoming a member of the European Economic Community. Here, in the eyes of Mao Tse-tung and Chou En-lai, was another potential counterweight to the power of the Soviet Union, with the added bonus that a united Europe could be expected to exert a modifying influence on the policies of the United States. A public display of friendship with the United States and with Britain was a useful move in an inter-Communist cold war.

The Chinese leaders were at the time suspicious of the French, because they had shown themselves too friendly to the Soviet Union, while in addition they had a past to live down as an imperialist power in South-East Asia. The Chinese thinking was that the British, once they were in the Community, would take the lead in the organization of European unity, and they calculated that we would harbour no illusions about the Russian Communists' intentions to expand at the expense of the West.

The question of the status of Taiwan had hitherto been an obstacle to full diplomatic relations with mainland China. General Chiang Kai-shek had been a friend in the war, and we and the other allies were reluctant to take any action which would seem to be ungrateful. But his claim that the Government of Taiwan was the legal authority for the whole of China had become more and more out of touch with reality, and I had reached the conclusion that it could no longer be sustained. Had the General been willing to lay a claim before the Credentials Committee of the United Nations for recognition of Taiwan as an independent country, we could have supported his claim, and I believe that he would have commanded the majority which was necessary for membership. He would have had to stake his claim before China was elected to the organization; for once there she would have exercised the veto on Taiwan's membership, but General Chiang was unwilling to surrender his title to be the Head of State of the whole of China, so the opportunity for self-determination and independence for Taiwan was lost.

The journey to China by air via Alaska is long and tiring, and one loses all sense of time. I found myself, therefore, washing down poached eggs and bacon which I had just eaten for breakfast on the aeroplane, with a double Scotch and soda at an American Air Force cocktail party. Elizabeth ought to have profited from my plight, but later on arrival at Shanghai she had to add a six-course Chinese meal to her recent breakfast. The good manners of the Chinese require one's neighbour on each side at meals to add to the original helping, and we had not then been told that it is not considered bad manners to leave food on one's plate. We arrived over-tired and over-full, and only the consideration of our hosts in allowing some hours for rest and abstinence restored a semblance of equilibrium. It was complete when we discovered on waking up that our guest-house was situated in 'Anti-Imperialist Street'.

It would be absurd to claim that it was possible in a short visit to come to any solid judgement of modern China and its peoples, but certain strong impressions remain.

The first was the sheer impact of the numbers. Huge as the country is, in town and countryside the people swarm. While we were in Peking the authorities were constructing a canal about two miles in length. In Europe we would have used a dozen or more mechanical scoops and bulldozers, but they from the first day put 77,000 men on the job with buckets and spades.

The problem of how to keep the millions in work is the greatest headache of the Chinese leaders. They simply cannot afford rapid industrialization, or the importation of labour-saving machinery on any significant scale. Present-day China is therefore essentially a 'do-it-yourself' society. They are natural farmers; growing corn in the north, and rice in the south; while around the cities the country-side is one large market garden. The agricultural Red Star communes are impressive, although there are exceptions, and the result is that the majority of the people are adequately fed and well-clothed. They are poor in material possessions – a bicycle being the con-sumer's highest status-symbol, and most useful asset. Wherever we went the place was spotlessly clean.

The paramount need to keep the adult people in work conditions the thinking of the administration on such questions as the acceptance of credit from abroad, and the importation of machinery. Their motto is 'Slow but Sure', and their policy that of self-reliance.

We saw an exhibition of modern art, which had been collected from all the provinces of China. There was some beautiful individual work in jade and coloured stone. There was one almond tree in blossom, about eight feet high, which was so realistic that I was deceived until I was less than a yard away. It had taken one family seven years to make. So far the output of such art is too limited to amount to a significant export trade.

My second impression was that of a completely disciplined people; for obedience to the thoughts of Chairman Mao appeared to be absolute. The focus of Chinese loyalty had traditionally been the family. How far that had been permanently eradicated by the Communist doctrine it is difficult to say; but on the surface the change from the old order to the new is complete.

We were in China soon after Lin-Piao had attempted to challenge the authority of Chairman Mao and Chou En-lai, and had paid the penalty with his life. It may be, therefore, that anyone who had thoughts of deviation had deemed it wise to go to ground. On the surface all was calm and content.

Wives and students and anyone not for the time being in work can be sent to any part of China to do any sort of task for a period of two or three years; and apparently no excuses are allowed.

The young are indoctrinated from a very early age. Elizabeth visited a children's school for four- or five-year-olds, and they all came running out of the class to see the 'foreign aunties'. They were all looking happy and singing, so she asked for the words of the song. They were 'How happy we are to be separated from our mothers, so that our mothers may serve Chairman Mao'.

One of the Red Army songs is typical of the propaganda which is always in the air.

THE THREE MAIN RULES OF DISCIPLINE AND THE EIGHT POINTS FOR ATTENTION

Revolutionary army men must know,
Discipline's Three Rules, Eight Points for Attention,
First, obey orders in all of our actions,
March in step to win victory;

Second, don't take a single needle or thread
People will support and welcome us;
Thirdly, turn in everything we capture,
Strive to lighten people's burdens.

Discipline's Three Rules, we must carry through:
Eight Points for Attention we must bear in mind:
First, we must be polite when we are speaking to the masses,
Respect the people, don't be arrogant.

Second, pay fairly for what we buy,
Buy fair, sell fair, and be reasonable;
Thirdly, don't forget to personally return,
Every single thing that we borrow.

Fourthly, if we damage anything,
Pay the full price, not a half cent less;
Fifth, don't hit people or swear at them,
Totally overcome over-lordism;

Sixth, take care, don't damage people's crops,
Either on march or in battle;
Seventh, don't take liberties with women.
Get rid of all habits decadent.

Eight, don't ill-treat prisoners of war,
Don't hit, swear at or search them.
Everybody must consciously observe the discipline,
Mutually supervise, and not violate it.

Know revolutionary discipline's every point,
People's fighters love the people ever,
Defend the Motherland and forever march ahead.
People o'er the land support and welcome us.

Such exhortations expressing admirable sentiments are everywhere. It is best to observe them.

In theory everything is open for public discussion, and we were told that there is a pattern of debate which starts at the Community Council level, and percolates through to the top. All over the cities and Community centres there are huge hoardings on which are displayed the Thoughts of Chairman Mao, which are the texts from which all discussion stems and all actions flow.

On my drive to the Great Wall with the Vice-Chairman of the People's Congress, I enquired as to how far the feelings of the people influenced the Executive; and what procedure was provided for the consideration of objections to any particular line of policy. He said that no such machinery was necessary because the decisions of Ministers were always accepted as right! Mao Tse-tung is the God, and the Thoughts are commandments written on tablets of stone. China is not only a 'do-it-yourself' but also a 'do-as-you're-told' society.

One of the main purposes for my journey to China had been to try and discover the real reasons which underlay the quarrel between Communist China and Communist Russia. On the face of it they should have been inseparable comrades, because they were brought up in the same school on the teachings of Marx and Lenin. Why then were they at daggers drawn? A judgement as to whether the dispute was superficial or permanent could be of considerable significance in terms of Western security.

That the distrust in China for the Soviet Union was complete was not for a moment in doubt. It was impossible for any length of time to talk to any Chinese on any subject without the conversation being brought round to the corruption in the Russian interpretation of Communism, and the way in which they had distorted its doctrine and brought its teaching into disrepute.

It is virtually impossible for a Westerner to disentangle the dialectics of Communism. When Mr Cheng-Yi, who was Chinese Foreign Minister in the early sixties, had to justify his deviations from orthodox Communism before a tribunal, I read such extracts as were allowed to be printed in the foreign Press. They were total gibberish. He was purged. I fared little better when I tried to discover from Chou En-lai and his colleagues the nature of any doctrinal difference which there might be between Mr Brezhnev's version of Communism and that of Chairman Mao. The Minister said that Russia's crime had been to use propaganda and subversion, backed by the threat of force, against governments with which they were in friendly diplomatic relations. That had given Communism a bad name all over the world.

Mr Chi Peng-fei, the Foreign Minister, was more explicit. 'The actions taken by a super-power to push expansion under façade of *détente* will definitely not be accepted.'

The Chinese had clearly never forgotten the 'treachery' of the Russians who had come in as partners in the adventure of a People's Revolution, and then let them down. But there was much more to it than that. Hatred is the only word which adequately describes the attitude to the Kremlin which I found in Peking, and it springs from deep-seated fear.

The leaders were afraid that the Soviet would, by a pre-emptive strike, take out their nuclear capacity, and while we were there Peking was being honeycombed with underground shelters big enough to take the whole population of the city.

Chou En-lai interpreted the Russian-inspired revolution in Afghanistan – the subsidies given to Iraq – the subversive activities in Oman and Aden – the defence Treaty with India, and their hugely expanded naval activity in the Indian Ocean, as designed to encircle China. Doubtless the presence of an external military threat to China was to some extent useful politics, but the fear seemed to be genuine and it was general.

I tried to persuade Chou En-lai that the Soviet Union could not be so idiotic as to make a permanent enemy of the Chinese people, and when the Foreign Minister, Mr Chi Peng-fei, visited London two years later I thought that the mood of near hysteria had calmed.

But he was still apprehensive, and still unwilling to believe that the Indian Government was not a party to a Russian plot of encirclement which was aimed at destroying Chinese unity.

The Russians are also afraid, to a point where they have placed a million men under arms on China's frontier, with tactical nuclear weapons.

The reason that the Russians have armed the frontier so strongly is that they fear that the Chinese have designs upon those provinces now included in the Soviet Union, which were once part of Imperial China.

The Chinese have constantly asserted that they will regain these lands, and they have made good their boast in the case of Tibet, and of the strip of territory on India's border. The Russians anticipate that as Chinese military strength grows the threat to their frontier will increase. The tensions will clearly last for a long time.

I did not find the Chinese explanation of the ideological dispute particularly convincing. Had not Chou En-lai boasted that the continent of Africa was ripe for revolution? Were they not busy in Aden and the Yemen and in Tanzania and the Sudan? Chou En-lai's answers to this amounted to the weak defence that any Chinese presence was acceptable to the country concerned, and anyway it was only a little one.

If my assessment that the difference between China and Russia is basically about frontiers and territory is right, then the world is unlikely to be faced with a renewed military alliance of the two great Communist powers.

The Great Wall of China is one of the most majestic monuments which I have seen anywhere in the world. It marches across the mountain tops disdaining all heights, contours and obstacles. The mobility of China's enemies who came down from the north was provided by the horse, and if in that arid and unfriendly land a man was parted from his mount, he perished. The Wall was built as a barrier to cavalry, and as such, until internal friction led to the neglect of the external defences, it was a success. Now, if the Russians were so rash as to attack, there is no such physical barrier. But the Chinese have already organized their plan of guerilla warfare. To invade China would be an act of suicide for the Russians, and unless they lose their heads, they will never attempt it.

My Chinese guides were impressed that I had walked further along the Wall than President Nixon. I am bound to say that it was an easy record to beat.

The Chinese Ministers were impeccable hosts, and we talked easily and long of everything under the sun. When Elizabeth and I were given a dinner by the Government we were greeted by the strains of the 'Eton Boating Song' immaculately played by two military bands; a song which, in Britain, would doubtless be denounced by the Left as the anthem of aristocratic capitalism, was received with acclamation and enthusiasm in the Great Hall of the People's Republic.

The first visit of a British Foreign Secretary since Palmerston had literally gone with a swing.

At home the winter of 1973 was largely consumed by speculation as to whether the militants among the Trades Union leaders would seek a confrontation with a Conservative Government, by forcing wage-claims to a point which it would be impossible to concede without wrecking the country's economy.

Few had any doubt that the rampant inflation was caused in the main by wage awards which bore little relation to productivity, or to the earning capacity of any particular business; but the question was whether the Government could arrive at agreement with the Trades Union Council on voluntary restraint, or would statutory powers have to be invoked.

No Prime Minister before Edward Heath had ever taken such trouble to bring Trades Union leaders into discussion, nor spent so many patient hours on formulae which would achieve moderation and result in constructive partnership between capital and labour.

It is often forgotten how nearly Heath's policy of restraint on wages and rents and profits succeeded.

1973 was successfully navigated, and it was only at Stage III that the economic package began to come undone. That it did so was largely due to the determination of Mr McGahey, the Communist leader of the Scottish Mineworkers' Union, and Mr Scargill of the Yorkshire coalfields. Both saw the chance to break a Conservative Government by strike action which, by withholding vital supplies of power for industry, would bring the economy of the nation near to a standstill.

The Government, faced with a run-down of coal stocks, with a probable shortage of oil supplies, and the chance that key electricity workers would come out in sympathy and paralyse the power stations, felt bound to introduce a three-day week to eke out supplies as far as they could be stretched.

Over Christmas and the New Year positions hardened and the question began to be posed – could the Conservative Government or any elected government allow itself to be blackmailed to a point where it was rendered impotent to govern? Would not that finish the authority of Parliament, and see the beginning of the end of the Westminster pattern of democracy?

I could not help feeling that we had moved a long way from 1926 when one sentence from Sir John Simon, declaring the General Strike to be illegal, was enough to throw the whole Trades Union movement into disarray, and to bring concerted industrial action against the State to an end, with the full approval of the British public.

So the straight question was increasingly formulated up and down Britain. Was the country to be run by the elected Parliament, or by some non-elected self-appointed section of people?

Before I went on a tour of East Africa in the second half of January, I talked with the Prime Minister. Neither of us liked the idea of an election in an atmosphere of emotion, intolerance and bad temper; but it had to be admitted that further talks with the Trades

Union leaders had little prospect of progress, and a running confrontation month after month, with increasing industrial trouble, was not inviting.

Both of us recognized the historical reasons for avoiding an election in which the coal miners were involved. There was, too, the important consideration as to what action any future government of any complexion would take, if the electors' verdict by misunderstanding or mischance went against the Government and in favour of the wild men.

Finally, every politician of experience knows how difficult it is to keep a 'straight question' before the electors for the duration of a campaign. To do so needs a high degree of skill, persistence and luck.

I left for Africa fairly sure that the decision would go in favour of an appeal to the Country, but I do not know which was the more unhappy – I or the colleagues whom I left behind. No election is easy to win – one into which one enters with only half a heart is not much fun.

The campaign started on 7 February, and for a week it was held on target with skill and determination, but our luck was out.

One development in particular threw the electors off balance. The Pay Board, under the chairmanship of Sir Frank Figgures had been asked before the election was called, to examine the miners' wage-claim in relation to the requirement of Stage III of the wages, prices and incomes policy. During the second week of the campaign an unofficial press briefing was given by the vice-chairman of the Board, Mr Derek Robinson.

The figures which emerged seemed, on a first interpretation, to suggest that the whole election might well be much ado about nothing. I had never in any election relied upon statistics, but such was the confusion, that I was thankful to be able to switch and talk authoritatively for a few days on Foreign Affairs and Defence.

From that moment the campaign, which had been going swimmingly on the 'straight question', began to slip out of our control, for the electors were muddled. I believe that this incident made the difference between a Conservative victory and defeat.

The country was spared the worst result which would have been a clear-cut majority, giving this or that non-elected section of society the green light to defy Parliament. That did not materialize because attention was diverted from the central issue, and because on a wave of emotion Scottish nationalists won a number of seats, and, with the Northern Irish members, confused the voting picture of Westminster.

The question 'Who is to govern Britain?' might have to be put again to the electors. But I hope that it will never be necessary, because the British public will have recognized that the only sure protection for the individual is that Parliament and the law are supreme.

XX

45 years of politics

Forty-five years is a long time in politics, and during my years in Parliament there have been changes in the social, economic and political structure of British society which are profound. As in all human affairs some are good and some are bad.

It is possible, for example, to measure with our own eyes the improvement in the well-being of children. They are better fed, better clothed and in better health. That is firm and welcome evidence that the conscience of the nation has been at work and the result is all gain.

Education too – and this is basic to the development of democracy – is available to a far greater number and in much wider variety, and that too is good.

Expansion in the fields of science and technology has clearly been right, as if Britain is to earn an adequate income the bulk of it must come from converting comparatively small quantities of imported raw materials into machines of the highest quality and value.

That the young should be technically equipped is essential if we are to hold our own in a world of ruthless competition. But if we are to make the best of ourselves we should beware of certain pitfalls.

With the decline in the teaching of the classics the standard of written and spoken English has undoubtedly fallen. That fall must be arrested, for English is sure to be the world language for science and technology.

But there is an even more important reason and it is that words matter. Any young person who goes out into the world without grammar or vocabulary is severely handicapped, for he cannot accurately and directly express his meaning.

As is often the case with a new broom, the good gets swept out with the bad. Doubtless there was much about the old school curriculum which was stuffy and we are better without it. But I trust that a corner will be found again for the classics, because they contained much wisdom and humanity, and he is an arrogant man who dismisses his ancestors as fools.

Another danger against which we must guard is the lowering of the standard required of teacher and pupil. Egalitarianism apparently demands a system of comprehensive schooling while the examination system is constantly under bombardment. Parents are apt to be trapped into supporting the abolition of examinations because without them none can ever say that their precious boy or girl is inferior in scholarship to another. But we should beware, because unless some system of effective selection on merit is retained, the pace of advance is bound to be that of the slowest in the school; and such a state of affairs would soon be reflected in the state of the nation.

In one material respect the contrast between now and the pre-war years is markedly unfavourable. The last budgets which showed no inflationary trend were those of the late fifties when Mr Selwyn Lloyd and Mr Heathcoat-Amory were Chancellors of the Exchequer. Ever since then, although some years have been better than others, we have signally failed to stabilize the value of money. The result has been that it has become more and more difficult for the individual or for a business to plan ahead with any confidence, and the national purpose and performance has faltered.

As investment has hesitated our competitors have stolen a march on us and we have slipped down the league of living standards. The result has been that governments of all parties have felt bound to intervene increasingly in the working of the free market economy. Their main purpose has been admirable; to establish an equation which would combine full employment with a steady level of prices. So far all efforts have failed and the plain fact is that the quality of life in Britain has fallen.

The economic theory which in my lifetime has been held in best repute was that of Maynard Keynes. The theory of it seemed to be impeccable, which was to modify a boom and to prime the pump in a slump.

The trouble has been that it is a matter of so nice a judgement when these delicate processes should be put in motion that few if any can mark the right moment to act.

But even if that science was exact, democracy in the present state of education has presented a crippling complication. Neither public nor politician have so far been willing to curtail a boom. 'We have never had it so good' has been a slogan which few have been willing to forego.

Can a democracy with one man one vote acquire the necessary political sense to allow its representatives to work these checks and balances and restraints? Or will it always cry for the moon? And will the electors reward with their votes those who promise to give it? The point is unresolved, but it is the 64,000-dollar question because it is becoming more and more clear that there are few halts between Keynes and Marx.

There can be little doubt which is the better way for the ordinary citizen. The economic performance of the Soviet Union, after more than fifty years of applied Marxism, is far behind that of those countries who have operated the capitalist system. Nor have the Russians been hampered in their experiment by anything like democracy. Agriculture for example has been practised according to the Marxist book without any interference and its failure has been abject. Those lessons we can learn.

There is another which, if it can be accepted by the non-Communist/Socialist world, would do a lot to restore that confidence and enterprise without which no society can be content with itself. It is the dictum of Abraham Lincoln, 'One does not make the poor richer by making the rich poorer.' Unless the truth of that is recognized, Britain will be condemned to dividing a diminishing cake. We cannot afford the politics of envy.

There have lately been some signs that understanding is beginning to dawn that there is an absolute relationship between work and reward, between individual productivity and the fate of the nation. If a democracy with one man one vote can accept and adopt these elementary economic truths, then Britain can resume a place of influence in the world. We have the opportunity, for we are partners in three associations which are of high importance. The European Community, the NATO alliance, and the Commonwealth. We should use them all to the full.

There have over these years been two changes which have had a measurable effect on what one may broadly call the character of the British people. The first is the decline in the practice of the Christian religion; the second the abandonment of the basic tolerances in and out of Parliament.

With the fall-off in Christian witness has come the weakening of belief in the sanctity of the marriage contract with the inevitable consequence of the loosening of the ties between children and home. The home and the loyalties which it cultivated had been seen as symbolic of the unity of community life. While it is too early to say that the concept is dead, it has without doubt been diluted as have many other traditional moral values. Not long ago I asked Harold Macmillan if he could put his finger on the point in time when the slide in values in Britain began to set in. His answer came without hesitation: 'The day when people stopped going to Church regularly on a Sunday morning'. It was an arresting reply, and I believe that it was not far from the mark. In my young days Church on a Sunday morning was a fixture. How many attended because they found renewed assurance of the salvation of the soul, how many from a sense of duty, or simply because habit was strong, I do not know. But for one reason or another the community was present. At its highest it was good for the spirit; at its lowest it was no bad thing for at least once a week to subordinate one's wishes to those of others.

My strong impression and recollection is that the great majority of the convinced and the doubters drew some strength from community worship – that the habit did something to help neighbour respect neighbour, and that the whole added fibre to the fabric of the life of the nation.

Of course it is easier for the countryman to recognize that man is not self-sufficient, for he is reminded of it by nature every day. In modern industrial society man can create so much for himself that he is apt to believe that he has all the answers.

Every now and again we are taken out of ourselves, as for example when the Queen was crowned, and was seen to pay homage to the King of Kings; or when the solemnity of the funeral service for Winston Churchill brought home to all that even the most powerful life is only lived by the grace of God.

With the decline of religious observance I believe that some virtue has departed from the British people. But I do not despair for if Christianity is the Truth then it will in due time once more command the allegiance of man.

If tolerance is the essence of democracy then Parliament should set an example. In recent years I believe that the House of Commons – the most representative and prestigious of all political institutions – has fallen short of the people's expectations. No body of men could have been more antipathetic to each other than the Whigs and Tories of the nineteenth century, and at the time of the Reform Bill Parliament was at times a shambles. But, although the protagonists and antagonists of reform would not enter into each other's houses, and bitter charges and counter-charges were made, the country did not lose faith in the institution of Parliament.

The reason was that, beneath all the sound and fury, there was a tacit understanding that no party would so outrage the principles

The Hirsel.

With all five grandchildren at the Hirsel, Christmas Day, 1971.

overleaf Tying a fly with David on the Tweed.

held by the other as to drive its opponents to pledge repeal of the legislation passed by the Parliament of the day.

In this century Mr Asquith came nearest to breaching the unspoken and unwritten rule, when he threatened to swamp the House of Lords with appointed Peers of his political persuasion; but he stopped short of the deed.

Mr Attlee's post-war administration proposed to nationalize the steel industry, and the Conservatives promised to repeal the Act if it was passed. But it was not until the latter part of Mr Wilson's first tenure of office between 1964 and 1970 that policies so outraged principle that they were frequently met with the riposte of repeal.

Tweedledum and Tweedledee knocked each other on the head alternately whether they spoke sense or nonsense. It was a sterile battle. If leaders of parties persist in this practice democracy will not survive. Sooner than later the electorate will get tired of such barren procedures. They will feel that party warfare is taking pride of place above the issues which affect them in real life, and their verdict will be 'a plague on all your houses'.

There are signs that we are uncomfortably near that situation already, and nationalism is to some extent an expression of the popular discontent. The call for a strong man will be the last and most dangerous manifestation of disillusion.

It is true that the 'function of Opposition is to oppose'. It is true that a democratic parliament lives by the cut and thrust of debate. But basic tolerance is an essential element in any democracy, and without it even the Westminster pattern of it will die. There is time for recovery, for Members of Parliament are still concerned that their profession should be one of public service.

The big difference between now and then is this. Then no one would have asked the question 'Is Britain governable?' Nor would anyone have doubted that the Westminster brand of democracy was the best. These are signs of which we should do well to take serious notice for there is evidence of less regard for politics and less respect for the law. This is change for the worse.

with Elizabeth at Carlton Gardens on my seventieth birthday

It may be that the system of Party government has served its purpose. I am reluctant so to conclude for until political intolerance and the cult of envy took charge it served us well. But now a party can be elected on a minority vote, and in spite of that gain a Parliamentary majority, and use it to force down the throats of the electorate policies which the majority do not approve. That is a caricature of democracy. It was never meant to be like that. Mr Solzhenitsyn has called it the 'strangled silence' of the majority.

I conclude, and this would be my preferred solution – that the party leaders should exercise that restraint in the use of the power of the majority to a point where it is not necessary for an Opposition to pledge itself to undo what the government of the day has done. It is not an easy assignment, but politics is a profession not for the bully with a bludgeon, but for the artist with a baton. Unless that rôle is accepted and within a measurable time, people will become tired of being a shuttlecock between extremes, and will insist on franchise arrangements which more accurately reflect the middle and moderate view. They will be right.

The remedy, so long as the democratic processes are allowed to continue, lies largely with the public. They must learn that democracy requires participation, and that for any individual to shirk that responsibility invites the destruction of the system on which he relies for his liberty.

Edmund Burke put the whole thing in a nutshell. 'All that is necessary for the triumph of evil is that good men do nothing'. There is a large majority of 'good men' in Britain. Let them be up and doing.

No review of these forty years can be complete or honest unless it records that man has become more violent. It is a world-wide phenomenon, but none the less of grave concern to Britain because forty years ago, although there were many flaws in our society, this was not one of them.

It would, for example, have been thought totally un-British forty years ago, that a young man should go to a dance-hall, or a football match carrying a knife; while it would never have occurred to any one of us that we were likely to be 'mugged' walking the streets of London at night.

Doubtless there are excuses. The hate let loose by war will take time to fade away. The threat from nuclear weapons contributes to uncertainty and encourages the thought that life is cheap; while the coverage of crime by the public media endows the criminal with a certain glamour.

There is no quick answer. The public will require, and rightly, that the punishment fits the crime; but deterrence is only part of the solution and violence will not cease until parents accept the responsibility for disciplining their children against it, and will support the school authorities in continuing that side of the child's education. It is an urgent task, for violence as it is practised today is the sign of a sick society.

Internationally how are the scales balanced as between war and peace? Is history repeating itself in that we are approaching a 1914 or a 1939 all over again?

Today a map of the world dotted with pins, marking areas of violence, looks like a patient with measles, and it is a sad commentary on man that he has not learned that force cannot pay. It is impossible, for example, to avoid the conclusion that the continent of Africa shows all the portents of a prolonged period of civil and tribal wars.

But there are signs that the existence of the nuclear missile is sobering those who have much to lose. Europe, which was the cockpit of battles, has deliberately buried its rivalries in a Community for economic and political unity.

Russia and the United States, with huge armouries ranged against each other, are careful to avoid a clash. Peace or war in the future largely turns on how far the Soviet Union is prepared to apply such pressure to the democracies that they find themselves squeezed to a point where their basic freedom will be lost. The choice then would be capitulate or fight.

That could happen if the Western democracies are so supine as to abandon one position after another to a Communist take-over. Mr Solzhenitsyn believes that demoralization has already gone too far. I find that judgement too pessimistic, for if the West shows guts and mobilizes massive opinion in support of its democratic ideals, then the opposition will be too strong for the Soviet Union to dare to make the challenge. A supreme effort will be needed, but it can be done.

I believe that my children and their children will be able to enjoy life, provided that they have learned the lessons of the recent past, and that the human mind can comprehend the problems of today.

As for that past there are many things which, if I could have a second chance, I would re-do; but there is much for which I am grateful. First that I was born a countryman. Many of my friends prefer the life of city and town, and I respect their choice because so much of civilization is to be found there, and so much of the colour of life is drawn from people and friends.

But although I understand that I can never envy it, for it is in nature that I find myself in perfect tune with creation, and can discover and rediscover peace of mind. Beauty in its purest form I find in the beasts and birds, the butterflies and the flowers. Nothing can take that away, and surely perception of it must be at least a part of the passport to the heart of the Creator?

Then I must testify my gratitude for the feeling of security provided by a loving and happy home. It is, I believe, impossible to overvalue the influence which parental understanding and discipline can have on the life of a child. Far into life confidence remains based on home. The home must not be possessive; it is enough that it should be there.

I am conscious of the supreme good fortune too that I found the perfect partner in life who was able to combine the hurly-burly of political life with that of bringing up four lively and happy children. I know that our path has been easy compared to that of many others, but I am convinced that there is a direct connection between the benevolent exercise of parental responsibility, and the content and happiness of a nation.

I have in politics had a fair share of the luck of the draw. I have enjoyed politics because essentially they are about people.

Finally, I am glad that I was brought up in the Christian faith and provided with the hope of a God who is a Redeemer. I do not think that I have been unduly influenced by the prospect, so to speak, of saving my own skin.

A man walking along the street was once intercepted by a zealous lady who asked, 'Sir, are you saved?' He answered, 'Yes', and tried to move on. But she persisted. 'Why then are you not dancing in the streets and crying aloud praises to God?' 'Because, Madam,' he said, 'I consider it is to be so narrow a squeak that I had better keep quiet about it.' Like him, on the question of personal salvation, I must be content to be quiet and to take pot-luck.

I have been more concerned that man should recognize the validity of the Christian code of conduct on earth. For, although I was ready to concede to my Bishop that the first duty of a Christian is to know his God; yet I believe that the practice of the code as between neighbour and neighbour provides the beginning of proof that the ultimate purpose of creation is good.

My belief may not be rational. It may be intuitive. It cannot be proved. But it is for me, for today, for tomorrow, and I trust for always, 'The way the wind blows'.

APPENDIX A

Suez

The noble Earl, Lord Attlee, once referred to me in another place, in a moment of irritation, as an 'amiable Lord'. In this series of debates I am bound to say that he has stretched my amiability. I should like to remind him, when he criticizes our action and all but, if not quite, dubs us as aggressors, that twice in a generation this country has expended all its wealth and many of its lives, because we have known for certain that not to deal with a dictator who wishes to dominate mankind is a fatal policy. The criticism to which we have been subjected in the past – I am not quite old enough to remember 1914, but certainly in the case of the rise of Mussolini and in the case of Hitler's policy in the Rhineland – was that this country did not use its power in time when it might have prevented a world war.

If I can do any service to your Lordships' House in this final speech – after all the arguments have been put backwards and forwards across the House – it may be to focus attention on the main themes which have been common to the majority of speeches. While noble Lords have discussed the rights and wrongs, the wisdom and stupidity of the Government's action in Suez, none has been able to isolate this action from the wider backcloth of world affairs, and in particular from three features: the post-war rôle of international Communism, backed by Russia's power; the collapse of the security system, as it was originally designed to enforce International Law; and the part which must be played by the United States of America if security and safety for the countries of the world is to be found.

My Lords, since 1945 Russia has adopted the conception of permanent hostility to the West, and her foreign policy has openly been advertised as a policy of world revolution. Your Lordships are familiar with the instruments of that policy; subversion within and military pressure without. I need not remind all those in this House this evening of the ruthless and unrelenting probing that there has been against what they conceive to be the weak spots in the structure of the Western world: Iran, Greece, Turkey, Berlin, Malaya – and I could continue the catalogue. The purpose has always been to extend Russian dominion, which is greater today than it was in 1939. There have been three prongs to this sustained attack; the physical occupation of Eastern Europe and the division of Germany; the use of Communism in South-East Asia to deprive Europe and the West of the mineral wealth of that area; and to deny Europe the oil of the Middle East. My Lords, what a prize if Russia could bring that off, the destruction of an industrialized Europe, the outflanking of Turkey and Iran and Iraq and Pakistan, and the opening up of the gateway to Africa!

Then to these traditional methods of political warfare and penetration they have, with diabolical cunning, added another, and that is anti-colonialism. I do hope that not many of our friends will 'fall for' this Russian game. Ever since representative institutions were given by the Crown to a colonial territory, the pattern of the British Commonwealth has been clear; a pattern of independent, free countries – in what contrast to the Russian Empire, as indeed must be plain to India and Ceylon and to the world at large! The Russian objectives are perfectly clear; to weaken the West, to use the confusion in colonial territories or Arab countries to dominate later. They preach coexistence and they practise anarchy.

When noble Lords opposite are inclined to twit us – and I take it in good part – that we have exposed a Russian plot, perhaps 'plot' is a misleading word. This has been the consistent and continuing policy of Russia, and the Baghdad Pact was designed to meet it. What was revealed in the recent operations was how near to maturity the joint Russian–Egyptian plan was. I have emphasized this aspect of policy because I do not believe it is possible to understand the action or, indeed, to explain it, and the recent events in the Middle East, unless one looks at them against this large feature of the background of Russian foreign policy in promoting international Communism.

The second fact from which none of your Lordships has been able to escape in considering this Suez situation has been this: that since 1945 collective security has been stultified. The United Nations, as at present constituted (I am going to respond later to the appeal of the noble Lord, Lord Pakenham) cannot guarantee the physical security of any one of its members. And, worse than that, not only can the Russian leaders block the processes of conciliation or the action of security which is necessary to protect one of the members of the United Nations, but any stooge on Russia's payroll can snap his fingers at treaties and conventions and International Law. The noble Lord, Lord Coleraine, has made some very significant speeches in this series of debates, and in the last debate he made the most penetrating analysis. He said that we have a complete system of International Law; it is logical, it is consistent; it is ascertainable. In fact it is quite watertight. There is only one thing wrong with it: the wicked will not obey it and the righteous will not enforce it. That is not International Law. All it means is giving an open licence to the criminal.

This is the background: the fact of Russia's ambitions; of the United Nations' inability to exercise its authority, and the unwillingness of the United States to do so. Here, let me agree with what the noble Lord, Lord Henderson, said (I am paraphrasing; I hope I am not misquoting), that the United States, in its membership of NATO and its membership of SEATO has recognized that it has a responsibility to underwrite the security of Western Europe and the security of South-East Asia. I am not criticizing, I am simply saying that the United States, possibly for its own very good reasons, has never thought that it need go so far in this area of the Middle East. A great many of our troubles, I am afraid, have flowed from that attitude. In these circumstances, the whole burden of ensuring the stability in that area has fallen upon the shoulders of the United Kingdom, and has been accepted by the United Kingdom over the years: in Jordan, the subsidy: in Iraq, help. In the Middle East, and in part in North Africa, the burden of maintaining stability has fallen upon us. In these circumstances, there was always the strong possibility that, if the balance were upset, the United Kingdom would have to shoulder the responsibility of enforcing order and of having to act perhaps to prevent a general war.

I should like, because I think it ought to be mentioned, to recall to your Lordships how over the years we have done our best to help Egypt. There was a series of political and economic agreements, and we withdrew from Egypt so that Egypt should enjoy unqualified sovereignty over her soil. What has been the reward? Colonel Nasser has used his sovereignty as a passport to illegality. He has seized the Canal. He boasted that Israel would be the next victim on his list, and there is no getting away from the fact that he gave notice to Israel, and perhaps wider afield, of war. Even so, with that background – and I do not think that many noble Lords will disagree with the analysis that I have given – we did not intervene between Israel and Egypt in order to remove Colonel Nasser; we did not intervene in order to impose a settlement for the control of the Canal. We intervened to stop them. We intervened to prevent the war growing. We intervened in order that the foundations should be laid on which there might be a permanent settlement of the Middle East.

I was interested in the speech of the noble Earl, Lord Attlee, because my mind went back to an occasion in another place, when we were debating the Middle East in the context of the Arab–Israel war, to a speech which Mr Bevin made on that occasion. I have refreshed my memory. He said, 'If there is any danger, or when we see danger, we must react quickly. I must ask for the support of the whole House and the nation to this principle that if this area is endangered we shall always react quickly.' An Honourable Member asked, 'Which area?' Mr Bevin replied, 'The Canal Area and the Middle East Zone.'

The noble Earl, Lord Attlee, was then Prime Minister, and presumably he agreed with his Foreign Secretary. Whether he agrees with his 'Shadow' Foreign Secretary today I cannot guess or know.

If the Government believed that a general war in the Middle East would cause economic and political chaos throughout the while of the Middle East, what was their duty? The noble Lord, Lord Silkin, said that this was a moral question; so did the noble and learned Earl, Lord Jowitt. I do not dissent. There must be a moral quality and quantity in British foreign policy. But if the life is to be squeezed out of the United Kingdom and the countries of Western Europe, if the authority which is set up to maintain International Law, to bring security and to see that justice is done between peoples, is to function, then I think – and it is only a personal opinion – I cannot argue it on a legal basis with the noble and learned Earl, Lord Jowitt – there is not only a moral right to prevent that but a moral duty to do so, because the first duty of a government is to bring security to the life of its people.

The noble Lord, Lord Pakenham, said that we suffered from illusions of grandeur. We were more concerned with our continuing life, with the threat of war over the whole of this area. The noble and learned Earl, Lord Jowitt, asked me certain questions and, in particular, one about consultation with the United States. My noble friend, Lord Reading, to some extent dealt with that matter, and the Tripartite Declaration and action under that, but Lord Jowitt also asked about M. Mollet's statement in Paris (I think it was) that the reason why there was no consultation was, in fact, that we knew that America would disagree. The reason was – and the Foreign Secretary has given it – that, at the time of the Israeli attack, speed was of the essence if this action was to succeed. I shall give to your Lordships in one moment the reason why I think that can be justified, and justified up to the hilt.

The noble Lord asked me again about something that the Minister of Defence had said in another place. I have looked up that quotation. It was a quotation at the end of a number of questions. It was in the third supplementary dealing with the Israeli mobilization, to the effect that there was an inconsistency, I think, in the reply. If the noble Lord will consult Columns 1258 to 1260 of Hansard of 5 December in another place, he will see the Foreign Secretary's answer, which states the position quite clearly; that on 26 October we knew of the Israeli mobilization but from then until the time that Israel attacked they might have attacked anywhere.

What results have we got from this action or for what results can we hope? A war has been stopped. Is that a 'disastrous consequence', as the Amendment suggests? A war has been prevented from spreading. Some doubts have been expressed from the Benches opposite as to whether this war would have spread any further. My noble friend Lord Rennell, last night – I am going to quote again from what he said, because many of your Lordships were not here and did not hear him – mentioned what the Egyptian Commander-in-Chief had said in a broadcast on 30 November. The Commander-in-Chief began by saying that the Kingdom of Saudi Arabia, the Kingdom of Jordan, the Yemeni Kingdom, the Syrian Republic and Egypt had a military agreement. Then he said: 'On the evening of 29th October . . . I issued instructions to put into effect the plans prepared to meet this treacherous aggression . . . Syrian armed units began to move . . . The Saudi forces were assigned to move to the Jordanian/Israel front to undertake a joint operation with the Arab-Jordanian Army . . .' Then he said: 'After the Anglo–French ultimatum . . . orders were issued to the commands of the joint forces to avoid taking part in substantial military operations.'

My Lords, that seems to be not only evidence but proof that a wider war has been stopped.

There may have been mistakes. No Minister of a Government in this situation, when events have not been of our own timing, can claim, or would claim, that every action has been perfect. But a war has been stopped: a war has been prevented from spreading. For whatever cause, a United Nations force is actually there on the ground, for the first time in an international dispute of this sort; and the United States for the first time has said that it will not tolerate interference with the integrity of the countries which make up the Baghdad Pact. I cannot equate any of these results with 'disaster'.

Then, indeed, what would the Opposition have done? The noble Lord, Lord Henderson, has been fair. He told us that they would have consulted more effectively than we did under the Tripartite Declaration, and that they would have sought action. Noble Lords opposite have said that they would have acted and sought agreement to act under the United Nations: and as I understood them, they would not have acted without that assent. My Lords, the United Nations is exactly as effective as its members choose to make it, and up to now the members have chosen to make it just as effective as this – a body which passes resolutions. Two hundred and two meetings in the Security Council on Middle Eastern affairs! What comfort to an Israel whose life was about to be squeezed out of it would meeting number 203 have been? What comfort to Turkey or Iran or Pakistan, about to be taken in the rear, meeting number 204? And what comfort to Hungary the strictures passed on Russia by the United Nations Assembly which Russia brushes aside as inconvenient to receive!

At long last, two nations, members and loyal members of the United Nations, have dared to assert that no moral law can be enforced unless it is supported and sustained by physical power. We wish to see this physical power exercised by the United Nations. I say this in response to the speech of Lord Layton, in particular, and to those on the Liberal Benches who have pleaded for this. We will work with the United Nations to make it no longer a sham behind which we all hide, but a reality in international affairs. My noble friend, the Leader of the House, made that most clear yesterday when he said, 'It is idle to shut our eyes to these harsh realities, but, at the same time, to say that is, of course, no reason for writing off the United Nations as a dead loss. That, I believe – and here I agree with the Opposition – would be a counsel of despair. On the contrary, it seems to me a compelling reason for looking forward and not back, for getting together with other like-minded nations and seeing what can be done to give to the Organization that life and strength without which it would not be a protection but a danger to the world.' I should like to say to the noble Lord, Lord Pakenham, that it is the unqualified intention of Her Majesty's Government to make the United Nations a reality.

With regard to the noble Viscount, Lord Esher, I cannot but comment on the delightful speech which he gave us today. He compared the Government to a lot of foolish virgins. Foolish we may be, my Lords! But which would he rather be – a foolish virgin, or a lady of impeccable virtue sitting on the fence while generation after generation pass by until she is desiccated and dead, and no good to anyone? My Lords, he said that he was an artist – he did not quite say this, but he meant it – an artist among virgins and vulgarians. But, if I may say so, after his speech, although he may vote the other way, I thought his 'art' was in the right place.

I have never disguised from this House – and perhaps Lord Tedder has already kindly given me some credit for this – that our action was a shock. It was a shock to the Commonwealth, to the United States, and to ourselves, that, as I have said before, a country, which built up the League of Nations and has done more than any other nation (I think we can say that without arrogance) to sustain the United Nations, should be compelled to take action of this kind. I am not going to apportion blame between ourselves or the United States. When there is a cleavage of opinion, I wish that the Opposition would not always assume that it is this country which is wrong. I am going to say that it is the intention of Her Majesty's

Government to co-operate fully and absolutely with the United States in NATO and SEATO and in any security pacts in any field, and in the United Nations Organization, because it is our profound belief that upon that co-operation the existence of the free world depends. So too with the Commonwealth, because the Commonwealth and the United States of America, peoples devoted to the ideals of democracy, must underpin any effective world organization.

On consultation, our purpose is always to find out each other's thinking. Our thinking cannot always be the same. My noble friend Lord Hore-Belisha pointed out, for instance, that India and ourselves have always disagreed about security pacts and about the Baghdad Pact in particular. But we will attempt always to keep each other informed, in the hope that the maximum understanding of each other's policies will lead to a basic appreciation of motives and aims. If on occasions there is not that basic appreciation, then a country must take its own decision; but we can hope that understanding will be intimate and complete. Some of the Opposition speakers have ended their speeches on a note of almost unrelieved gloom. But this may be one of those turning-points where the free world will begin to live and to breathe again. For China has not become a Russian satellite; Eastern Europe, with incredible bravery, is breaking the grip of Russia upon it, and in the Middle East Russian policy has had a setback which may have lasting consequences. I greatly welcome this opportunity to exorcise international Communism which has been the curse of mankind.

The noble Viscount, Lord Alexander of Hillsborough, said – and the noble Earl, Lord Attlee, agreed with him – that there were two remedies: one was to change the Leader of the Conservative Party. Well, I would hesitate to make any such suggestion to another Party. It would be very difficult if I had to make any suggestion about his Leader. I should have to ask him, first of all, which one? The second suggestion was that if Her Majesty's Government felt so confident in their policy we might go to the country. My Lords, I do admire his bravado; but beware we do not take him at his word!

Speech at Harrogate
October 1970

Since the General Election we, as Conservatives, have set out to apply in international affairs, a coherent view of Britain's interests. There are certain areas of the world where Britain is directly involved; there we have to set out to define our commitments, and to give a balance to our priorities so that our resources may be deployed to maximum effect. In other areas, Britain's interests are less direct. But as a trading nation, with many of our resources of supply vulnerable, we have one overriding interest, and that is stability and peace. From that point of view there is one problem which is the most dangerous and difficult of all those with which your Government is faced in Foreign Affairs. It is not new; indeed, there is a sense in which it is one of the oldest problems in the world.

The Middle East is the cradle of Western civilization; but it is also the oldest battlefield in the world. The nineteenth century saw the European powers drawn into the rivalries of the region – at first the French, and then ourselves, the Russians and others following.

These interventions began a process of tremendous change. New Arab States were created, exposing traditional societies to the new tensions that come with political independence and economic growth and international contact. Then the emergence of Israel as a State with ideals to capture the imagination, but with a troubled history which has resulted in dangerous tension with her neighbours;

tensions which have given rise to war on three occasions in the last twenty-five years. Finally there has been the spread of a political revolution through the Arab States, with violent change and drastic shifts of alignment.

Throughout this turbulent period the Great Powers have retained their deep involvement in the region. Partly this is a matter of historic commitment. Partly it is a matter of vital oil reserves on which the Middle-Eastern economy is based. And partly it is, as it has always been, a question of strategy, in the context of international politics and security; because in spite of the changes our century has seen in transport and communications, and the art of war, this region still lies across Europe's way to the east and Russia's way to the south. That is part of the background to twenty-two years of emotion, religion and ideology, with each side sure of the justice of its own cause.

The Arabs believe that Arab lands have been usurped by Israel. They point to the sufferings of the Palestinian refugees now swollen to nearly a million and a half, as evidence that their land was unjustly taken. The idea of Arab unity, which in its modern form has grown up in our lifetime, has become linked with this cause; and the status of Jerusalem is once again a rallying call for Muslims, just as it was for other religions in earlier centuries when they too felt dispossessed. That is why Arabs for long refused to recognize Israel; that is why some have on occasion pledged themselves to Israel's destruction. And since the war of 1967, it has seemed legitimate and necessary to many Arabs to drive Israel by violence out of Arab territories, occupied at that time, which Israel seems determined to keep. That is why the guerilla activities of Palestinian nationalists find ready support in Arab countries, however much their activities may be condemned in the international community, as adding fuel to fire – an international community which recognizes in stateless freedom-fighters a new threat to peace and security.

On the other side, for the Israelis, as an elected member of the United Nations, the main and rightful concern is their own survival and security. They feel that the very existence of their State is threatened; to them this justifies the use of force in self-defence, something for which the Charter of the United Nations provides. Since the 1967 war, they have believed that the Arabs will make peace only if they see that every attack is met by deterrent force. This determination is strengthened by a mixture which is just as potent as the Arabs' own, of history and nationalism and religion.

So both sides believe they are right. Both sides believe that force is legitimate and necessary for them to achieve their goals. And so the dispute drags on from crisis to crisis, with all the waste and bloodshed that it involves. Above all, waste of opportunities for economic development in the region, which would relieve poverty, but instead is being squandered on unparalleled defence expenditure.

And waste is not the only evil. For it is this dispute which has enabled Soviet influence to penetrate the Arab world – a penetration which will continue as long as these tensions are not resolved, and which brings the area of the Middle East, and perhaps more than that area, to the brink of a major conflict; for it carries with it the appalling risk that any future war between Arabs and Israelis will involve the Super Powers.

How can these tensions be resolved? An equilibrium is needed in the Middle East which both sides would be prepared to accept. The actual issues in dispute are of a kind which can be solved. The fabric of a settlement consistent with the Security Council Resolution of November 1967 which would be fair and should be workable can easily be produced. Agreed solutions on all the separate elements would have to be incorporated into a formal and binding agreement which would be endorsed by the United Nations Security Council. But like the Resolution of November 1967 any such settlement must be based on two fundamental principles: the inadmissibility of the acquisition of territory by war, and the need for a just and lasting peace, in which every State in the area is guaranteed the right to live in security. This means, as the Security Council Resolution said, that Israeli Armed Forces must withdraw from territories occupied in the conflict; and that, on the other hand, the state of belligerency which has existed in the Middle East must be ended, and the right of every State to live in peace within secure and recognized boundaries, free from threats or acts of force, must be recognized.

At its simplest, the Arab/Israel dispute has been about two things, land and people. I believe that a settlement would establish a definitive agreement on territorial questions. Such an agreement would be the answer to Israel's fear for her existence and, at the same time, to Arab fear of Israeli expansionism. That is why the balance between the provisions for Israeli withdrawal and secure and recognized boundaries is so important.

No outsider can prescribe exactly where these boundaries should be. If they are to be recognized, they must first and foremost be agreed by the countries concerned. Between Israel and Egypt an international boundary has existed for a long time. I believe that this boundary should once again be recognized in a settlement, subject to whatever arrangements might be made to deal with the special problems of Gaza – problems that derive from the immense concentration of refugees in the Gaza area – whose future would have to be resolved by a settlement. Between Israel and Jordan, the problem is more difficult; there has never been a recognized boundary between the two countries. But I believe that the Resolution implies that secure and recognized boundaries should be based on the Armistice lines which existed before the war of 1967, subject to minor changes which might be agreed between the two countries. Between Israel and Lebanon there is no problem; the present boundary, though troubled by fighting like so many other areas in this troubled region, has never been questioned and should remain. Between Israel and Syria there is of course the very sensitive problem of the Golan Heights. Syria has not accepted the Security Council Resolution; it is therefore impossible yet to discuss how the dispute between Israel and Syria should be resolved. But I would expect that, once Syria accepted the Resolution, the general principles governing the location of the other boundaries would also govern the boundary between Israel and Syria.

There is one special problem, which in some ways symbolizes the Arab/Israel problem as a whole; I mean the problem of Jerusalem. The complexity of this problem, and the depth of feeling about the city are so great as to make any compromise between the positions of the two sides hard to conceive. Some agreement providing for freedom of access to the Holy Places, and for their protection, seems to be the only answer, and will be an essential part of a settlement. But this may have to be almost the last problem to be tackled.

The second main pillar of a settlement would be the binding commitments which the Arab countries and Israel would make to live at peace with one another. These should include the establishment of a formal state of peace. They should cover an obligation on all States to refrain from any act or threat of hostility, and to do all in their power to prevent the planning or conduct of any such acts on their territory.

There are, of course, other problems. One, which I should like to emphasize, is that of the Arabs who were refugees from Palestine during and after the fighting of 1948. When I spoke earlier of the Arab/Israel dispute being a problem of people, it was above all of the refugees that I was thinking. For many years the international community as a whole has agreed on how this problem should be settled. It is agreed that those refugees who wish to return to their homes and are prepared to live in peace with their neighbours, should be allowed to do so; and that those who choose not to should be enabled to settle elsewhere with compensation. The need for a just settlement of the refugee problem is pressing, although it is unrealistic to suppose that a settlement will be reached before the other issues of which I have spoken are resolved; it must be a part of the whole. And we must now ignore the political aspirations of the Palestinian Arabs, and their desire to be given a means of self-expression. We cannot support any political programme which would involve the disappearance of the State of Israel; and this is what the Palestinian resistance organizations at present demand. But we must work for a settlement which will attract the agreement of all the people of the area, including the Palestinians, and which takes account of their legitimate aspirations – resettlement in dignity and honour.

There is also the problem of freedom of navigation in the Straits of Tiran, the Gulf of Aqaba and the Suez Canal. Firm guarantees will be required for all three.

All these are matters which are capable of solution. They are matters on which practical action can be taken, action which would remove the distrust which has so far stultified progress. Now that for a time the shooting has stopped, now that the fighting has ceased in Jordan, now that the four major Powers and all the parties agree that peace should be made, now is the opportunity; and it should be seized.

There are many problems ahead. There is the problem of how a settlement would be achieved. There is a more important problem of the charges and the counter-charges of violations of the military standstill in the Suez Canal. These are all questions which must be resolved. I believe that a simultaneous effort by all concerned, a simultaneous decision to grasp the opportunity of making peace which I think exists, would allow progress to be made. Britain launched the Resolution on which Dr Jarring's peace mission rests. If this opportunity to relaunch it is lost, we may face another twenty years of tension and strife – twenty years or more in which the peace which the region so desperately needs will be lacking – and with the risks of confrontation between the major Powers increasing. This is a price which I believe none of us, neither Arab nor Jew, neither Russian nor American, certainly not we in Britain, should be prepared to pay.

APPENDIX C

Rhodesia

Hon. Members will by now have had time to study in more detail the proposals for a settlement of the Rhodesian dispute with Britain. The main point for decision today is whether or not they should be placed before the Rhodesian people for their verdict.

Before I come to analyse the substance of the terms I should like, as a background, to give the House some general observations and conclusions which I drew from the many contacts that I made during my visit to Salisbury. Many of the Africans whom I saw – groups of Africans and individual Africans – were certainly concerned about their political future, but the problem which presses on them more and more as time goes by is the search for work and the dignity that work brings with it.

I went one day – completely unannounced – to an African township to talk to those people who wished to talk to me about a settlement and very quickly a large group of people assembled. There was a lot of interest in a possible settlement. Without exception the questions were on the same theme, particularly from the young Africans – would a settlement help to bring them work? I met a delegation of African businessmen from Salisbury and from African Trade Unionists. Their concern was with work for the Africans – would a settlement bring investment, stem and then reverse the great unemployment growing so fast in the African Tribal Trust areas?

Their concern is not surprising. The birth-rate in the African population is increasing very rapidly. Boys are coming into the labour market at the rate of forty thousand a year and at present there simply is not enough capital for the expansion of agriculture or the introduction of labour-intensive industries on the scale that is needed to absorb the growing and alarming pool of surplus labour.

In that context it is possible to argue that sanctions have bitten, but only a few Africans have suffered. It is, unhappily, the Africans who are the witnesses to any success that sanctions have had. Some rather airily detached critics of a settlement have said that Mr Smith might be forced, in two or three years' time, to concede better terms than those available now to the British Government. I can only say that I could not be, that I would not consent to be, the one who went back to that township and advocated such a delay to the thousands of Africans who are today pleading for work and who, because there is so much competition in the labour market, are forced to accept a wage which is miserably low. All the Africans, and the many Europeans whom I saw who are sympathetic to the plight of the Africans, testified that the priorities for the well-being of African-Rhodesians were: first, capital to spend on the infrastructure in the Tribal Trust areas, to facilitate modern farming and other developments such as minerals and country industries. Second, investment in labour-intensive industries in the cities, vital for the future of the Africans. Third, funds for African education directed in particular to the provisions of technical training colleges in agriculture and in engineering.

I do not think that enough attention has been paid to the development section of the White Paper which contains the British offer of substantial aid which is to be matched by money from Rhodesia additional to that already voted for the development programmes. That programme will be directed to three sectors in particular of Rhodesia's economic life – to the development of African Tribal Trust areas, to education in technical colleges and to the general development of industry in the cities of Rhodesia.

All the evidence is that many countries are only waiting for a settlement to invest heavily in Rhodesian enterprise. Such expansion would transform the prospects for the Rhodesian African and, incidentally, as his education and income increases have a significant effect on his political status and the pace of political advance under the First Principle. I cannot stress too strongly that the African's priority is for work, and work now.

There is a second broad impression which I gained. I spoke briefly last week of the deep concern of almost all those to whom I talked – African and European – with the trend which they saw towards the South African pattern of life. Thus until now among the moderates – both African and European – there has been a certain fatalism as they have watched this creeping . dvance towards apartheid. So the alternative to these proposals is, in my mind, a certain and rapid move to apartheid and that surely cannot be a thing which any Honourable Member in this House wants to see.

There is not yet the fear in Rhodesia which one finds further south, in South Africa, but there is a widespread apprehension about the spread of discrimination by Ministerial decree against which neither African nor European has any effective appeal at present.

There was no doubt whatever, therefore, as to the second priority for the African. It was a justiciable Declaration of Rights, through which there would be restored to the individual the protection of the Courts – an appeal beyond and above Ministers who today have the last word. The request for a Declaration of Rights, to be made justiciable, was universal from all those whom I saw on my visit to Rhodesia.

The Act which has caused most alarm and distress is undoubtedly the Land Tenure Act. Here one broad qualification of the condemnation of the Act has to be made. Whatever such an Act is called – whether Land Apportionment as it was when we still had reserve powers in Rhodesia, or Land Tenure as it is now – there must be a law which requires that large areas of land are reserved for African farming and ownership.

If there were today a free market in land in Rhodesia, all the good land would be bought up by those with the money who are the Europeans and possibly some Asians. I can tell Honourable Members opposite who may not have been to Rhodesia lately, that young South Africans, young Afrikaaners are coming into Rhodesia and buying up any land which they can find. Unless there is a law which protects the African and reserves his farming land, the African has no defences whatever against those who come in and buy it up.

A bad feature of the Land Tenure Act – this is where much of the trouble lies – is that it enables the Minister to prevent, for example, professional and qualified Africans – as qualified as any European – from conducting their business in white areas, and to prevent the European from conducting his business in an African area or, for example, to do such things as to restrict admission to multi-racial schools.

If we are honest with ourselves, we must admit that in the past there were restrictions under the Land Apportionment Act which we operated, for example, on Africans working in white areas. But in 1961 the whole trend was towards multi-racialism and a non-racial state, and the difference now is that the trend in the last five or six years has been reversed and is towards discrimination. That is the position now. The discrimination which is made is always petty, very irksome and very unfair and unjust.

That brings me to the Commission which is to examine and report upon all discriminatory legislation. It will have to pay attention to all discriminatory legislation, but pay particular attention to those matters of discrimination which I have mentioned, which cause most of the trouble in the Rhodesia of today.

There has been criticism that the Rhodesian Government are not pledged to accept all the recommendations of the Commission. Whatever they may be I cannot think that Honourable Members who considered it for a moment can really believe that any Government anywhere could be asked to accept all the recommendations of a Commission blind. But the wording of the proposals clearly carries an obligation to act and to change the law in respect of those recommendations which are made in the context of improving and fostering racial harmony.

Hon. Members opposite who criticize these arrangements should compare the Rhodesian obligations under these proposals with the absence of any commitment whatever in the case of the similar Commission proposed in the *Fearless* terms. Furthermore, under our proposals there is to be an African on the Commission, and our agreement to the composition of the Commission is required. This was not so under the *Fearless* terms which required only consultation.

As to the political attitudes in Rhodesia, it is much more difficult to judge. One eminent Churchman said to me that a few years ago, when he arrived in the country, he was sure that he knew all the answers to Rhodesia's problems. Now he was filled with uncertainty. The outlook of the extremists on both sides is clear. The extreme African Nationalist approach – apart from adherence to NIBMAR – was vividly expressed to me, as I have no doubt it will be to the Commission which is to carry out the test of acceptability. It was, and for some it still is, that Britain ought to have used force, that we ought still to be prepared to use force to quell the rebellion, and that they, the African Nationalists, are only prepared to do what Britain ought to have done and ought to be doing now. They still want to use violence and some of them are still prepared to advocate it.

I told them that I could understand this point of view, but could not accept it or recommend it, and that is why in terms of release from detention it is impossible for any British Government to lay down which individual should or should not be released.

Twenty-three detainees have lately been released, and thirty-one are to follow shortly. There will remain in detention sixty-two, and a tribunal on which we shall have an observer is to make a special review of these cases. I can tell the Hon. Gentleman how the situation now as regards detention compares with the situation when the Right Hon. Gentleman the Leader of the Opposition was conducting the *Fearless* talks. There were then one hundred and thirty-three in detention. There are now sixty-two. There were then three hundred and eighteen restrictees. There are now two. This is an advance, although a great deal more has to be done. I shall return to that matter later.

At the other extreme, there are some Europeans who told me plainly that they wished to retain the right to use additional discrimination and to perpetuate minority rule. They were a small number, but they told me this quite plainly. To them I had to make it crystal clear that it was Britain's purpose not to freeze but to thaw racial relations. That there could be no agreement of any kind with a British Government on their terms. I made that absolutely clear.

For the great majority of Rhodesians, black and white, the future is seen as one of evolutionary change in which the African gradually and on merit assumes his rightful place in society and on the franchise. For that reason, with the exception of the extremists on either side – the African Nationalist on one side, the extreme European on the other – there was unanimity that Rhodesia must work its way back to a common role as the only true political expression of a nation which seeks to live at peace within itself.

If a settlement which is fair can be reached, the siege mentality can be lifted. It is far too easy now in Rhodesia for an ordinary critic to be accused of rocking the boat. Even further to be accused of being treasonable to his country. Many men of goodwill who do not now like to speak, will begin to do so because there can be a fair settlement. Indeed, in recent days, a good many have been gaining courage to speak up and say what they believe the future of Rhodesia ought to be. Not before but after the Rhodesian Parliament has embodied these proposals in its law. Not before but after Mr Smith has put all his authority behind constitutional changes – not till then does Parliament have to legislate here for independence. These exchanges which Mr Smith has to put through his own Parliament with his own authority are very extensive indeed as far as the Constitution is concerned. When this is done, and only when this is done, will the way be clear for the lifting of sanctions.

I will now turn to test the proposals in the White Paper against each of the Five Principles. Principle One is the essence of the whole matter. Power in any country stems from Parliament, and it was clear to me therefore that it was in the Constitution that the major changes had to be sought and made. It had to set the Rhodesian Parliament and Constitution on a new direction and on a new course. First, it was necessary to decide the essential changes that had to be made. The Income Tax arrangement which governed the rate of increase in African representation had to go. It was a hopeless unjustifiable arrangement. A new blocking mechanism against retrogression had to be installed and entrenched because the present one is totally inadequate. The express provision forbidding progress beyond parity – the creed of the Rhodesian Front Party – had to be replaced by firm provision for majority rule.

All these essentials necessary to turn the signpost in the opposite direction to that at present pursued by the Rhodesian Front have been achieved, as well as the provision that at parity before the election to the common role seats a referendum will be held among enrolled Africans as to whether or not they wish to be represented only by directly elected members.

I think it is essential to recognize that these are major changes in the political opportunities for Africans. There will be all the difference in a few months' time, as these arrangements go through the Rhodesian Parliament, between the position as it is now and the position when this legislation is passed through the Rhodesian Parliament. They will have entirely new opportunities.

The statisticians are doing their sums as to when majority rule may be reached. Those calculations cannot be more impressive than guesswork. Our own statisticians on matters of population are not too clever here. There are too many variables. There is the question of how many Africans will register. There is the question of how many under the new education drive will receive secondary and technical education. Above all, it depends on the pace of the agricultural and industrial qualification. Under all those headings the prospect for the African advance is good.

The Right Hon. Gentleman the Leader of the Opposition said that one cannot measure this by the calendar or the clock but by achievement and this is right. Achievement, I hope, will tell.

Next we have Principle Two. The essential safeguard of the sanctity of Principle One which must be taken with it. I come to the second of the Principles. In the proposals there is from the start a blocking mechanism of the elected Africans alone. I repeat that. There is a blocking mechanism of the elected Africans alone. In the event of a discriminatory or undesirable legislation being brought to Parliament they will undoubtedly receive reinforcement from the indirectly elected Africans. I will say why. Hon. Members have sometimes equated indirectly elected Africans with the Chiefs. In all cases since 1969 when there has been a division in the Rhodesian House of Commons, the indirectly elected Africans have voted with the directly elected Africans against the Rhodesian Government. In fact – I do not know whether this is known to Hon. Members – the tribal Election Colleges contain a majority of elected councillors. So the elective process governs the situation as far as the indirectly elected Africans are concerned.

I have seen it suggested that this mechanism would depend on the Chiefs. In fact this is not the case. The Chiefs have no status in this matter. After parity is reached, the ten common role seats will be created. Any change, any departure from that course, to be carried, would have to have the assent of at least seventeen out of the fifty Africans who by then would in all probability be all directly elected members, and such a number would be a very ample blocking vote. Some of the newspapers have suggested that the creation of these ten common role seats is dependent on the recommendation of the constitutional review Commission and on a two-thirds majority. The reverse happens to be the case. The ten seats are created unless two-thirds of the Assembly, including seventeen Africans, at least, vote for some alternative which they themselves prefer.

It is complicated, I agree, but a Commission will sit and that Commission may propose certain alterations to the Constitution. If it does so propose, then that alteration can only be carried by a two-thirds majority of the House. It also has to include the assent of seventeen out of the fifty Africans present in the House at that time. It is governed by Parliament, but the blocking mechanism operates in that way. I shall ask my Right Honourable Friend to explain that more clearly later on.

It has been said that at the first election after parity, there may be equality, that the seats may be divided five and five. If the qualified voters were, at that time, exactly equal and proportional representation was applied, that would get that result. Proportional representation was one of the methods suggested and discussed – what is certain is that from the first election onwards the basis on which Africans will come on to the register would ensure majority rule. It must be hoped that by that time the divisions would be those of political parties and not of races.

The blocking mechanism, the return to objective criteria for the increase of African representation in the House of Assembly, the accession of African members to the Parliament at each election as qualified members grow, the provision of the referendum when Africans can decide to be all elected, the transition through and beyond parity to ten common role seats – all this amounts to 'unimpeded progress to majority rule' under Principle One.

Principles Two and Four reinforce each other. The blocking mechanism in Parliament to prevent the introduction of new discriminatory laws should be taken with the Declaration of Rights which allows not only new laws – this is a very important point – and new regulations to be challenged in the courts, but new regulations which might be made under the old laws. For example, new regulations made under the Land Tenure Act could be challenged in the courts.

The matter of subordinate legislation is of particular consequence in relation to the Land Tenure Act. The trouble with the present

Land Tenure Act is that the division of land is too rigid. There is too much power to discriminate in the hands of the Minister and of the landlord, and particularly of the urban landlord.

The attention of the Commission, which is to review all existing legislation, is specifically drawn to those areas in which Africans and many Europeans feel that the discrimination is particularly unwarranted and offensive in a society which should have as its standards merit and responsibility.

Under Principle Three there will be an immediate improvement in the lot of the African. If the Africans register, there will be at least four African seats added to Parliament immediately – a twenty-five-per-cent increase. There will be an extended franchise for the lower role. Economic help for development and education will hasten the pace of political advance.

I have dealt with the Fourth Principle in connection with the Second. Finally I come to the Fifth Principle as the test of acceptability. It is important from every point of view that it should be thorough and seen to be fair. The terms of reference are designed to meet this end. That the Commission shall satisfy itself that the proposals for a settlement have been fully and properly explained to the population of Rhodesia to ascertain, by direct contact with all sections of the population, whether the people of Rhodesia as a whole regard these proposals as acceptable as a basis for independence and to report to me accordingly. Mr Smith has agreed that the Commission should have every facility to conduct its enquiries as it thinks best, after the members have decided how they want to proceed and whom they want to see.

In the context of normal political activity a number of questions have been asked as, for example, who might be allowed to broadcast or which detainees may be released in addition to those already released.

It was impossible for me, and it would be impossible for anyone else, to say whether an individual will be released. No such proposal was made on *Fearless* and it would be impossible to make it. But the Commission will be able to hear the opinion of anyone it wishes and if it feels it is handicapped in its work it will say so. I have no doubt that their wishes will be met.

It has to be remembered that there are in Rhodesia unrepentant advocates of force and violence. They will be heard by the Commission, as I was able to hear them and talk to them, but it is clearly desirable that the Commission should conduct its business in an atmosphere where it can hear and be heard in peaceful conditions.

I have had the advantage of meeting Mr Nkomo recently and having a conversation with him only a short time ago. I have no doubt that the Commission will be able to see him and to hear all his views.

I have been very conscious during these last years that Britain's influence on the Rhodesian situation was running out but that we must exercise it while anything of it remained, to try to obtain the best deal we possibly could for the Rhodesian African. That is the sole reason why I assumed the responsibility of trying to find a settlement with Mr Smith's Government. It was a heavy responsibility because one cannot but be conscious of the limitations on the 'best' which is involved in compromise. In Africa perhaps more than any other place in the world one is deeply conscious of the fallibility of man.

I can only say in conscience to this House that I do not believe that better terms could have been negotiated and I was interested that Sir Robert Tredgold, who is held in the highest opinion in all quarters of this House, has said that he regards the settlement as honourable. Sir Robert has been a Liberal all his life and one of very advanced views. I can only add my honest conviction that if the proposals are accepted all the races in Rhodesia have the chance to build a new, non-racial country.

Such a non-racial community in the centre of Africa if it could be established cannot be over-priced or over-prized.

Members of the Constitutional Committee 1970

The Rt. Hon. Sir Alec Douglas-Home, KT, MP (Chairman)
Sir David Milne, GCB (Vice-Chairman)
The Rt. Hon. Lord Avonside (1)
Henry Ballantyne Esq. CBE (2)
The Rt. Hon. Viscount Dilhorne (3)
Brigadier Sir Bernard Fergusson, GCMG, GCVO, DSO, OBE
Professor A. L. Goodhart, KBE, QC
Michael Joughin Esq.
Professor J. D. B. Mitchell
Sir Ronald Morison QC (4)
The Rt. Hon. Lord Polwarth
Lady Tweedsmuir
Sir Charles Wilson
The Rev. Dr. Ronald Selby Wright, CVO

Advisers:
The Rt. Hon. Sir Robert Menzies, KT, CH, QC
Professor Sir Kenneth Wheare, CMG

(1) Resigned August 1968.
(2) Appointed October 1969.
(3) Resigned June 1969.
(4) Appointed September 1968.

Index

Abdication crisis, 52–3, 63
Acton, Harold, 36
Aden, 146
Adenauer, Konrad, 149–50, 154–5
Africa, 51; *see also* individual countries
Aird, R., 32
Aitken, Sir Max, 251
Alexander of Hillsborough, Lord, 165, 295
Alexander of Tunis, Lord, 165–6
Alington, C. A., as Headmaster of Eton, 31; nature, 55–6; and teaching of Christianity, 76–7, 80
Alington, Elizabeth *see* Home, Lady
Alington, Mrs Hester Margaret, C. M. Wells and, 31; on Lord Hugh Cecil, 49; nature, 55–6
Allen, G. O., 32, 34, 39
Allingham, Margery, 87
America *see* United States of America
Amery, Leo, 45, 70, 74
Amin, Idi, 80
Anders, Wladyslaw, 88
Anderson, John, 202
Anguilla, 238–9; *see also* individual statesmen
Anstruther-Gray, Sir William (*later* Lord Kilmany), 183, 221
Asquith, H. H. (*later* Earl of Oxford and Asquith), 281
Attlee, Clement (*later* Earl Attlee), and Chamberlain, 75; and NATO, 145; verbal brevity of, 202; and nationalization, 281; and Suez, 287, 290–1, 295
Austen-Leigh, R. A., 30–1
Australia, 107–10, 146, 244; *see also* individual statesmen
Avonside, Lord, 313

Balfour, Arthur (*later* Lord Balfour), 194
Balfour of Inchrye, Lord, *Wings over Britain*, 67
Baldwin, Stanley (*late* Earl Baldwin), speech of, 24; and Eton and Harrow rivalry, 33; as Prime Minister, 47–8; Lord Hugh Cecil on, 49; and Abdication crisis, 52–3; resignation as Prime Minister, 60–1; and Tom Jones, 69
Balewa, Sir Abubakar Tafawa, 120–3
Ballantyne, Henry, 313
Bandaranaike, Solomon, 37
Baring, Evelyn (*later* Lord Howick), 36
Baring, Maurice, 44

Barrie, J. M., 34–5
Basutoland, 226
Beck, 88
Ben Gurion, David, 229
Berlin, Russian occupation, 94–5, 97; the Wall, 95–6; and allied air-space, 95–6
Bevin, Ernest, 145, 204, 232, 290–1
Bird, W. S., 25
Birkenhead, 1st Earl of, 45
Blake, George, 177
Blakenham, Viscount, 190, 212, 214
Boothby, Robert (*later* Lord Boothby), 70
Bowes-Lyon, David, 41
Bracken, Brendan, 70
Brand, David, 32–3
Brandt, Willy, 150, 233–8
Brezhnev, Leonid, 270
Bridgeman, William Clive, Viscount, 33
Bridges, Lord, 195
Brook, Sir Norman (*later* Lord Normanbrook), 192, 195
Brooke, P. V., 27
Brown, 'Bunko', 25–6
Brown, George (*later* Lord George-Brown), 174, 232
Bruce, David, 244–5
Buchan, John, *The Path of the King*, 87; *The Thirty-nine Steps*, 87
Bulteel family, 20
Burgess, Guy, 178
Burke, Edmund, 282
Butler, R. A. (*later* Lord Butler), and India Independence Bill, 50; and Home, 71; and Rhodesia, 133–4; and Home as Prime Minister, 185

Caesar *see* Julius Caesar
Cahn, Sir Julien, 39
Canada, 20, 105, 117–18; *see also* individual statesmen
Caradon, Lord (*formerly* Sir Hugh Foot), 239, 243
Carrington, Lord, 177, 244
Carter, A. T., 37
Casey, Richard Gardiner (*later* Lord Casey), 107
Castro, Fidel, 147
Cecil, Lord Hugh, 49–50
Cecil, Lord Robert, 44
Ceylon, 110–11; *see also* individual statesmen
Challenor, G., 39

Index

Chamberlain, Mrs Annie Vere, 60, 71-2
Chamberlain, Austen, 60
Chamberlain, Joseph, 20
Chamberlain, Neville, bird-watching, 14;
  and Abdication crisis, 53; as Prime
  Minister, 59-75; fall of, 74-5, 85
Channon, Sir Henry ('Chips'), 72
Cheng-yi, 169-70, 269
Chi Peng-fei, 270
Chiang Kai-shek, 264-5
China, 169, 174, 247, 263-72, 295; see also
  individual statesmen
Chou En-lai, 263-4, 267-71
Christie, Agatha, 87
Christie, John, 30
Churchill, Lord Randolph, 20, 143-4
Churchill, Winston S. (later Sir Winston
  Churchill), as back-bencher, 49; and
  India Independence Bill, 50-1; and
  Abdication crisis, 52-3; and wish for
  peace, 54; and rearmament, 55, 63, 70;
  on 'appeasement', 67; and Lindemann,
  69; under Chamberlain, 73; and Norway
  expedition, 74; as Prime Minister, 75-98;
  on thought, 84; at Yalta, 90; in
  Commons debate on Poland, 91-4; and
  Berlin, 94; and voters, 100; and Scottish
  Ministry, 102; and James Stuart, 104;
  resigns as Prime Minister, 105; enthusi-
  asms of, 116; and Alexander, 166; clarity
  of, 202; in Opposition, 217; funeral, 280
Clark, Kenneth, Lord, 39
Coleraine, Lord, 289
Collingwood, Mr (butler), 24
Collins, Sir Godfrey, 59
Collins, Wilkie, 87
Commonwealth, and Second World War,
  64; examination of, 105-37; nature of,
  163; creation of, 174; Britain in, 279;
  and national sovereignty, 288
Congo, 129
Constantine, Sir Leary, 34
Cooper, Duff (later Lord Norwich), 49, 70
Courtauld-Thomson, Lord, 201
Crawley, Cosmo, 41
Cromer, Earl of, 36
Crookshank, Harry, 49
Cyprus, 146, 172, 243; see also individual
  statesmen
Czechoslovakia, 64-5, 250

Daily Herald (newspaper), 142
Daily Mail (newspaper), 142
Daladier, Edouard, 73
de Courcy, Kenneth, 243
de Murville, Couve, 151-2, 233
Denmark, 171
des Portes, Mme, 73

Desai, Morarji, 112
Diefenbaker, John, 117-18, 135-6
Dilhorne, Viscount, 181, 183, 313
Disraeli, Benjamin, 87
Dixon, Sir Owen, 115
Dobrynin, Anatoly F., 244-5
Douglas family, history of, 14-21
Douglas, Archibald, 1st Duke of, 16-17
Douglas, Duchess of, 16-17
Douglas, Sir James ('The Good'), 14-15
Douglas, Lady Jane, 16-17
Douglas Castle and estate, 12-13, 15-17, 23,
  28-9, 40, 45, 102
Douglas-Home, Sir Alec see Home of the
  Hirsel, Baron
Douglas-Home, Bridget (author's sister),
  bird-watching, 12; egg-collecting, 13;
  early education, 22; as nurse in Second
  World War, 85
Douglas-Home, Charles Alexander (author's
  grandfather), 12th Earl of, 12, 17
Douglas-Home, Charles Cospatrick
  Archibald (author's father), 13th Earl of,
  as naturalist, 11-12; advice to author, 21;
  nature of, 22-3; in First World War, 43;
  and politics, 43-5; and wish for peace, 54
Douglas-Home, Edward (author's brother),
  birth of, 14; as Japanese P.O.W., 22-3,
  85; schooling, 26
Douglas-Home, Elizabeth see Home,
  Elizabeth, Lady
Douglas-Home, George (author's brother),
  birth of, 14; schooling, 26; death of, 85
Douglas-Home, Henry (author's brother),
  observation of, 12; egg-collecting, 13;
  early education, 22-3; at Oxford, 36;
  and field sports, 40-1; in Scottish
  Command, 85
Douglas-Home, Rachel (author's sister),
  13, 55
Douglas-Home, William (author's brother);
  birth of, 14; nature of, 25; schooling, 26;
  in Second World War, 85; The Chiltern
  Hundreds, 24; The Reluctant Peer, 183
Drummond-Moray, Andrew, 186
Drummond-Moray, Mrs Andrew, 186
du Cann, Edward, 220
Dugdale, Tommy (later Lord Crathorne),
  52
Dulles, John Foster, 109-10, 138-40
Dunglass, Lady (Lilian. née Lambton;
  author's mother), and Lambton family,
  19; and Christian education, 22;
  housekeeping of, 24-5
Dunn, Arthur, 25
Durham, Earl of, 19-20, 105

Eban, Abba, 229, 258

Eccles, Sir David (*later* Viscount Eccles), 117

Eden, Anthony (*later* Earl of Avon), as Foreign Secretary, 61; and Russia, 68; relationship with Chamberlain, 69-71; ability of, 97; as Prime Minister, 105; and Suez, 139; and Vietnam, 168

Edward VII, King of England, 144

Edward VIII, King of England, 52-3, 63

Egypt, and Suez Canal, 138-41, 287-95; and Israel, 228-32, 299; *see also* individual statesmen

Eisenhower, Dwight, 95, 139-40

Elizabeth, Queen of England, Consort of George VI, 53

Elizabeth II, Queen of England, 185, 198, 201-2, 280

Elliot, Rt-Hon. Walter, 46

Emrys-Evans, Paul, 70

English, Sir Crisp, 85

Esher, Viscount, 294

Ethiopia, 139

European Economic Community, de Gaulle vetoes British entry, 154, 177; British negotiations in 1970, 248-9; Britain in, 279

Evatt, Herbert, 108

Feiling, Sir Keith, 38

Fender, P. G. H., 32

Fergusson, Sir Bernard (*later* Lord Ballantrae), 313

Figgures, Sir Frank, 274

Fletcher (of Selkirk), 19

Flodden, Battle of, 17-19

Foot, Sir Hugh *see* Caradon, Lord

France, fall of, 62; and Czechoslovakia, 64; and Second World War, 68; and 'Soames affair', 233-8; *see also* individual statesmen

Franco, Francisco, 171, 243

Fraser, Sir John, 85-6

Fraser, Sir Michael (*later* Lord Fraser of Kilmorack), 187

Froode, Mr (butler), 23-4

Frost, David, 216

Fry, C. B., 31

Gainsborough, Thomas, 16

Gaitskell, Rt-Hon. Hugh, 131-2, 138, 142-3

Galbraith, T. G. D., 177

Gamelin, Maurice Gustave, General, 62, 73

Gan, 146

Gandhi, Mrs Indira, 51, 114

Gandhi, M. K., 56, 112

Gaulle, Charles de, treaty with Stalin, 93; and Germany, 149; nature of, 150-1; and 'Polaris' submarine, 152-3; and USA, 154; and British membership of

EEC, 154, 177; and European security, 155; and 'Soames affair', 233-8

George III, King of England, 174

George V, King of England, 47

George VI, King of England, 53

Germany, and Italy, 61-2; position of, 64-5; and Second World War, 68; and Russian occupation, 94-5, 250; and NATO, 149-50; and 'Soames affair', 233-8; *see also* individual statesmen

Ghana, 119-20; *see also* individual statesmen

Gibbs, Sir Humphrey, 224

Gibson, Clem, 40

Gibson, C. H., 32

Gilliat, (*later* Sir) Martin, 108

Gladstone, William, 20-1, 87, 105, 206

Goering, Hermann, 66

Goodhart, A. L., 313

Goodman, Arnold, Lord, 251-3

Gordon Walker, Patrick, 234, 236

Goschen, George Joachim, Lord, 104

Gow, A. S. F., 28-9

Gowon, Yakubu, 123

Graham, Billy, 77

Greece, 172

Greenhill, Sir Denis, 249, 253

Gregory, J. M., 32

Grey, Lord, 19-20

Grey of Fallodon, Lord, 44

Grey, Lady May, 20

Grivas, George Theodorus, 172

Gromyko, Andrei, and Berlin, 95-6; Home and, 158-9, 250; and Vietnam, 169-70; and Russian ambassadors, 245; and spies in Britain, 249

Gromyko, Mrs Andrei, 159, 250

Gudmundsson, Gudmundur I., 173

Guise, J. L., 33

Gulf States, 261

Haig, Sir Douglas, 43-4

Haile Selassie, Emperor of Ethiopia, 199

Hailsham, Mary, Lady, 180

Hailsham, Lord (*formerly* Quintin Hogg), 180-2, 185

Halifax, Lord, 75

Hamilton, Duke of, 16-17

Hankey, Lord, 72, 195

Harriman, Averell, 170

Harris, Kenneth, 184

Hastings, Stephen L. E., 234

Headlam, G. W., 28-9

Heath, Edward, and author, 71; and Scottish devolution, 104, 205, 207-8; and EEC, 177, 248-9; and Resale Price Maintenance, 189; as Prime Minister, 202, 240-75; and Conservative Leadership, 272-3; and 1974 General

Heath, Edward, *(cont'd.)*
 Election, 273
Heathcoat-Amory, Derick *(later* Viscount
 Amory), 117, 142, 277
Heathcoat, Amory, Dick, 37
Henderson, Lord, 289, 293
Henderson, Sir Neville, 243
Hendren, E. H., 39
Henry VIII, King of England, 17
Hill, Mervyn, 32
Hill-Wood, W. W., 32
Hirsel, The (estate), 12, 17, 20, 23-4, 40-1,
 43, 45, 71, 80, 85, 102
Hirst, George, 32
Hitler, Adolf, desire for war, 63-4, 113;
 meetings with Chamberlain, 64-7;
 Vansittart and, 70; behaviour of, 138,
 147; aggression of, 287
Hoare, Sir Samuel, 50
Holland, Sidney, 106-7
Home family, history of, 17-21
Home, Alexander, 3rd Baron, 17-19
Home, Alexander, 9th Earl of, 21
Home of The Hirsel, Baron Alexander
 Frederick Douglas-Home (*formerly* 14th
 Earl of Home; Sir Alec Douglas-Home),
 bird-watching, 11-12; egg-collecting, 13;
 love of nature, 14; given Freedom of
 Selkirk, 19; early education, 22-3; at
 Ludgrove, 24-6; and cricket, 25, 31-4,
 39-40; at Eton, 26-35, 44; at Oxford,
 35-9, 49; and field sports, 40-2; and war,
 43; enters politics, 43-6; as PPS, 58;
 as PPS to Chamberlain, 59-75; as
 Foreign Secretary, 71, 142-55, 241-75;
 as Prime Minister, 71, 182-90; and
 Christianity, 76-83, 276-85; illness, 85-8;
 on Communism, 88-97, 250-1; in debate
 on Poland, 91-4; and Berlin, 94-7;
 Under-Secretary in Foreign Office, 97;
 defeated in 1945 General Election, 98;
 electioneering, 99-100; succeeds to title,
 100-1; retires from politics, 102; as
 Minister for Scotland, 102-5; as
 Secretary of State for Commonwealth
 Relations, 105-42; and Khrushchev, 156-7;
 and Gromyko, 158-9; on UN, 160-5;
 on House of Lords, 165-6; on NATO,
 167-8, 171; on Vietnam, 168-71; on
 Cyprus, 172-3; on Iceland, 173-4; on
 Britain's role, 174-5; on EEC, 176-7, 248-
 9; and Vassall affair, 177; and Profumo
 affair, 178; and nature of Premiership,
 191-7; and Kennedy's assassination,
 197-8; and Nehru's funeral, 198-9; and
 Nasser's funeral, 199; at Chequers, 200;
 and the Queen, 201; and 'public image',
 202-4; on Scottish nationalism, 205-11;

and 1964 General Election, 212-15; end of
 Premiership, 215-17; as Leader of Opposition, 217-22; resigns leadership, 222; as
 Shadow Foreign Minister, 222-40; and
 South Africa, 223-4, 226-8; and Rhodesia,
 225, 251-8, 302-12; and Israel, 228-32,
 258-60; and 'Soames affair', 233-8; and
 Anguilla, 238-9; and 1970 General Election,
 239-40; and role of Ambassadors, 242-5;
 and families of Foreign Service officials,
 246-7; and Russian spies, 249-50; and
 Arab Gulf States, 261; and China, 263-
 72; on Trades Unions, 273-4; speech in
 Lords on Suez, 287-95; on Israeli-Arab
 conflict, 296-301; member of
 Constitutional Committee, 313
Home, Douglas *see* Douglas-Home
Home, Elizabeth (lady, author's wife), and
 author's frugality, 25; marriage, 55-7;
 electioneering, 100; in Ceylon, 111;
 and Godfrey Huggins, 126; and Home's
 succession as Premier, 184-5; and official
 entertaining, 196, 216-17; at Chequers,
 200; and 1964 General Election, 203;
 enjoyment of Foreign Service, 246;
 visit to China, 265-6, 272
Homer, 26
Hong Kong, 146
Hore-Belisha, Lord, 72-3, 295
Huggins, Godfrey *(later* Lord Malvern), 126
Hume Castle, 17

Iceland, 173; *see also* individual statesmen
Ikramullah, 141
India, independence, 50-1, 119; Home
 visits, 111-14; and Suez crisis, 140-1;
 see also individual statesmen
Inskip, Sir Thomas, 63
Iran, 139, 261; *see also* individual statesmen
Israel, 228-32, 258-60, 296-301; *see also*
 individual statesmen
Italy, 61-2, 70, 88; *see also* individual
 statesmen
James IV, King of Scotland, 17-18
Jamieson, Tommy, 40
Japan, 174
Jarring, Gunnar, 301
Jay, Douglas, 191
Jewell, Maurice, 39-40
Joicey, Lady Joan, 41
Jones, Tom, 69
Jordan, 299
Joughin, Michael, 313
Jowitt, Lord, 291
Julius Caesar, 26, 191

Keitel, Wilhelm, 66
Kennedy, John F., Rusk and, 96; and
 'Polaris' submarine, 152-3; Macmillan

Kennedy, John F., *(cont'd.)*
and, 155; and 'British colonialism', 160;
and Vietnam, 170; and Nuclear Test Ban
Treaty, 179, 212; assassination of, 197–8;
and British Ambassador, 244; as President,
244
Kent-Hughes, Wilfred, 36
Kenya, 129, 137
Kerr, Captain, 16
Keyes, Sir Roger, 74
Keynes, Maynard, 278
Khama, Seretse, 132
Khama, Lady Seretse, 132
Khama, Tshekedi, 132
Khan, Ayub, 115, 135
Khrushchev, Nikita, 95, 155–7
King, Mackenzie, 117
Kissinger, Henry, 165, 264
Knox, Ronald, 49
Kotelawala, Sir John, 110–11

Lambton family, history of, 19–21
Lambton, Lord Freddy, 20
Lambton, Geoffrey, 26
Lambton, Jack, 20–1
Lang, Cosmo, Archbishop of Canterbury, 76
Lansbury, George, 47–8
Larwood, Harold, 39
Laughton, Charles, 59
Layton, Lord, 293
League of Nations, 54, 144
Lebanon, 299
Lee Kuan Yew, 116
Lenin, Vladimir Ilyich, 245, 269
Lennox-Boyd, Alan (*later* Viscount Boyd),
36, 126, 128
Lin-Piao, 267
Lincoln, Abraham, 279
Lindemann, Frederick Alexander, 1st
Viscount Cherwell, 37, 69
Llewellyn-Davies, Nico, 34
Lloyd, Selwyn, 142, 183
Lloyd George, David, 45, 48–9, 58
Luns, Joseph, 155
Lyttelton, 4th Lord, 56
Lyttelton, Edward, 56
Lyttelton, Oliver (*later* Lord Chandos), 126

Macaulay, Lord, 87
McBride, Sir Philip, 107
MacCanlis, M. A., 39
McCorquodale, Malcolm, 36
Macdonald, E. A., 32
MacDonald, Malcolm, 52, 244
MacDonald, Ramsay, 46–7, 52
McEwen, John, 107
McGahey, Mick, 273
McGovern, John, 48
Maclean, Donald, 178

Macleod, Iain, 185–6, 189, 215
Macmillan, Mr (gardener), 23
Macmillan, Lady Dorothy, 191
Macmillan, Sir Harold, succession to as
Prime Minister, 11; and Eden, 70; and
Home, 71; and Commonwealth Prime
Ministers' Conference, 108; and 'wind of
change', 123–4; and Rhodesia, 131, 133;
and South Africa, 136; and Suez, 139;
appoints Home Foreign Secretary, 142–3;
and 'Polaris' submarine, 152–3; and
Kennedy, 155; and Khrushchev, 156;
and EEC, 177; and Vassall affair, 178;
and Profumo, 178; and Nuclear Test
Ban Treaty, 178–80; illness, 180–1;
resignation, 182–3; Cabinet of, 185;
nature as Prime Minister, 191–2; and
British decline, 279
Makarios, Archbishop, 172, 242
Makins, Roger (*later* Lord Sherfield), 35, 37
Malan, D. F., 135
Malawi, 226
Malaysia, 115–16
Mao Tse-tung, 263–4, 267–70
Margesson, Henry David Reginald, 75
Marsh, Ngaio, 87
Marten, C. H. K., 28–30
Marx, Karl, 269
Masterman, J. C., 37–8; *To Teach the Senators Wisdom*, 38
Maudling, Reginald, 185, 213, 222
Maugham, Somerset, 87
Maxton, James, 48
May, H. Erskine, *Parliamentary Procedure*, 49
Meir, Golda, 229, 258
Melbourne, Lord, 20, 87
Menon, Krishna, 140
Menzies, Sir Robert, 107–9, 139–40, 313;
Afternoon Light, 140
Milne, Sir David, 313
Mirza, Iskander, 114–15
Mitchell, J. D. B., 313
Mollet, Guy, 291
Molotov, Vyacheslav, 68, 159
Monckton, Sir Walter (*later* Lord
Monckton), 131–3
Montgomery of Alamein, Lord, 165–6
Morgan, Charles, 87
Morrison, Sir Ronald, 313
Morrison, Herbert (*later* Lord Morrison), 75
Mossadeq, Mohammad, 100
Mountbatten, Lord, 147
Muirhead, A. J., 59
Mussolini, Benito, Chamberlain and, 61,
69–71; and Italy's entry into war, 62; at
Munich, 66; behaviour of, 138; aggression
of, 287

Index

Nash, Walter, 106
Nasser, Abdul Gamal, and Suez, 138-41, 290; intentions of, 147; and Israel, 230, 232; nature of, 243
NATO (North Atlantic Treaty Organization), as safeguard against Communism, 62, 176; USA and, 96, 146, 245, 289; need for, 113-14, 148; formation of, 145; Germany and, 149-50; France and, 154; Russia and, 157; Salisbury and, 156; Home on, 167-75; and Vietnam, 232-3; de Gaulle and, 235-6; Britain in, 279, 295
Nehru, Jawaharlal, given Freedom of City of London, 107; and Home, 112-14; and South Africa, 135; and Suez, 140-1; funeral of, 198-9
New Zealand, 106-7, 109, 146, 248; see also individual statesmen
News of the World (newspaper), 143
Nigeria, 120, 123; see also individual statesmen
Nixon, Richard, 264, 272
Nkomo, Joshua, 134, 253, 312
Nkrumah, Kwame, 119-20, 130, 135
Norway, 74
Nyasaland, 125, 128, 133
Nyerere, Julius, 146

Observer (newspaper), 184
Ormsby-Gore, Sir David (later Lord Harlech), 244
Otterburn, Battle of, 15
Ovid, 26
Owen, S. G., 37

Pakenham, Lord (Francis Aungier Pakenham; later Lord Longford), 289, 291-2, 294
Pakistan, 114; see also individual statesmen
Palmerston, Lord, 174, 272
Pandit, Mrs Vijaya Lakshmi, 140-1
Pant, Govind Ballabh, 112
Pearce, Lord, 256
Pearson, Lester, 117-18, 141
Peel, Sir Robert, 87
Penney, Sir William, 179
Percy family, 15
Perrin, Percy, 39
Philby, Kim, 178
Philip, Prince, Duke of Edinburgh, 198
Pitman, Jim, 36
Plato, 26
Playford, Tom, 110
Plowden, Lord, 246
Poland, 88, 90, 92, 94, 250
Polwarth, Lord, 313
Pompidou, Georges, 248
Powell, Enoch, 181, 185-6, 189, 192, 215

Profumo, John, 178, 192
Radhakrishnan, Sarvepalli, 111
Rahman, Tunku Abdul, 115-16
Ramsey, Arthur Michael, Archbishop of Canterbury, 77
Ranjitsinhji, K. S., 31
Rawlinson, Sir Peter, 253
Reading, Lord, 291
Rennell, Lord, 292
Reynaud, Paul, 73
Rhodesia, 123-34, 222-6, 233, 243, 251-8, 302-12; see also individual statesmen
Ribbentrop, Joachim von, 63, 68
Robert the Bruce, King of Scotland, 15
Robertson, John, 222
Roosevelt, Theodore, 68, 90, 94
Roxburgh Castle, 15
Ruanda Burundi, 129
Rusk, Dean, 37, 95-6
Russia, revolution, 51, 54; and Second World War, 64; aggression of, 68, 88-97, 167-9, 250-1; military strength of, 174, 247, 283; and Middle East, 230; diplomatic behaviour of, 245-6; see also individual statesmen

St Kitts, 238
St Laurent, Stephen, 117
Sadat, Anwar, 242
Salisbury, Lord, 165
Sandys, Duncan (later Lord Duncan-Sandys), 70, 134
Saudi Arabia, 261
Sayers, Dorothy L., 87
Scheel, Walter, 150
Scotland, 14, 102-5, 205-11
Scott, Jimmy, 24
Scott, Robert Falcon, 34
Scott, Sir Walter, 15, 87; 'Marmion', 18
SEATO (South-East Asia Treaty Organisation); weakness of, 109; and British presence in Singapore, 146; USA membership of, 289; Britain in, 295
Shepherd, Lord, 239
Shirlaw, Nanny, 57
Silkin, Lord, 291
Simon, Sir John, 47-9, 65, 273
Simpson, Mrs Wallace, 52-3
Singapore, 116, 146; see also individual statesmen
Skelton, Noel, 58-9
Slade, Miss, 56
Slim, Sir William (later Viscount), 108
Smith, G. O., 25
Smith, Ian, and Rhodesia, 134; and Unilateral Declaration of Independence, 223; talks with Wilson, 224-5; nature of, 242; talks with Home, 252-7, 307, 312

Index

Smuts, J. C., 135
Snowden, Philip, 46-7
Soames, Sir Christopher, 233-8
Solzhenitsyn, Alexander, 282
South Africa, 134-6, 222-3, 226-8; *see also* individual statesmen
Soviet Union *see* Russia
Spaak, Henri, 155
Spain, 88, 171; *see also* individual statesmen
Spears, Sir Edward, 70
Springhill *see* Hirsel, The
Stalin, Joseph, 89, 93-4, 113, 245
Stanley, Oliver, 49
Stansgate, William, 1st Viscount, 143
Stanyforth, R. T., 40
Starzenska, Count, 88-9, 94
Starzenski, Countess, 88
Steele, Tom, 98-9
Stephen, Campbell, 48
Stevenson, Adlai, 161
Stewart, John, 16-17
Stewart, Michael, 232-9
Stirling-Maxwell, Sir John, 99
Stuart, James (*later* Viscount Stuart of Findhorn), 102-4
Suez *see* Egypt
Surrey, Earl of, 17-18
Sweden, 139
Swinton, Lord, 53-4, 62
Syria, 228, 299-300

Talbot, Father Ted, 49
Tan Siew Sin, 116
Tanzania, 137, 146
Tedder, Lord, 294
Telfer, Mr (game-keeper), 24
Thomas, J. H., 46-7
Thomas, J. P. L., 70
Todd, Garfield, 124-5, 253
Tredgold, Sir Robert, 312
Tree, Ronnie, 70
Trend, Sir Burke (*later* Lord Trend), 195
Trevelyan, G. M., 87
Triplow, Miss (governess), 23
Turkey, 172
Tweedsmuir, Lady, 313

U Thant, 157, 172
United Nations, Commonwealth and, 118; Balewa addresses, 120-3; on Rhodesia, 130, 223; and Suez, 141, 289, 293; as peace-keeping force, 148, 293-4; Russia and, 156-7, 160-5; and British security, 167; and Vietnam, 171; and Cyprus, 172; and Britain, 174; and Israel, 230-1; Sir Hugh Foot as Ambassador to, 243; and China, 265; and Arab-Israeli conflict, 296-301

United States of America, and League of Nations, 54; nuclear power of, 62; and Second World War, 64, 68; and Suez, 139; and NATO, 145-6, 149; military strength of, 174, 247; and Israel, 230, 260, 283; and Vietnam, 232-3, 244-5; *see also* individual statesmen

Vansittart, Sir Robert, 69-70
van Thal, Herbert, *The Prime Ministers*, 70
Vassall, John, 177-8
Verwoerd, H. F., 135-6
Victoria, Queen of England, 144
Vietnam, 232, 245
Virgil, 26, 28
Voce, W., 39
Vorster, John, 223-4, 227

Waldheim, Kurt, 171
Walpole, Hugh, 87
Warner, Sir Pelnam F. ('Plum'), 39-40
Ward, Barbara (*later* Lady Jackson), 78, 81
Webb, Mary, 48
Webster, Ronald, 238
Weizmann, Chaim, 229
Welensky, Sir Roy, 126-33
Wells, C. M., 28, 30-2
Welsh, J. C., 45-6
West Indies, 248
Wheare, Sir Kenneth, 313
Wheeler-Bennett, Sir John, 243
White, Henry Julian, 37
White, J. C., 39
Whitehead, Sir Edgar, 130
Whitworth, A. W., 27-8, 38
Wilhelm II, Kaiser of Germany, 113
Wilson, Sir Charles, 313
Wilson, Harold (*later* Sir Harold), and Home as Prime Minister, 184, 186-7; and 1964 General Election, 213; in Parliament, 217; and Rhodesia, 223-5, 306-7; and 'Soames affair', 233-8; and EEC, 249; and evacuation of Aden, 261; political conduct of, 281
Wilson, Sir Horace, 69
Winterton, Lord, 49
Wolmer, Lord, 70
Wolsey, Thomas, 39
Wontner, Sir Hugh, 215
Wright, Matt, 32
Wright, Ronald Selby, 313

Young, R. A., 31-2
Younger, George, 186
Yugoslavia, 88

Zambia, 137